DEAR WORLD & EVERYONE IN IT

Children should not sing. The Anthem / is mightier.
Static instead of words. The / Flag is not there. Behold
the empty / sky

I am your paper

    beyond me

        out of them

        dropped   arms

SUCH PASSIONS   ABOUND
in the CYBERSPHERE !

On the <u>Have Your Say website</u>,

Pitt-Palin **Pacified** Rice Thatcher's

face is *embroiled* in a **botox debate** about one

hundred and sixty four people having a debate debate

about the <u>Have Your stick insect Say</u>

debate where a good cross-section of social strata are

embroiled in a **patriotic debate**

about themselves,
a digital mirror sputters,
the lines rage aimless,
the passion is aimless.

Nathan Hamilton is one of the UK's leading young poetry editors. He runs Egg Box Publishing and has co-edited the anthology series *Stop Sharpening Your Knives*, as well as numerous other pamphlets, books and poetry projects over the years. He is chairman of the board of Inpress, representing over 40 independent UK publishers. He has been published in a number of places, in print and online, including *The Guardian, The Manhattan Review, The Rialto, The Spectator* and *The Wolf*.

I think half of commercials begin with the words *are you*
and the other half
are useless and remote

DEAR WORLD
& EVERYONE IN IT
NEW POETRY IN THE UK
EDITED BY NATHAN HAMILTON

walked in / with economic / wish fulfilment
playing in their ears / cathartic slide / as i hallucinate
our escape / through these steel walls / we are sold
down / the river / and drift off smiling

BLOODAXE BOOKS

ISBN: 978 1 85224 949 6

First published 2013 by
Bloodaxe Books Ltd,
Highgreen,
Tarset,
Northumberland NE48 1RP

www.bloodaxebooks.com
For further information about Bloodaxe titles
please visit our website or write to
the above address for a catalogue.

Supported by
**ARTS COUNCIL
ENGLAND**

Cover design: Neil Astley & Pamela Robertson-Pearce.

Printed in Great Britain by
Bell & Bain Limited, Glasgow, Scotland.

CONTENTS

space distribution between words and lines
must fulfil not only feng shui symbology but also
provide a statistical analysis of the training market

FOSSILS ON MARS

NH, 2012

Dear World, Today, as I try to write an introduction, I have received numerous newsletters and The Olympics is on. Specifically, water polo. It is USA vs Team GB. USA wins, easily. I am jealous of the straightforward, instinctive moment of the good goal, of indisputable victory and the pecs. I don't want to be a poet. It is too complicated and too vague and the rewards are so small. And I don't want to edit a poetry anthology. Today, I want to be a water poloist. I imagine walking into the dive bar across Grand Street with my big pecs and, when someone asks me what I do, I say 'I play water polo' and instead of looking kind of surprised and sorry for me they look interested and look at my pecs.

*

'Please forgive us for not producing a STUFF newsletter since the Spring. This gap does at least mean we've got lots to share! And with our new in-house marketing professional in post (along with other recruits) you'll be hearing a lot more from us (and more regularly) from now on. So here goes... lift off!

We know the picture shows the rocket about to crash back in the sea, but its smoke trail inadvertently happens to have drawn The Poetry Trust logo – so we couldn't resist using it!' [1]

*

Dear Wordle, You tell me, disappointingly, the most common word by far in this anthology is 'like'. How can 'like' be interesting?
1. Propose it is symptomatic of a fundamental uncertainty in the young.
2. Assert it emulates and demonstrates the influence of American speech.
3. Consider that it shows how often a poem compares a thing to another thing and makes a new thing, as if breeding.
4. Something about Facebook.
5. Forget about it and move on. ✓

*

---

[1] From Poetry Trust Newsletter, August 2012.

Dear Reader, Today The Editor received an email from The Publisher asking about Young Poets not included in The Anthology. He asks whether this is covered in The Introduction, so: the reason some are in this book and not others is because some new Young Poets still write Old Poetry.

Just being young and proficient doesn't mean your writing is new and interesting. Some Young Poets seem to write to appeal to Old Poets, like a creepy family picture where all the kids are dressed in smaller versions of their parents' clothes. Everybody has a horrible, graveyard smile on their face. You sense something sinister will happen as soon as the camera is gone. We'll have less of this sort of thing in The Anthology.

*

Dear World, I later complain about the water polo to a good friend 'but will a water poloist be remembered in 100 years?' he says. 'Yes', I say. 'Yes, I think some water poloists will be remembered in 100 years. By water polo fans. And fans of water polo probably outnumber poetry fans.' And he says: 'But poetry is remembered by the language.' Smart ass.

*

Dear Old Editors, Recent poetry anthologies and magazine selections edited by you have paid uneasy lip service to a greater spirit of cooperation, experiment-ation, and 'hybridisation' taking place in young UK poetry. To say such things suggests you still see divisions rather than a spectrum. Such self-descriptions mask a prevailing conservatism: few selections, if any, have actually included work that is 'more experimental' with your 'mainstream'. As an excuse you cite the spurious General Reader for whom poetry needs to be sanitised, a sort of insipid dust phantom who dissipates at too strong a poetry fart. The Anthology says it will represent a plurality: not mean but be. The Audience will define and reveal itself in response to The Anthology.

*

Dear Craig Saper, In *Networked Art*, you address the ways that an earlier rhet-orical approach to literature, which demands 'the presumed a priori existence of a "probable reader"', has changed. In contrast with the anxiety voiced by the Romantics at the disappearance of this 'probable reader' you identify an opportunity to make work that goes further towards defining its own readership.

The world of readers consists of multiple, diverse groupings difficult for the practitioner either to identify or attempt to include. Contemporary poetic practice might therefore depend 'on receiving the strange and the stranger'.

Increased awareness of how a text is received, and by whom, prompts consideration of text as performative and participatory, involving interaction between reader and text.[2]

*

'It has mostly been my own aspiration, for example, to establish relations not personally with the reader, but with the world and its layers of shifted but recognisable usage; and thereby with the reader's own position within this world.' J.H. Prynne, September, 1985.[3]

*

Hello, Stranger…

*

Dear Old Editors, The Editor hears Young Poets complain that poems winning competitions judged by Old Editors are boring. He hears young poets say they write different 'sorts' of poems they feel will appeal to different Old Editors. He hears Young Poets complain that tutors don't 'get it' and ask for too much certainty. He hears you Old Editors are limited in your scopes. In the 80s, more innovative poetries were marginalised in hard-to-find small UK presses, or were hard to reach overseas. Now, it is all over the internet. Something has stirred as a result.

*

Dear NASA, I saw today your Mars rover, Curiosity, landing. I would like to be a Mars rover, parachuting onto other worlds, eating chocolate. I would like to work for you and think that poetry can't give such a sense of an unquestionable job well done: you curious guys at mission control waiting for the word 'touchdown'. Score! Whoop! Hugs. The little dance in the end-zone.

#

The Editor had the idea that some new terms were needed.

So, let's say there are two general modes in UK & US poetry: 'Product' and 'Process'. And that the young choose between these as 'poles' as opposed to 'camps', which conjures a Gulag. Then let's say the product-focused aesthetic relies on clarity of context, presenting self-contained, more or less complete thoughts and evincing a concern for descriptive accuracy when considering the external world. It is preoccupied with realising recalled events, sometimes through memory's distorting effects, while keeping failings of language under discursive control. It often assumes the fundamental reliability of an expressive self-hood, readable as individual poet or as a character in a novel – either through direct address or through persona. The 'Product' relies on pragmatic assumptions of 'common sense', or a 'common knowledge' realm of reference.

---

[2] Taken from emails between the author and Elizabeth-Jane Burnett, March 2012.
[3] Quoted by Martin Stannard in *Stride Magazine*, October 2005.

After that let's say 'Process' is the approach that instead enjoys non sequitur surprises aimed at highlighting formal relationships between words. Fundamentally uncertain about the reliability of the self as organising principle, it is concerned with poetry as a way of speaking about the world that simultaneously presents the difficulties of doing so. It feels suspicion towards, or attempts to make strange, subject-object correlatives. Rather than present a self-contained thought, it enacts the poem's or poet's own processes; highlights or ironises these processes, or the thinking that produces the poem-text.

So 'Product' seeks to build in mimesis while 'Process' seeks to enact in and through language. Product would understand realism as representing the physical world through verisimilitude in 'good language' or 'the best words in the best order'. Process would define realism as a textual performance of the drama of language, self and world.

But 'Product' and 'Process' represent the modern creep of business and corporate language and ideology into all areas of thought and work – dismiss them from your mind entirely.

*

Dear UK, Book production became easier and cheaper for more risk-taking smaller presses. Digitisation made it easier to organise readings and cooperate and publicise widely more cheaply. In a saturated market, financial rewards are smaller, which encourages a focus on other rewards. An increase in creative writing courses allowed more protected time to write and brought diverse ranges of writers together. A period, now gone, of wealth allowed more relaxed choices about careers. It is easier to find previously obscure poetries. Younger poetry – which has always been a little more likely to be experimenting, changing, playing around – is generally more visible for these reasons, before it has been groomed by established Old Editors. Cooperation and mutual curiosity and experiment and play are more common. The Anthology believes that the UK Poetry Establishment needs restructuring.

*

Dear Jean-Luc Picard, This afternoon I read an article on the BBC website about 5 planets like earth that are only 20 or so light-years away which makes them feel so close. Tonight, looking at the constellation Orion from a cobbled street in Norwich, I want to live on the *Starship Enterprise* and look back fondly on an age when we had just sent a rover on an ambitious mission to Mars and found five Earth-like planets nearby right at the point that our own was heating up.

*

Periods of great change or upheaval trigger species knowledge that things need to be new. This encourages more copulation and increased birth rates. Grrrrreat!

*

Dear The Anthology, It is impossible, and silly to pretend, to be comprehensive or impartial as The Editor. It is impossible to be comprehensive in representing the amount and the variety of the activity in the poetry scene. Conversely, it is impossible to be impartial in a world this small, where many of the individual poets will be known to you and a number of them may be friends you don't want to make sad.

*

Dear Poetry, Scientists find new human species! Mars rover Curiosity lifts its mast cameras!

*

Perhaps my grandchildren will live for hundreds of years. Maybe forever. If they do, here we are in the last two properly mortal generations.

*

Dear Olympics, Today I was thinking again about your opening ceremony, which floated a crazy bunch of unconnected cultural vegetables around a spiky salad bowl. It was sometimes moving.

*

This morning, taking a break from choosing between poems to choose between a cappuccino, an espresso, a mocha, an americano, a latte, a latte with cinnamon, a... The Editor thought again that some terms were needed... he wonders, after reading Jo Crot's poem, whether the UK Poetry Scene could be divided into *Star Trek* aliens – he means in terms of its characteristics. So, fame-hungry poets or mainstream publishers would be like the Ferengi. J.H. Prynne would be a sort of Vulcan. Or maybe Data. Or would that be The Editor? People like Basil Bunting might be Klingon. Fiona Sampson would be Cardassian. Or maybe also a Ferengi. Perhaps a half-breed. But could a Cardassian and a Ferengi ever actually mate? It might not even be possible. Each poet The Editor thinks of starts to fit into one category or other if he thinks hard enough. Then he could research all the minor alien races that pop up in one-off episodes ... he realises that the girl at the counter is still waiting to hear what he wants to choose and there is a line behind him all also waiting to choose. He wastes at least two days on this on Wikipedia and uses it to justify a week spent re-watching all seven series of *Star Trek* TNG on Netflix.

*

The Editor later thought that perhaps poetry could be divided into Poetry Austin Powers and Dr Evils – in terms of how it is popularly imagined. Poetry Austins are the sort of older poet who tried to be more accessible and 'groovy' in the 80s but now look lamely anachronistic. Dr Evils would then be academy-based intellectuals. The Editor jettisons this after writing 2,000 words on the subject. Perhaps categorising poetry is just a bad idea. The Editor then considers describing poetry in terms of colour groupings, with Luke Kennard being a sort of greeny-orange...

*

Eddie Izzard in a dress saying 'BUnch of flowerrrrrrrs!'

#

Dear sun and moon, the way you are both exactly the same size in the sky intrigues. You fit so well despite the distance. This coincidence sometimes gives people big ideas about their perspective.

*

Dear Poetry,

WEB

I am ravelled here
to the live field, in a rig of stress.

Turned on my new axis to a swathe
of shriven grey, I remind myself
of a cork float in a fishing-net spread out
to dry in the sun, waiting for the fisherman
– both *retiarius* and *secutor* –
to attend to what is broken and undone.
I watch now as the spider unknots itself
slowly, and elbows out of the dark.

ROBIN ROBERTSON

Unknown

As we know,
there are known knowns.
There are things we know we know.
We also know
there are known unknowns.
That is to say
we know there are some things
we do not know.
But there are also unknown unknowns,
the ones we don't know
we don't know.

DONALD RUMSFELD

In February 2002, Donald Rumsfeld performed an accidental homage to Gertrude Stein at a Department of Defence news briefing, on the right. On the left is an extract from Robin Robertson's poem, 'WEB' (original capitals). Is it possible to write 'WEB' in this way without semantic dissonance? What is Robertson missing? What is successful about 'Unknown'? Slavoj Žižek, in *The Reality of the Virtual*, adds another category to Rumsfeld's list, that of *unknown knowns* as relating to disavowed beliefs. Is this is a useful way of

categorising what is needed for some persistent practices and public expect-
ations of poetry in the UK and wider, relating to the presentation of self? Can
Donald Rumsfeld be considered a more interesting poet than Robin Robertson?
If so, how and why? And what does that say about UK poetics?

*

Dear surface, you are like a water surface and the way it speaks of the river
bottom at the same time as the wind and the moon but is its own place and
its own thing and different when viewed from elsewhere.

*

'A dictatorship would be a heck of a lot easier, there's no question about it.'
George Bush

'I do think that the poorest man in England is not at all bound in a strict
sense to that government that he hath not had a voice to put himself under.'
Col. Rainsborough, *The Putney Debates*, 1647.

'For diplomacy to be effective, words must be credible – and no one can now
doubt the word of America.' George Bush

'By an unfortunate use of the reduplicated plural, the Sussex country people
confuse the ideas of fairies and Pharisees in a most hopeless manner.' Rev. W.
D. Parish, *A Dictionary of the Sussex Dialect*, 1875.

*

The collapse of the liberal classes has historically always presaged spam and a
lot of death.[4]

*

The Department of Culture, Media and Sport.

*

In *New Lines* (1956) Robert Conquest advocated 'a sound and fruitful attitude
to poetry', after the self-expressive 'excesses' of the poetry of the 40s, the
mistake of which generation was to give 'the Id, a sound player on the percussion
side under a strict conductor, too much of a say in the doings of the orchestra
as a whole'. Instead, felt Conquest, a 'new and *healthy* general standpoint...
[demonstrating a] reverence for the real person or event' was required [my
italics]. Robert Conquest is 95. His latest volume is *Blokelore and Blokesongs*.

*

---

[4] Paraphrasing *Death of the Liberal Class*, Chris Hedges, October 2010.

General Reader says 'Eyes forward, quiiiick mArch!' Spam, spam, spam, spam; spam, spam, spam, spam...

*

Dear Marjorie Perloff, you said: 'suppose [instead] we regard "poetry" as the language art, parallel to the composition of music, the making of visual objects, or dance? However original the art work may be, there is a discipline to be learned: a discipline that cannot encompass personal effusions like...the magazine verse that now dominates the poetry scene.'

You also said: 'in the Internet age, where we are at liberty to download such a plethora of texts – to reproduce them, recycle them, change their appearance by altering font, typeface, spacing, size – context and framing become the key elements. The poet's role has become, in the literal sense, that of a *word processor*, finding how best to absorb, recharge, and redistribute the language that is already there...confronted with an unprecedented amount of available text and language...context replaces content as textual determinant.'[5] *Language processor* might be a better term.

*

Dear Denise Riley, you said: 'Unease about the pretension of writing poetry at all is something one expects to find in young poets manifesting itself in violence, obscenity perhaps, and mockery.' These impulses also serve as an extra creative spur to originality.

You also said: 'however much [the poet] strives for originality, she's merely parroting the accumulated insights of others... every time I open my mouth, I'm insinuating myself into some conversation which pre-exists me and to which my contribution is only a rustle of echoes – on paper, which is where we all must live.'[6]

*

Dear Roland Barthes, you said: 'A text is...a multidimensional space in which a variety of writings, none of them original, blend and clash. The text is a tissue of quotations... The writer can only imitate a gesture that is always anterior, never original. His only power is to mix writings, to consider the ones with the others, in such a way as never to rest on any one of them.'[7]

*

So, the 'writer' has in fact becomes an 'editor', of sorts. And the reader is an editor, too.

*

---

[5] 'Towards a Conceptual Lyric', *Jacket*, 28 July 2011.
[6] *The Words of Selves*, 2000.   [7] *Death of the Author*, 1967.

The Editor has read some 1500+ poems written by around 300 poets over the last couple of years in compiling The Anthology. The Anthology reveals the Young Poet is less likely than previously to be concerned with the construction of a coherent assertive character/persona or self with reference to a presumed world of common knowledge. They are more likely to be engaged in conducting linguistic dramatisations or ironisations of the tensions between a notional self and the world. This is a reflexive response to the media-rich world in which they live; its exerted social/corporate pressures. A poetry not attuned to this in some form – not self-conscious as, or at least self-conscious about such processes in, and as they relate to, language – simply feels, exhaustingly, like another attempt to persuade or advertise: Poetry Spam.

*

Tony Lopez described W.S. Graham like this: 'He saw the concept of a coherent self (that which is bound up in consistent chronological narrative) as a problem requiring examination through performance in language.'[8] W.S. Graham and other poets with similar concerns might be set to become more popular.

*

Eddie Izzard in makeup, though blind, can see.

\#

Dear Simon Armitage, yes, all poetry is political, in that it involves a counter-current decision to not be a banker or a lawyer, but consider also arrests without charge ahead of the royal wedding; the crackdown on the Occupy movement, curfews during and force-sales of property ahead of the Olympics; the Cultural Olympiad; 'corporate message', 'defamation', 'marketing', 'sponsors'; consider how the interests of corporate-capitalism select for a state more like China, and less like the UK and the US in the 70s (Zizek). Consider declining literacy rates and civil rights, apathy. Why would anyone write poetry that doesn't question itself and the language it uses?

*

Dear *Star Trek*, why are TV series just not as optimistic any more?

*

Dear Chris McCabe, your two pieces in The Anthology demonstrate political anger, and rebelliousness; they are uncertain, destabilised texts. The location and dates of each are those of the original playhouse and year first performed of

---

[8] 'The Life and Works of W.S. Graham', *Edinburgh Review*, 75, 1987.

the play of each title. There are curious oscillations with players dragged between theatre and street; the desires/anger/concepts of the plays also happen in a 'real' London. Through this and other oscillations – from the 1600s to now, and still further oscillations between Jacobean language and a contemporary/future language of Jacobean influence – a V For Vendetta-style anachronism is at work. In the historical (dis)placement of each poem – the Jacobean Age mixing with modern London and its language of banking and capitalism, and into the future, reworking Jacobean words through modern contexts – a sideways incitement is made to uprising, in the face of corporate ideology (replacing royal or religious) and its greed and corruption. This reminds me of the Fawkesian OWS mask meme. All the while, the speakers are still aware that they're in a play, even as their emotions are killing them, and sometimes confuse their political anger with their sexual/romantic equivalents. They are still fundamentally uncertain texts, aware of themselves as texts, enacting a drama of self, language, text and world.

*

Dear John Wilkinson, the work of young poets in the UK often fits what you describe as *frostwork* poets, frostwork being window glass that is semi-opaque through its decoration. That is, poets whose writing exhibits a sustained balance between linguistic surface and reference to an external or internal world. Clearer referentiality is mostly eschewed as less interesting, cliché, or old-fashioned.[9]

The more linguistically opaque younger poets seem still to remain 'voiced and corporeal' in their linguistic procedures, as opposed to purely textual in the manner Perloff advocates. This seems to characterise a difference between experimental tendencies or trends in US and UK poetry.

Marianne Morris' poems generally enact an expansive tragicomic drama with a presiding fear that somewhere there is a battle being lost. Amy De'Ath's poems have an infectious strut to their turn of line and phrase, and poke fun at and pick and juggle around with the word-stuff of human relationships. Sutherland, Critchley; McCabe, Cremin; many others – their poems variously contain collage and recontextualised text, or mixings of font and size, or generally opaque language, or destabilising or disruptive devices, but, as opposed to the purely text-based experimentalism/conceptualism described by Perloff, their work is still 'voiced and corporeal' in a drama of self-and-language in a recognisably modern world.

*

Dear Patrick Coyle, your work is more directly the sort of language art discussed by Perloff. It is shot through with delights of linguistic coincidence,

---

[9] 'Frostwork and the Mud Vision', *Cambridge Quarterly* (2002), 31 (1).

collisions, sense-making, and formal discoveries from textual play. It joyfully enacts a self-and-language in the world. But it still remains voiced, not purely textual. Dear Patrick Coyle you are also responsible for the fact that the second most common word in The Anthology is 'therefore'.

*

Dear Luke Kennard, you stated in interview that you write out of 'Anger. And wanting to make that anger into something funny.' You describe using 'a fairytale-like [quality] to comment on society.' (*Observer*, 2007) Frequently highlighted is your poetry's surreal, or absurdist, aspects; commonly overlooked is its political thrust. Your ironic lyric modulates between manic despair and personal farce in response to a world of maddening or tyrannical forces. It constructs and popul-ates a surreal, humorist mise-en-scène as a reflexive poetic gesture designed to reassert personal responsibility or agency in a reductive, relativist modern world. This ironic, absurdist bent, when married to more traditional poetic forms, in effect parodies them. This succeeds in redefining the poet's 'identity'. It pulls faces in poetic 'identities' assumed for the 'identity parade'. You are reflexively reclaiming the terms of your social 'packaging' and role, and establishing your own.

*

'Rather a Few Mistakes than Fucking Boredom.' Tom Raworth.[10]

*

'If a new reader were to open your book at this poem, and say: 'Mr Ashbery, this is stranger than I had ever imagined any poem to be. Where do I begin? Can you lead me into it, please?' What would you say to that?'

'Well,' says John, staring and staring at his handiwork, 'I'm frequently asked that question, and... I'd just tell him to sort of read it if it seems to interest him, and not worry about what it means. Perhaps it will all mean something when he's finished – or some time later...'

And what sort of meaning would that be if and when the reader finally chanced upon it?

He sighs with a heartfelt, let-this-cup-pass-from-me-Lord sigh. 'It's very hard for me to say since I'm not the reader, you see. I often wish I could have a perspective on my own work. We all long to see ourselves as others see us – which, unfortunately, is not possible. Or perhaps fortunately...' [11]

*

---

[10] *Windmills in Flames: Old and New Poems*, 2010. [11] The Luscious Dependability of Chocolate Shrimps' http://www.bowwowshop.org.uk/page5.htm

The Anthology thinks using Facebook and Twitter a lot also makes people more aware of text and self as performance.

*

Spam
Poets
After
Meaning

*

'Many still believe… that thinking in images… is the chief characteristic of poetry. Consequently, they should have expected the history of "imagistic art", as they call it, to consist of a history of changes in imagery. But we find that images change little; from century to century, from nation to nation, from poet to poet, they flow on without changing… The more you understand an age, the more convinced you become that the images a given poet used and which you thought his own were taken almost unchanged from another poet… The works of poets are classified or grouped according to the new techniques that poets discover and share, and according to their arrangement and development of the resources of language; poets are much more concerned with arranging images than with creating them.' Viktor Shklovsky, 1917.[12]

'Nothing changes from generation to generation except the thing seen and that makes a composition.' Gertrude Stein, 1925.[13]

'With nothing can one approach a work of art so little as with critical words: they always come down to more or less happy misunderstandings.' Rainer Maria Rilke, *Letters to a Young Poet*, 1902-1908.

#

'Psychoanalysis should be the science of language inhabited by the subject. From the Freudian point of view man is the subject captured and tortured by the language.' Jacques Lacan.[14]

*

Eddie Izzard, in Tesco, foresuffered all.

*

---

[12] 'Art as Technique', translated by Lee T Lemon & Marion J. Reis in 1925, reprinted in David Lodge, ed., *Modern Criticism and Theory: A Reader*, 1988. [13] Composition as Explanation, 1925. [14] *The Seminars of Jacques Lacan*, 1968.

Advertising (perhaps 'the' mainstream media) often ironises its own attempt to manipulate or persuade; is already 'self-conscious' as well as outward-facing and engaged in the contemporary moment. That advertising in general could be a step ahead of the normalised practice of poetry in the UK, instead of the other way round, is a major cultural failure (but not necessarily a poetic failure).

*

Has there been a time when poetry was potentially more important? And, yet, perhaps not coincidentally, has there been a time when the disjunction between the public image of it, and its actual uses and practices, has been so marked?

*

Poets aren't able to talk publicly about themselves and their chosen artform without articulating this in terms other media are prepared to accept. Consider much of the BBC's Poetry Season of 2009: the preponderance of rural or coastal scenes in which poets spoke wetly of memory and emotion and of 'finding the right words to express'; poets talking straight to camera with furrowed brow, or, worse, actors doing so for them. Rarely, if at all, did it present a proper debate about poetry, other than about its demise or not (both implying a demise). The level of discussion about 'modern-ness', or 'relevance', rarely rose above such observations as the fact that mobile phones or computers or comics or brands are now being mentioned in poems. Or that poetry connects us to history (without an examination of whether that is always A Good Thing). Or that poets sometimes use Facebook or the internet like *normal people*. Compare this with the modern art world: its theories and ideas are generally engaged with in public through a response to a specific piece of artwork; to acclaim or outrage, either way, the terms are that of the concept and what it might, or might not, mean. Perhaps this is because the visual art object is more easily commodifiable, and so fits with the commodified everyday.

*

Things have gone too far when you encounter the slogan 'keeps the body warm' in a jaunty font next to the corporate logo on a recently redundant, state-funded, life-support machine. At what point does marketing become psychological abuse?

*

Late Beastie Boys member Adam Yauch has used his will to stop people from using his music or image in advertising.

It read: 'Notwithstanding anything to the contrary, in no event may my image or name or any music or any artistic property created by me be used for advertising purposes.'

The phrase 'or any music or any artistic property created by me' was added in handwriting.[15]

*

Fuck off, pantywaist hedge-funders, the Republican party, evil corporations – get out of my fucking face, I'm trying to watch TV.

*

Dear World, The Anthology thinks you should sue Saatchi & Saatchi for depression.

*

Pussy Riot, I almost cannot see you because of the Olympics. Syria, the Olympics has blocked out the sun, where are you?

\#

Now crowd-sourcing and collaboration is easier, it is difficult to justify not doing it when compiling The Anthology. If you are not doing it, The Anthology would like to know why.

*

The Anthology is collaborative: a first wave of poets asked to provide work were asked also for three nominations, based on 'gut instinct' of who 'had' to be included. These nominations were asked for work and three further nominations. The final group were asked to provide work and no nominations.

Some poets declined to offer nominations. Others offered 50 +. Some 6, some 4... In each case, 3 were taken. Some poets came up more than others. Eventually the recommendations gave the sense of a 'landscape' having more or less defined its own boundaries. This was the theory.

*

The practice deviated. Poets were discovered by accident. The Editor tweaked and fiddled, selected, interfered and corrupted, as editors do. Anyone receiving more than 2 nominations was approached for work. Some stumbled upon were still asked for nominations. Some who received only 1 nomination were not approached. For various reasons, both wrong and sound, others were.

Participants were asked to try and avoid second-guessing or conferring on who had been selected or contacted already. A few, or many, did not stick to

---

[15] BBC News website, August 2012.

this. Some flounced and denounced and refused in response, others thought it a good idea.

*

In a lot of cases it was surprising how few poets knew about poets other than themselves and two or three friends. If they like each other's poetry, poets tend to end up friends.

*

'An anthology' is awkward to say.

*

Saying The Anthology is an anthology of the 'best young poets' is also awkward to say, for different reasons: the terms of that assessment remain invisible and bias is hidden from the uninitiated. This takes away the terms of discernment from the reader and makes them, essentially, passive consumers of a hidden editorial agenda.

So, this is NOT an anthology of the *best young poets* in the UK.

This is as good an anthology of good poetry being written by as varied a group of poets and poetries as The Editor could have compiled currently and in the time given and for the money paid. That seems fair.

*

This text thinks /
it would be better /
with hyperlinks.

*

The Anthology is described as containing work from young poets in the UK. The Anthology includes work from poets born, or stationed, overseas. The Anthology challenges a notion of UK poetry as parochial. The Anthology represents what and who young poets in the UK are reading as well as what they are writing.

The Anthology has broken most of its own rules. The Anthology grew from a series of *young poetry* features for *The Rialto*, the guideline age for which was 35 (based on spurious neurological notions). In deciding to follow poets' own recommendations, The Anthology has included people *as old as 37*. In short, The Anthology stopped caring. 'In the UK and more or less 35 when *The Rialto* feature started' just about covers it. But also doesn't. The Anthology remains unconcerned.

*

Dear Stranger in the restaurant the other night: Actually, poetry *does* make things happen. We know from neuroscience that reading a text, or interacting with language, causes changes in the brain. Thought patterns are wired and rewired through neurones forming and reforming and reinforcing neural pathways based on a brain's regular activity patterns. A behaviour, a habit, a pattern of thought, a personality, can be rewired. It is a process called 'neural plasticity' attaching to cognitive behavioural therapy. An art that creates new links between words, disrupts old links, reworks ideas, dismantles clichés, or received histories, or highlights latent biases in language, can therefore *literally* and physically change, however slightly, a mind. It can liberate.

*

Karaoke: a portmanteau and a form of interactive entertainment or video game in which amateur singers sing along with recorded music.

*

The Anthology is polyphonic. The Anthology is a collage of different, or opposing, voices, some enhanced by The Anthology, others working with or against The Anthology. The Anthology does not await the anointment of a Great Poet of The Age to speak for it. The Anthology believes this is an old way of thinking critically in the UK informed by the nation's attachment to monarchic ideology/Ted Hughes. The Anthology will have none of that Spam.

*

'I have gathered a posie of other men's flowers, and nothing but the thread that binds them is my own.' Montaigne, 1533-1592.

*

This crispy mandarin orange chicken says 'I'm meat free!' Why would anyone want to eat this? It is both vicious and sanitised.

*

Eddie Izzard in a dress saying 'BUnch of flowerrrrrs!'

ÉIREANN LORSUNG

The Book of Splendor

Egg cartons encrusted with gilt.
In the last days of the last emperor, the tsarina trains ermines.
They wind about her feet as she walks.
Everything that lives in those rooms to be beheaded.

While we believe silver we paint scenes inside perfume bottles.
Our century hands illuminate the margins of everything.
We use radium to paint our tongues.

We find certain series more useful than others.
The four colors of the off-air signal and the semaphore that keeps airplanes up.

Inside the book things are starting to move.
There's no Poland where there was a Poland. There's no sash
           on the tsarina's chest.
Wind ignores the book.
Birds won't touch it.

Come on, the book says. As though it knows what it's waiting for.

The book knows there's something coming.
Our parents' births hover over us like dirigibles.

The 20th Century strikes a match.

Grey Century

On the first grey morning of the grey century
spiders have put webs on the windows.

By the time you wake up the morning procedures
are going on. A tiny forest of cyclamens

in the backyard. You can't say, Did I sleep
for a hundred years? You know that's ludicrous.

The milkman looks at you funny.
The century wants you to enjoy the little plants

that flower in the shape of ghosts. It hates
to remind you everyone you used to love is dead.

Pink list

When I make lists of names, I dread the ones I forget.
ÉDOUARD LEVÉ

Pink a condition of the text, not a particularly *feminine* condition
in the sense that feminine said that way is originary, fixed, and becomes
        necessary of us.
The common expansion of the thing in an uncontainable fashion.

*

I'm running my hands over the bodies of Roland Barthes and Jacques Derrida,
same hands that picked strawberries in a field in eastern Minnesota
next to a girl I'll call Chelsie.

I'm running through the corn in St Paul at midnight with boys whose names
are a mystery to me now, next to whom I slept, with whom I ate,
whose music I stole.

In a red smock I am touching the bodies of Roberto Bolaño and Haruki Murakami,
Jean-Michel Maulpoix, Walter Benjamin, Cummings, Rilke, Nabokov, Proust.
In a gray smock I am touching Marc Chagall.

A girl with vines in her hair accompanies me. I call her *S*.

*

I put my hands in the jar of honey.
I walk through the old orchards calling for the ones I know.
Things in flower: clover, lavender, thyme, rosemary, black locust,
        alfalfa, linden, appletrees,

hawthorn, goldenrod, eucalyptus, heather, tea-trees, musk thistle,
      tulip-trees, sage, tupelo.

The bees are coming in and out as they like, teaching me how to be in the world.

*

Condition of the text perpetual forgery.
Intercession, a woman in a long turquoise dress wearing the sun on her head.
I'm running my fingers through their words, the woman's words.

Pink an indelible fruit, entrail of the world.
Among women. Entre les fruits de ses entrails.

*

I've been paying attention to embroidery on plain houses here.
When I said feminine before I meant something I'm not sure you can understand.

*

In a hallway I stood under a chandelier and Caroline climbed a ladder
to pick the big, round crystals like it was a fruit tree.

*

I'm hoping that the poets and other people in the world will
find time to fall in love more than once and *not* descend the basement stairs

saying they've forgotten something, and shoot themselves in the head
while outside the rare blush dogwood blooms a pale peach like the inside of a leg.

Pink the almond trees blooming, and constellations.
Pink in your old photograph, the one in which you are already certainly dead.

*

What would I give up in order for this to happen?
– A narrow bed covered in quilts in a single room.

Pink is the solitude of being in love or of being alone,
the bed with quilts and books or a bigger bed.

JAMES WILKES

Welcome to the Show

ladies and gentlemen
please give it up
ladies and gentlemen
your cause is lost
please give it up
please give it a warm reception
ladies and gentlemen
to the jury
to what you're about to hear
playing live
in the theatre-on-the-air
ladies and germs
i'm sorry the atmospherics
atrocious tonight
the atmosphere
let me try to convey this to you
the crowds
the baying
the anticipation
the laurels
the atmosphere
electric
a kind of green / greyish-green soup
a sort of cloud if you will
connected to everyone else
in this world and beyond
if you can just picture it

we are speaking to you
from the future
from the fireside
from the bottom of our hearts
from a bunker several miles
beneath the smoking ruins
of chicken cottage
on Tottenham Court Road

as was
from one machine to another
from the cosmic ether
from beyond
we are speaking to you
yes, just you
from the wireless operator's cabin
in a small caravan
on the Isle of Sheppey
from a cottage inside the woods
from chicken cottage, as was
please give it up

this is the future speaking
if we knew then
what we know now
we would never have done
what we did
but we didn't

so welcome all
to this tiny independent
nation of sound
dreadful atmospherics
you can almost picture us
if you will
in a tiny radio shack
pitching and yawing
in extra-territorial waters
please extend your hand
of friendship
and lend us your ears
the res publica
of the air
so breathe

i repeat
rabies and settlement
what you're about to hear
i'm sorry
the heavy pressure tonight
lets me converse this with you
the crowds

the chickens
the payday
the payday
the antiseptic
the antique sovereign
the lawless atmosphere
you can just pinch it
we are speaking to you
from the frontline
from the fume cupboard
from the bottom of our listening wells
several miles from the surface
and naked to the stars
which are hard radio
if you will

and if we weep then
what we weep now
we would never have bleeped
what we bleeped
but we bleeped
i repeat

germs and coagulants
from the bottom of our arteries
from our widest res publica
what you're about to hear
is a sovereign nation
is a tiny airspace
freaking and jawing
around its own axis
is a smoking ruin
connected to other
smoking ruins
we make no apologies
only I'm sorry
it's the ether talking
after the news
the atmosphere
atrocious tonight
so lend us your wireless
so hades and betterment
so breathe

must i repeat
germs and jellytots
our jurisdiction's limited
a sort of theatre if you will
atrocious cruelty
atrocious mercy
please extend the band
playing live tonight
and air's running out
the payday
the payday
listening well
we are speaking to you
the future is a sealed chamber
connected to everyone
who's given it up
if we do next
what we do now
if we welcome the dreadful
atmospherics
of hard radio
of wireless organ
of breathe and breathe
of listening post
of buried bunker
of tiny speaking
of atrocious sound
of coming up next

so breathe

RUE

i got the virgin squints
in the rue garden
in beaconsfield
eating with strangers
and dear friends
the newly pregnant
clamber over each other
away over the grass
we blotch with pleasure
keeping our capillaries
trim & laughing
painters of bluish-green
& greenish-yellow
light, for friendship
& grace of evening seen
clear in the herb patch

Radio Margate

Dreamland burned down. The dreams of Dreamland burnt too. I tried explaining the penny arcade to my hunting pack. They snapped and they clinkered and one by one they died. Ranter and Ringwood, Bellman and True.

Oto   Petr   Božena   Ypsilon   František   Oto

Radio rust over Dreamland, over. Shortwave static grows through the scaffold of the coaster tracks, propagates slowly in the evening tide. Echoes of the ghost train. Right well I served my master, said the voice.

Zola   Frederik   Yvonne   Arthur   Qualite   Telefoon

One voice from the bunker. Female uninflected, smudged by atmospherics, generated by machines. Whiskey stained. Foxtrot and tango as sprung dance-floors into powder. Dreamland attracted over two million visitors a year. Perhaps

Two   Two   Six   Two   Eight   Eight

Dreamland attracted me. As you will plainly hear, smudged by sunspots. In the public language of numbers, though this is not, shall we say, for public consumption. I spent many nights here as a young buck.

Lorenzo José   Francia   Kilo   Inés   Yegua

Perhaps fifty times larger than a man, Dreamland was potential. Its ruins lie all around us, in burnt out sierras, of dandelion, sorrel, jack-by-the-hedge. I tried explaining seaside architecture to a dead gull. From its bill whispered Kursaal, Washington, Hotel, Napoli.

Palermo York   Torino   Livorno   Xilófono   York

Poaching the ruins for steel struts and coddling them for coaster rails. Dreamland was a controlled explosion. Dreamland was my delight. I tried to explain this to the numbers as they pulsed over water and tangled in the scaffold. Dreamland burned down. Dreamland burned down. Dreamland burned down.

Niklas Sigurd   Erik   Ludvig   Tore   Bertil

TOM WARNER

Magician

After dropping in a second fizz of Alka-Seltzer,
I hold the glass to the kitchen's fluorescent tube
and ask myself why on earth I carry on with this
in our age of mentalists, reality shows and rolling news.

The magic's gone. A puff of smoke: the primetime slots,
the hairspray, the sold-out nights at the Albert Hall,
assistants with high-cut legs and spangled jackets,
and one last bow to the minor royal in the Royal Box.

From here on in, it's gigs that smell of squash and biscuits,
and mornings with eyes a shade of Hammer-Horror-red.
One of these days I'll shave the 'tache, ditch the wig,
and write my resignation to the Circle in invisible ink,

then run a finger along the guillotine's razor edge,
push a hand through the air beyond to demonstrate
the honesty of the trick (one last time, for old time's sake),
before lying down beneath that fucking blade.

Day Thirty-two

More wrecked fuselage washed up this morning.
Biggest section yet, like a whale carcass in the breakers.
There's a corpse still belted in a seat, the face bloated
in its oxygen mask. He has a beard. None of us recognises him.

Jane's still not talking. Mainly she cries and hugs her knees.
When she really gives it some, her shoulders shake slightly.
She's sunburnt raw and her lips are scabby and dry.
I've moved my shelter further down the beach.

Marcus spells out HELP in rocks on the white sand.
Filippo says it should be SOS. The universal sign for distress
is actually a large triangle; I know this but don't say.
I read it once on MSN; *How to survive a desert island.*

Rev. Biddle is losing weight, but remains a true believer.
His sermons are beginning to chew at people's nerves.
I don't fancy his chances, not long term.
Since Bryony ran off into the trees, nobody's seen her.

Marcus came over today to ask how I was getting on
with that radio set. It's going to take some time, I said.
Salt has eaten at the circuit board. I must have looked the part,
wearing the big headphones like I was trawling interference

for a voice, a signal, anything (*are you there, survivors?*).
Truth is, I've got the Test Match on. It's the second day
and we're batting well, but I keep it to myself, obviously.
When rain stops play, I listen to commentators filling air

and whittle at the bails I'm carving from a piece of driftwood.
Sometimes I lie back with one hand under my head,
like a gorilla in a zoo, and think of my red-faced boss
clearing my desk and struggling to cover the hours I've left.

The Levy of Distress

Whether he comes as a woman or she comes as a man,
do not open the door to the bailiff.

Do not bring in the horse the bailiff trundles up the path.
Do not eat the glassy seeds dripped through the letter box.

Do not believe the bailiff's eely words;
the bailiff does not love you.

The bailiff cannot cross the threshold without invitation,
but once across all things the bailiff brushes are lost.

Do not open the door even though the bailiff answers
your dove with a hawk, your hare with a hound.

Sunlight and Rain

They drove in silence
and brightness of dawn.

They drove in the strobe
of dawn bright in trees.

They drove in brightness
through brightness

into a whale like a storm
like clouds humped black
at the motorway's end.

They drove in silence
and brightness
and blackness
into a whale
into rain as fat as pennies

into the white noise of rain
as fat as pennies
into the static fuzz of rain
and brightness
where flyovers were gasps
in the white noise of rain as fat as pennies
gobfuls of air
grabbed in the grapple of drowning
in the white noise fuzz
of rain as fat as pennies.

They drove in silence
over miles of worn pelts and feather
flattened beneath a black anvil of cloud.
They drove in silence and rain

through silver pennies
and smudged pelts
into the gape of a whale

and a crushed wing
lifted in their windy wake

turn around
come back.

ÁGNES LEHÓCZKY

Rememberer
(Nagyszüleimnek)

They warned you about the edges of the season, of the next on its way. About rims of the months, the years, fictitious, nearly impalpable. They muttered words about margins. About the stimulus it takes to cross them, the spur of inching from one season into the next without any drastic alterations, grotesque metamorphoses. The tattered body of the old summer boat reeled smoothly through the water a few metres above an underground city shaped geometrically like the river, curling like your own meanderings across another city built overground on hot tarmac. You scanned passing landscapes through the dis-coloured windows of the boat, pages of what's outside, folios of the hour, coated and folded like an architectural ghost, a geometrical memoir of tarred rooflines, manuscripts scraped off and used again, marks of removed stairways, dust-lines of former wholeness. Shadows of floorboards pared pale yellow as hot sand. Static and moving your face conversed with the filthy glass as the hydrofoil trickled the water down out of the season like a hollow shell, a curled up carapace of an insect, a metal cocoon with two rudimentary wings, two antennae on each side, stroking the surface of its own liquefied context. Its diluted circumstance. Shedding quiet conversations about the sudden ending of summers. You then learnt their conversations by heart, unfinished sentences about approaching hot Septembers, floating down the millennium old sky, the river, the city, the body. Under railway bridges and over deck bridges passing by abandoned boatyards cramped with dysfunctional kayaks, superfluous mops and buckets, paddles with chipped blades, peeling gloss. One envies the mouldy patience of these shed-objects, the apathy of summer and winter bric-à-brac. Their idle being there. But then one envies the river diver too. His sporadic rota of diving underworld, down into another labyrinthine city. The cryptic wealth and the riches he finds underwater. Digging through the impenetrable, the strata of dusked river beds. Lost key rings, forint coins tangled with river weeds and moss, wire hair combs, rust-eaten compasses, sunken yachts, empty telephone boxes reeking of once raucous messages imparted in immaterial moments, their inaudible hieroglyphs, the objects' danse macabre, their un-corrodable presence. And then the bones. The skulls. Inhabited by snails and river worms. The abstract carcasses of the once anthropomorphic. It took you one never-ending hour to float down the Danube from one point of the city to another, from one gangboard to the next. To comprehend the caesura between two sentences, the glottal pause you take half a breath before exchanges of seasons. Bare footed, you hopped off the deck. Leather sandals in hand. How long is this river? you asked them, and held the sandals up in the air. You'd once seen this in a fresco of a high ceiling, an old man holding up his flayed skin in his right hand. You hoped one day he would tell you about what he could remember. About the syntax-less second when it reverses into artless forgetfulness. About the distance between the body and its long wintershadow, between the skin and the glossy album, the deck and the land. The late night walk back home led you across the aqueduct. Heading towards the city. Metre by metre trudging above the debris of the river, above cardboard corpses quietly flowing down the liquefied city. The day was as complete as the first pear of the autumn. (The water police was searching for someone. They mistook the body of a seal for the man's who had gone missing, here and there occasionally emerging on the surface of the sea. From a distance the body looked substantial, its glossy skin now and then shimmering on the water in the winter sun. You photographed maps of yellow lichens unfurled on rocks, brown bladderwracks washed out by the tide, entangled with themselves. Beyond the multiplied horizon red and blue cargo ships were queuing. After circulating for an hour, the lifeboats, one by one, vanished from the view.) Then deliberating between a plum poppy seed pie and a pudding sundae you overheard newer configurations of former conversations, their familiar anxieties of running out of words, running out of the season. Hiding in tiny patisseries from the heat these were soundless whispers about comets' swift departures. Your face smeared in the glass case, jammed between towering tortas, mini Kugler mignons and pompous rows of bonbons, then all at once faded in the thick aroma of freshly ground Karaván coffee. Invisible, you eavesdropped as usual on the small talks of cafeterias. On choices between the seasonal and the static, between wintering and migrating. The key is to have a companion as an alibi for walking solitarily, they said. Perhaps a small black dog or a ghost. For one's manic pursuit of nameless courtyards and cobbled cul-de-sacs. Assembled, like small stacks of autumnal flora, they talked about lacks, puffs of nothing, regurgitating air bubbles, memories of draughty stairways and dark elevator shafts. Souvenirs of the millennium shrouded with dark linen. They gathered together with anatomy transparent. They spoke with coarse voices, conversed with anaemic lips. They listened with elastic lobes stretched by heavy silver earrings for many years plaiting otherworldly tête-à-têtes about the heat that flooded those late summer city afternoons. That brimmed over the rims of porcelain. They predicted one everlasting summer storm, they said it was on its way. Then their words died away into quiet murmurs about lichthofs and enormous fire walls exposed vertically to the world. Silhouettes of ghost trams, their ostentatious midnight apparitions every winter clad in a thousand silver light bulbs. But these tête-à-têtes weave the vegetation of the world, you decided. Because it's hard to dig through the stratigraphy of fallen leaves, the thick autumnal carpets of camouflaged inhabitants forever dormant, pupa, cocoons, bugs, bones, mud, carapace, carcass, mud, then carapace again. To learn dimming evening horizons by heart and then remember the courtyard where they were last enclosed. Faces you are unlikely to find in morning mirrors, copper-coloured mascaras washed away by the turbulence of late summer storms erasing contours, breaking bones, filtering through the calcium of words. That night, as they'd foretold, the sky cracked open and drowned the city, flooding the fin-de-siècle firewalls, dawn-lit corridors, alleyways and elevator shafts, pouring the pitch black night into ear tunnels, throat tunnels, arteries as hot lead. Into canals of maps. Scaring crow families off the tops of gigantic silver birches. These clumsy birds help to step over thresholds, they said, into new nightscapes already forgotten. These details, the crows, the umbrellas, the twilight lamp posts, the half-dead light bulbs: are all necessities of the coming season. Museal cityscapes of reminiscing, quilted then unravelled into newer patterns. The abandoned circus sites after rain, the watered-down merry-go-rounds, the other-worldliness of shooting galleries, the plastic puppets' reluctance to perform, to play, to remember anything at all. An old regime's peeling hotels, pale ochre. Graffitied changing cabins with eternal rhetorical questions: 'meet me here tomorrow and tell me, how I will get from the North Pole to the South, what I mean is from one inch to the next without you.' After a lightning followed by the familiar thunder, the city tilted from the tropic of Capricorn toward the tropic of Cancer. You found the bus stop in the end after the first downpour. It stood there stagnant, between two thunders and a lightning. You were left to climb the last hundred muddy metres on foot. The elderly up there talked with inconsolable fear. They lived above sea-level, town-level, above world-level. Beyond the white house only the layered velvety texture of dark green conifers. Around the trunks small heaps of pine cones. They complained about dysfunctional doorbells and the tautology of sudden summer storms. About visitors who would lose patience and give up waiting on their doorsteps. Then they sent you away loaded with their early autumn harvest, grapes and plums, pears and pallid pumpkins. One morning, you said, all grandmothers' faces would slowly turn into stones. Then into torsos. Their skin would peel off, like yellow cities' walls, crumbling tufa, colourless ash. These stone-faces would one day charge you with their own continuous existence, their staying here, pottering about on the top of the hill, warming their thin lilac veins in the winter sun, prehistoric fossils, sundried lizards, forgotten parchments. Trudging in puddles of fallen leaves, discarded cocoons of former homes, you left the hill with the first pear of the season rolling down three hundred metres of copper-coloured clay accompanied by solo dog barks and the sharp whistle of wind. Downtown. Fishing for the deposits of the river in your palm to find out if memories had bones. Under-water. On your way across the green cast iron bridge a grand piano blocked the pavement. Residues of the busker's melody, wet trunks, water rats and corpses, dark bodied ducks, slooshed down the river spinning in oily currents for seconds before they vanished. These residues anchor this bottomless city, she said. She had a piece of old cardboard with a message: 'You can play the most daring combination of cacophonic planets.' It was radiating like the early morning news warning the entire capital of constellation Perseus. That night the sky would drop meteor showers, rain clutter of a thousand year old dust of the solar system. The air one breathes in every second in downtown. One must look upward toward the North and wait for the comet to pass by like a sudden flock of swifts or late night bats which touch the top of skulls but intend no harm. Nuclei composed of rock. Of rock faces. Faces of rocks, dust, water ice and frozen gases. These faces are tens of kilometres long. Faces of giants. This means that the winter would be long – perhaps thousands or even millions of years far out in the cold dark of interstellar space. (And you spotted winter on the bridge for a second and saw it arriving in cargo wagons driven by wordless train drivers pulling heavy tons from one season into another through a snowed-up continent. With faces lit up every time they pulled into a station.) Slices of summer melons swam down the river between the two far ends of Europe. And you thought of the hill, the liquefied afternoons you spent with them levitating a few hundred metres above the city. But what does one do with these unidentifiable details? you urged them. The Budapest parks, evaporating. The nameless omens scattered under arches of aqueducts, the small, fictitious failures. Green girder railway bridges arced under skies cracked open. Dogs' midnight panic after each thunder and lightning. Child- hoods' sleepwalking among dusty attic objects. Have you been venturing in a panoptikum or a planetarium all this time? (The bonnet of the old Mercedes crumpled under the weight of the sky at dawn.) They said some sentences eventually would have to be erased. Then they recalled the hot yellow sand of old vines, threshers, creaking road rollers. What language were they remembering in the end? Did they in fact say anything at all? Under dark green conifers. Descending the hill you hid a cone in your pocket and turned round. Their prophecies drifted into blurring figurines of bronzed autumn parks. Their silhouettes crumbled into two small heaps of tufa, loess then clay warm and sundried like the deck you stood on barefoot flowing down the Danube for an hour, almost eternal.

Balaton 2: *Spiral*

We spent the very last hour of the day under an unreal starry sky. A dizzy experience. A kind of dying: of fright. Upwards. Imagine vertigo, in reverse. But was it us or the planets who felt lightheaded that night? You say, we too are made of the same solar material. Of the same chewy red clay. The spiral in our lives, you say, is so obvious that one must be blind not to see it meandering whirling the deposits of years, silts of belated afterthoughts. Look at the web of helices braiding the young and the old. Did you know? That even stars and snails have something in common? It is in this land's curling characteristics, domes of basilicas, flights of stairs, layers of geology, chalk, bath stone, basalt, slate, lava, tufa, dolomite, calcium, magnesium carbonate, loess, silt, wind-blown, the abbey in front of us with two spinning spires, your whirling visits to the Copenhagen port, the Copenhagen you, the 'you' you could have been, the you 'you' passed by twenty five years after you passed by the Copenhagen port twenty-five years ago, this zigzagging to and fro and up and down. Did you know that in this lake Central-Europe drowned? Imagine Central-Europe as a water corpse. And, in search of the minute worn-crested Miocene shell, the tiny crescent nail of a goat, *Congeria ungulacaprae*, we dive down to the bottom of its basin with the children, for the tiny skeleton of the shouting girl, the water corpse of her shepherd and the bones of the shepherd's thousand golden haired goats, lost in the bottom of some kind of a hollow and concave vessel. They say they had turned into loess, basalt, magnesium carbonate, lava, tufa in the end. Then they turned into an abbey. Then into a manuscript, old and long-forgotten. Then into a bishop. We are made of remnants of each other. If you pass by this lake at night-time, you'll see an empty eye, as gigantic as the universe. This eye is a city made of endless stairways, a city which had long been drowned. Around it flickering houses and clapping sailing boats encompass its bright black pupil. Their chime is metallic as the boats in a bay of the North Sea. If quieter. Look, this snail, the one with the round mouth, is crawling onto this page, leaving a vapour trail across the paper.

phantom poem

(in conversation with Geraldine Monk)

one midsummer night   she says   carrying
a huge grey bird on the sleeve of her mac
(darling – it's a barred owl *strix varia* in *other*
words) we saw a dark colossus descending over
that hedge   the silhouette of an old aeroplane
    lights on the wings each cabin lit up
flying so close to earth – to us   nearly touching
the hair on our skull   that   we thought it
was doomed to crash into the moors   I am
sure   she adds   *I saw* what I saw   I *saw*
propellers simultaneously still   *and*   rotating
can you *imagine* she gesticulates with the globe-
eyed bird   claws caught in the coat
and not *only* that but   *the*-de-*de*-de f*o*g moment
when the giant faded   like people *do*   into
forests or behind *moons* as quiet as a   mouse

AMY EVANS

Collecting Shells

as if trying on comforts,
       relationship-brittle,
a sturdy skin of similes
       similars an only
path through what is: so hard
       it is mute

*

see sure...

*

look(ing), glass only
       just emerged
blown   upon an out-breath   *sigh*,
       as if, when you too quickly cool (grow
cold), I'll shatter
       in an in-
breath *gasp*   no (longer) matter

*

family, huddled left margin
       as [9 or so] thumbnails on a screen,
as if [12] years of silence in the hard [copy] world
       could be [naught: 0]   ether
-ial steps heavy from either
       sighed in the social engine
gathered herd   numb:erred

*

what word-burrowing to unfurrow
     brow   via typo over volition   [*ovulation* ~
ova revelation] I resist the *wed* in *we'd*
     and try not to scoff when I [don't] find
earning in *learning*

*

     yet the centre
of a flower
     will unfeasibly turn to fruit, straw–
or someberry burst forth further
     than anything that worries of,
     knows, its
shape

*

and she-blossom, a child
     's rank breath on waking,
like inhaled knowledge: of her poverty
     – strangled as
she hangs herself
     round my neck –
I too stir
     to the rarity of fetid intimacy

*

as if *shell* is not a word for
     the sheath of that which is
b u l l e t
     and can be spent

*

soft rubbing cleverness
        of skin as it blisters
but does not split
        spitting forth fluid only
when forced,
        happy to bud or burst:
options before breakage,
        when pushed

*

and the simple shout
        ing of love
AS IF
        annoyance: NO[,] EXI[S]T
the only [st]utterance

*

This, my a(r)mour:
        an accretion
of misguarded splendours
        rendered silent :text
/ure. Touch ing perhaps, when
        surface
only sufficed, but grown
        harder : still
to that touch. Such
        creaturing   :   I

*

      acknowledge mine, a home,
at the least, a shore. Seen
      wrack
as the scene as
      if gone back
and back for more,

  *

      [left
with less]

  *

     t i r e d a l,
whoreding treasures
    she'll-like
         drift *would*
: matterial

ANDREW BAILEY

Delight

Dear you, delight, feed me delight. You were
supposed to love me, lovely stuff, and you're a lie.
Swimming with small arms through this tenth-
best world I am soft, little kraken of me, short
of a casing. There's no such place as Super Mario World
or Paris, the least you could do is exist. Such games,
such music, and and and. And love despite. Andrew x

She is quite joyous, exploding on radio stations
everywhere. Tomorrow's beauty is significantly larger
and more universal; she represents the life force,
pointing to a glass of before. In Milky Way,
my appetite unspoiled, I have become the couple,
lucky and private. Reality shows multiply,
mobile conversations blare, secrets are
to talk about. I am soft, I am fine, dressed
in celestial sea. Stars. Starfish. Lovely stuff.

That we are, loving rats marooned
from her performance as if by sea, she is
the shore and I tweet our atomised
telegraphic contact. Delight on delight, no I want
to hear seagulls somewhere around me.

Dorodango

I was engrossed in mud balls
when it came upon me, how
the strong attachment to the ball
I was making, how the act
of making, makes us one. We
must, say specialists, understand the forces

that lead to a Big Ball
of Mud. My name is man,
clay, one can place too much
stress on personal relationships. I am,
indeed, having a ball. Some children
devote themselves to making them; feelings,
say the specialists, may change once
you leave them somewhere. Never, then,
let them go, leave them skulking
in a drawer like rescue cats
avoiding hope and thus disappointment – there
is always finer dust, this is
the code, always a smoother surface.
When I have somewhat different feelings
I turn to clay, ask it
why? When I dreamed I dreamt
the same, stuff and wet everything,
a casually haphazard structure. The forces
once understood may be resolved in
alternative ways, neither sweat nor attention
need be craft though they may
seem so. To make is always
to change, say, handfuls of mud
to cabochons shined in their dust;
I am one who has specialised
in high level software architecture, who
has observed the irredeemable, insoluble soil.
Who has rolled his dorodango dry.

Lit

I tell you what I saw last night; I saw a man with a cigarette get stopped by a
man without and asked if he could sell a cigarette to the second, and he smiled
and pulled the whole caboodle out, filters papers Cutter's Choice, but he without
said no I cannot, cannot roll. So the one that was with held out the other hand
that had the cigarette in it and gave it, lit, to the other. You're an angel, said
the one now with and the one without now walked off rolling another. I could
extemporise upon this but I leave it with you lit.

JAMES MIDGLEY

Influenza

A cabin breathes above the earth
and a well is for putting into, and drawing nothing.

A tree is a very quiet place for living.

I read that the lyrebird can mimic any sound.
Car alarm and chainsaw surround the wood
and I round upon them.

Nightly imports from floating townships of owls:
I hear inside of inside,
my hearing the smallest matryoshka doll,
and air is influenza.

I reread that the lyrebird has no sound at all
but the voicebox is a vacuum flask, and must be filled:
when it calls, you are already within,
as the dog alarming with barks
brings you to its underworld.

What is seen records what saw it.
I look at the hearth fire until it is tiger

or stir a stick about stirring.
A well shouts into me and listens for the echo.

Mine

> *That which mourns feels itself thoroughly known by the unknowable.*
> WALTER BENJAMIN

Wait long enough and the body is most things

Clothes fitted so close it's like being on fire

To believe in a dynamo concerting elements

To break this rockhead down to constituents

All day looking into the dark
the dark didn't look back

Other than: here is my carbon,
my ticking springwater

Other than: that's the mind's closed circuit,
no? thought as the opposably thumbed-in eye

There they are pulling something up in a harness
which slips out before reaching the light

The Invention of Faces

Do you remember the invention of faces?
Someone does but it's no longer me.

These celluloids washed against the beach
like jellyfish.

Remember the boy lifting food to a mouth
and finding none,

opal grapes shed upon a board before him,
a fish looking surprised.

Remember the woman combing her hair,
a mirror making a displaycase of her features

and the brush's needles knowing and reknowing.
So the eye bloats

and the sun's atavistic orb flexes and focuses.
So the mouth is an apple's afterthought.

Recall with me: silhouette and knife edge,
the hand's uncanny language,

another way of meeting, as acrobats under the lamps.
I don't want to be human any longer.

AHREN WARNER

from **Lutèce, te amo**

I. Here

The pigeons are *désinvoltes* like, I guess, the old slum shacks
    of the Carrousel were once dis-*involvĕbántur*,

their ramshackle awnings unwrapped, packed off, their vendors
    sent north of this *palais* wall.

Expelled I guess, like these pigeons, casual, expelling mid-air:
    piss-shit combos let fall,

land and dribble, bake and harden on the rock-hard foreheads
    of Murat, Molière and Voltaire.

V. How

to square the barricades, the *FFI*, the jimmying of rocks
    from boulevards –
those *appareils* of Baron H's anti-communista vistas –
    with Papon
or Pétain; the sandbags, the barbed-wire, the rifle cocked

and gripped, incongruous – a hand-me-down four-quarters
    violin
resting on the shoulder of some prodigious tot –
    and the trains
trundling out of Drancy, the *gendarmes* waving *au revoirs*.

And then, come to think of it, the only part of the plot
    of Baldwin's
Another Country I remember – Yves, I think, remarking
    that all
Americans are racists, exhibiting his Gallic *amour-propre*

and here, on the Boulevard, this black woman pushing
    white tots.
How indeed. The bakers fill the street with *un parfum*
    of buttered wheat;
a pregnant beggar slumps near-by, slowly starving.

Downriver, *Les raboteurs* awaits my rapt attention.

IX. Between

the *barre* and the *grand battement en cloche*,
    the *en dedans*
and the *en dehors* of last night's night-off
    fuckathon:

her room at the Grand Hotel, the *première*
    danseuse
and me (mere *sujet*) grinding through first
    to fifth

and on to two positions in which she led,
    never
myself having studied – under or on top of –
    J.G. Noverre.

XV. 'However deep,

this is no river of the dead or Lethe', or Rubicon,
    but a vast
and writhing cat we fondle our way along

to where the arches span, the *clefs de voûte* are set,
    the abutments
wade or bathe, to where the *pont*

straddles, struts, pontificates between the Rive
    Droite
et Gauche, to where the river takes its leave

of Paris, passing the last in that long *histoire*
    of walls –
the Périphérique, heir to those of Charles Valois

Philippe Auguste, Louis 'the just' – a scrawl
    of tarmac,
beyond which the Seine stretches its paws,

flounces its tail, licks its lips and arches its back,
    skitters north.
Elsewhere, others sleep, slumber on the banks

of the Rubicon, the Nile, the Med, the Chott
    El Marej,
while we leave Javel, bus it to the pont

de Bir Hakeim, to *pontificare* how Fernand Léger
    is way too *lite*;
to hold, to *invólvere*, each other beneath *les nuages*;

knowing, that for us, 'there will be sunlight'.

XVIII. Before

Soutine had left Smilovitch, had left Minsk, had left Vilnius.
    Long
before Soutine had left Paris, left Céret, had left Paris
    again,

before he had left Champigny, slept rough in the forest:
    a Jew
and Slav, trying to avoid his *billet simple* to Auschwitz.
    And,

therefore, even longer before his hematemesis,
    the blood
chucked up, the ulcer that ruptured, the peritonitis,
    the covert

agony of a night-time drive, northwards, towards Paris;
    the success
of avoiding the Gestapo. Thus, long before Soutine's
    exsanguination:

the *bobo* idyll of *Le Bateau-Lavoir*, its half-starved artists.
    Et après?
Matisse, radiance of crêpe, cancer smarting like a bitch.

AMY DE'ATH

Just Handcuff Me

Then paint me the sum of polygamy.
Tender brawny snippets, pear pips
& a drainpipe running down to the
sea. Not you not me.

With night you come stomping,
It's kristallnacht in my dream—
why did you shave our heads?
When will we reinvent love?

Look at me orbiting the earth:
cool extreme organic oil.
I tower above the Shard wearing my
new raspberry jeans and orange t-shirt.

Some worlds still purr apart
a fly   or fact   or loaf
some people are just called bodies
but I'd like to die clean on the spot!

Some feel a baby kicking.
Asterisk nipples the real September
I began and where I started. With
shining intuition. Esoteric holler.

Vertigo Valley

You arrived – it was unanticipatable, some bees even sang
into a future cloud very far away and yellow.

You are never perverse. You have never been perverse. You can!
A dog takes up loving on the empty gate just as other things happen
like you fall asleep, Shakespeare dies but Noroit is resurrected.

How will I know the heat from the cold and his pirate gang?

I feel the cold. I have a statue of my self that looks atonal
speaks   'the most lovable of all'   'once the reader
learns to respond'   'abate one tot'   ... I respond too.

*

I mean I don't swap souls eg. I don't see how accidentally
touching excuses this, I wasn't sure how to lift Spring into flight
and learned to respond by
              studying seagulls hard
wanting their pecks to last through hunger *and* forever amen, ugh
all the kindness, pseudo-Buddhism I want to totalise or live in, by
the world without books, pornographic bibliographies or
Turkish cuisine I respond by saying blanks out loud
embarrassing all types of metal strip clubs as well as bedside lamps
and cats eye honey wells, but what does the flower say?

Flower, what is it you want to do – boy oh la la, *les chapelles*
de mes elles! Invincible Flower, Let this Spring be the one, let notes be dogs,
              is the body time
the time when your assiduous eyeball meets mine and our breastplate
glows on the surface of a retrograde moon?
O my flower O my rodeo.

Listen to my kiss, let me have this joke on you and sit on it
                                        listen to my ass
the start of a new heart which does heart your curry-stained destiny.
Does swell the lake. Does heart your ass then sit on it. Keeps me off the street,
              springs two animals at peace.

*

Now I'm real nakedness some kind of hay bale girl a goofball
actress jumping rivers in the Comic Adventures of Boots.
Coming to terms with nearly two million people revealing
London's Caribou to be not *me* but *you*,
still for some time I am yours, for
              some life let me make this

                              s'up to you

I can't, I'm so moved by the Pacific furniture. That we have
              never spoken that we
might meet in a poem one day maybe even this one I have

stood next to you that night, simple phrase-boy, you have sat down next to me.
You banged your head on your cat mask then came up with100 sexy ideas.
Your kisses were even better live   snapping in the ocean
                                           out of love cream floats.
What relief, to relinquish all fauna
give it up to the vague princes who used to be my enemy
but lately just bounce my stare back through the windows of hydrogen buses.
Because I have the golden ticket   plus coupons and vouchers,
what cannot be achieved I am not sure exactly   watching hot ducks quack,
                    shiny compact duck bodies swept along the road.

*

It doesn't matter I'm your syndicat d'initiative, go bounce
          in the night—
hug me, I'm your girl. I will not talk tonight when you are in a spell.
When you are land and sea tending to huddle in your
treetrunk counting rivets I always find you are over 2,000 years old
and without fail I already know this but am always shocked.

What are you doing now I hope you will come back,
                    I ah   oh,
my gorgeous girl, to resume and get closer to the present
          I will I ever be here
with you? Perhaps we'll die before the bats come back.

Ice Land is expansive it makes sense to make me your Miss Lonely
and I will be Lonely too I will disintegrate happy into dust &
settle on your skin and form diamonds with you. Will I ever write
a Poem will you write this with me I don't think so I can do it.
          I don't think poetry
I don't think, the difference is important on the hardly seas
not to a new ghost.
                    I'd like to know I am always present I always
          sing to you
even when you're spelled
all the wild things wild leaves suddenly make me welcome.
Now I am conducive to everything.
Note today outside of notebooks in the
splayed plumage of our shared brain,
it doesn't matter even what I am doing if your head is turning
          beautifully to the left is
turning beautifully.

64

In Case of Sleep

Sitting on a retro toilet that once belonged to Geena Davis
I stand for what I pee. A mighty maze speaks Olivia

through its annals & look! Her apology implodes.
I came to see you to tell you that the weather is finally listening

when your chest bleats into the cul-de-sac, but dining into the human
species and their revolving loopholes all I hear is your blood

and see it flooding out on a doubly romantic dream of mine which
the poets say is beautiful but is really glamorous and tiring.

Sleeping with my childhood wardrobe in a garden centre
responsibly and respectfully sharing my angst with the lobelia

I might recline like a cat but I wouldn't sell my wares openly
I wouldn't want to be that memory-cat with the power to die the power

to be put back on my feet I came to see you'd been eaten by tar sands

and cat didn't exist   what kind of a country is this

what did you say   I missed that

I miss that cat

LAURA KILBRIDE

AFTER THE UNITED STATES, THE UNITED STATES
(for Ian Heames)

1

official subjects of the deepest rolling
news that stays
on the surface, the reception
noisily catches

like oil, the news decays

– the bodies were burnt –

after they frayed
particles blown by current snatches
match of the day

2

New research into bone immunity
The physiology of the sign O.K.
An attack on our community

The presses are incendiary

Say:

No confirmation
from the marine, a unity
gathers the force of information

No confirmation yet

from the marine
inordinate loss

– Ordinary ratiocination to toss
an artificial flower –

3

laser fall across my goggles
the punctum indolently
bossed
the sea throws again, redolently

our sole enemy
attacked
now rollingly shot
changes tack

who in the first
flowering of war attacked;
what is attacked
now fills our hours anew

4

The water-resistant flower
at the appropriate hour
has dutifully done;
its leaves home-spun

as the keen grass, the barely audible
hum of man, falling from
the fiftieth, tenth, or second floor become
official subjects of the rolling deep.

ANDY SPRAGG

Municipal Services

I

the dump is actually an apparatus for taking all our things away, and through those things being there and not here, we remember the deposit of these things and look to the spaces they left for us. See the shape in the dust, that is where my plant pot resided, and see the print in the soil that's where the coal scuttle grew a patina of green. See this line that's where the baby one day rolled away.
We could follow it if you like.

II

Singing from the top bunk:
what is this cabinet
and where are the cabinet makers
o why is this cabinet
and when are the cabinet makers
which is this cabinet
&c &c

III

mine was the brown envelope
prepaid now dutifully lost
what is this little shelf for
bringing little though holding all else.

Shorts
For Love

I

in interior briefly
but then the whole is a fan of fennel tea.

From being told what is happening, and claiming it
satisfactory or at least as an own of sorts. Shown up

and in the room, for you being there
fills it with raw nerves,

desired endings and
furniture already in use.

II

So to what the affair
heart-wise taught?
All neat tricks
set all sudden and like
motion become glorious,

the slip of silence
in every manner, and every eye
works neat catches,
spun fly-wheel and counter weight, what
embrace pairs down to its finest.

When held
what affair was this?

III

A then to a better place
things rush by
too swift to measure

IV

For some of us, already ingrained
with the dearest and most peckish
of hearts, there is a range of things

for the fondling – stay late or suspended
by the clock – so there sleeping then
a hot channel of blood.

To the Beneficiary

okay then maybe not mendacious but
you'll enjoy telling all who is
but bring scurry and favour   gap appetites

tickled by a void or in the lamp light of
passing year refrain
script the shedding legend   there's the airspace

and even in deep space   they will be listening
left stock and phrase
oh yes and then there's the many things

foot patrols and information concerning
talking earth and print
acts seen coming to earth is now wait

let's observe the mellow old folk
phrased that time doing heaps on their own
give me a little prairie   on which to grow old.

ANGUS SINCLAIR

FROM **In Place Of**

A Letter

Dear Mister _____
I have come to realise that you and I are in the business of absences.
I find myself – excuse me – find you, not in these apartment-block windows,
not even in their half-shaded courtyards where sunlight greases linden leaves.
Mister _____ this window where I sit looks down on potholes puddled
with yesterday's rain. Let me tell you that you – excuse me – we, us two,
dwell in the kingdom of surfaces. This morning at my window I am looking
            for space
that you or I have left in these uncircled images. Mister _____ are you
            listening?
I said it's like finding coins I know you left for me because I put them there.
There are some certainties in this space between us; time is unhidden here
and twinkles in the beer bottle glass of pothole puddles.

The Fence

at the border of this field is a fence
or section of fence   attached as it is
  to nothing but miles of invisible
fence   today you wear a red skirt a red
sweater   and try to square your hips against
a memory of fence and field   try to
imagine or remember   wet feet sucked
into new boots   or was it dry   it was
twenty years ago   now you find
  a smell of petrol in the turf   cold sky
    recollection   at the edge of purpose

Causal Relations

genealogy brought you here   romance
of paper trail and ordnance survey map
there are bedsprings in the bracken   a wire
fence punctures scotch ash   you take light readings
    the meter's needle skips and settles   noon
    flat   overcast   lines are clean   your shutter
claps   like an unnoticed bird taking flight
    as though you have a right to more   this edge
place   envelopes another silence   not
mister _____   but records of soft moss
    vanished birds   and improbable brown light.

from The traditional formal logic

assembled from the text of the same name by W. Angus Sinclair

Chapter One, Propositions

These books are books whose leaves have not been cut.
The subject is Boys, man from his birth, his wishes
and ejaculations and so forth. Several involved with one another
or incompetently mismanaged, reading in other
orders. Boys are not interested in games but grammar
the living organism, our own estranged tongue.
We have now reached the stage of seeing
not virtue but persons. Mortal as mortal being,
hard stones or diamonds or very hard things.

Chapter Two, Symbols and Distribution

I should explain. That blue-tits
are lovely little creatures
is such remarkable simplification.
I might take the inquirer out of doors
for the long songs of round vowels,
and entirely confine ourselves to forms
as forms. I no longer deal with how simple
it really is. A bluish tint on the wing,
is a consequence on the one hand
of the necessary use of a given subject,
a symbol between four and five inches
of the class of birds. On the other hand,
when I am asked, I deny their olive-green
backs. Saying something like the following:
the bird emerging upside down
on the top branch, blue and white
and so forth, is without
regard to specific meaning.

REBECCA CREMIN

To be on a page [1]

Begin here as a rested action.
Clothed in a mouth. Her she
attempts to move toward a
better'd homology and distill a
reading in per/for mance. Bend
now and break a reading
practised at a seated edge.
Please to follow me, like, is an
emobodied that resists yours to
rest.

Read here as a rested unction.
Pleasant and without now. Enter
a hooded place equipt with
rupture. Notice your window,
tied to memoried. Brakage. At
needle point. Appliquéd.
Rustling your page. Tinned like
eye. Sowed buckling up now. Be
pleased. Presence. How   to
read.

Spoken   here   as   a
rested   lection. And taught in
a soft breath.   Invitated.
Became midts choken. Strum
refrain. Left the road on the
left. Align. Is present. You talk
again. Transitional dried pen .
Read and touch. Pass. So low
here. Speak now. Alloud. Speak
as   page.   Kindling   of.

[1] An invitation to be here on this page. As a being rather than an off action. Am I addressing you directly? Please place your ear against me. Am I addressing you now more frequently? Please place your lips against me. Am I addressing you as yourself? Please place your face against me.

To begin: sit[1]: sit[2] at[3] edge[4] of[5] seat[6]: To begin: sit[7]: sit[8] at[9] seat[10] of[11] edge[12]: To begin: sit[13]: sit[14] of[15] edge[16] at[17] seat[18]: To begin: sit[19]: sit[20] edge[21] of[22] at[23] seat[24]:

[1] setel please setel
[2] setel please setel
[3] flexible a'breathed fore
[4] one voice, two steps forward, slowly tonally embroidered
[5] it   out the   to a

[6] the place is
place he dusted
seat she place

[7] setel please setel
[8] setel please setel
[9] flexible a'breathed fore

[10] the place is
place he dusted
seat she place

[11] it   out the   to a
[12] one voice, two steps forward, slowly tonally embroidered
[13] setel please setel
[14] setel please setel
[15] it   out the   to a
[16] one voice, two steps forward, slowly tonally embroidered
[17] flexible a'breathed fore

[11] the place is
place he dusted
seat she place

[19] setel please setel
[20] setel please setel
[21] one voice, two steps forward, slowly tonally embroidered
[22] it   out the   to a
[23] flexible a'breathed fore

[24] the place is
place he dusted
seat she place

To read: point [1]: point [2] rustling [3] like [4] eye [5]: To read: point [6]: point [7] like [8] rustling [9] eye [10]: To read: point [11]: point [12] eye [13] like [14] rustling [15]: To read: point [16]: point [17] rustling [18] eye [19] like [20]:

[1] physical restraint limiting privacy
[2] physical restraint limiting privacy
[3] movementing softly pulsed exasperatedly
[4] he seems fondly resembling. pleased to be affection ally.
[5] he seems fondly resembling. pleased to be affection ally.
       milled form available for this
       threaded centrally sightedly
       an mostly calm

[6] physical restraint limiting privacy
[7] physical restraint limiting privacy
[8] he seems fondly resembling. pleased to be affection ally.
[9] movementing softly pulsed exasperatedly
       milled form available for this
       threaded centrally sightedly
       an mostly calm

[11] physical restraint limiting privacy
[12] physical restraint limiting privacy
[13]   milled form available for this
       threaded centrally sightedly
       an mostly calm

[14] he seems fondly resembling. pleased to be affection ally.
[15] movementing softly pulsed exasperatedly
[16] physical restraint limiting privacy
[17] physical restraint limiting privacy
[18] movementing softly pulsed exasperatedly
[19]   milled form available for this
       threaded centrally sightedly
       an mostly calm

[20] he seems fondly resembling. pleased to be affection ally.

To spoken: strum [1]: strum [2] and [3] touch [4]: To spoken: strum [5]: strum [6] touch [7] and [8]:

[1] chordedly in hands
[2] chordedly in hands

[3]

    con   finite   con   as value junction logic as   con   us of two con   the per operands

[4] with the of the
[5] chordedly in hands
[6] chordedly in hands
[7] with the of the

[8]

    con   finite   con   as value junction logic as   con   us of two
    con   the per operands

BEN BOREK

Bezwład

My cousins (whom I have never met) are visiting for some reason
I will bring them here to the little cottage in the middle of the bypass.

One bright morning in the middle of November, the sky grey and dull,
Night already encroaching, Benjani Benjani B awoke at lunchtime.

My cousins (to whom I hold neither ill will nor candle) are visiting
For some reason I will cook the table and serve it on itself.

One day at midnight Benjy BB was so hungry he smoked a packet
Of Paramount Finest rolling tobacco. And I mean he smoked the packet.

My cousins are visiting twice, once today and once yesterday.
Yesterday I will take them to the places we didn't make it to today.

One night when the moon was hiding fearfully behind its own shadow
Bennius B Ben threw his cousins out for arriving uninvited, and five minutes late.

A Poem Written Between County Hall and Parliament

Oh you can't imagine anything more beautiful
In the whole world than this, and you'd be
Dead of spirit if you didn't feel touched by
The loveliness of it all. Like a big coat
London is wrapped in the morning,
Which is quiet and empty. Boats, office blocks,
Churches and other buildings are exposed to
The countryside and the sky. Everything
Is shiny in the clean, clear air. The sun
Has never risen as prettily on any hill, stone
Or ditch, I've never felt so calm!
The Thames is moving gently by itself,
Jesus! It's like the buildings themselves are
Not awake yet, and the pulse of it all lies flat.

Lavender

In a dream I saw a donkey
riding a lady. Big donkey dick,
furry donkey balls like
'Get you gone, you dwarf,
you minimus!'
Oh womanhood
denies my tongue to tell
more details but I heard,
'Please tumble me, o beastly
creature!'
Should I strike her,
kill her dead? My brother
will cut off her hands.
Who will not
change a raven for a dove?
Not me and not down
Hampstead tube and not
in a French sink full of savon.
My other brother will cut
out her tongue, wash it in
the French sink, prepare
to feed it to the swarthy old
Titan down Hampstead tube.
The donkey is gone.
The queen is dead.
All my brothers think they're in love.
Drink a silly drink and that's what happens:
Everything smells of a knicker drawer.

Cisse Windsor Knot

Dear Djibril you kept your word
and all world's weeping again under its own architrave
there was mad punching on outward bend but
But I'm thinking I still feel your *tatuage*
rounding on my shadow

79

like it would on anyone who was in your loft
with you when you called it out so clear.
Had I been one with that weird curve
flooring all other lovers in the outhouse
of general boating and conversation
I might have also chosen a new slant
on that athletic wave or maybe no.
Thing to think is that road is nowhere
And bus is crashing right about now.

Dear Elzbieta you're all gone already
and the weft is through us both like the Bakerloo line
in rough summertime. I suppose the piano
makes it easier, just like the tuner said
when he rouched up all the feathers in the bowl
but I can't help feeling you knew me better
when you say for us all light fades off the spectrum
first red then the rest all gets unsewn holistically
backward, 'like a Deptford barge'. The staircases
here loop up like tulips with a baseline of
genuine *Kölnisch Wasser* and hidden nerves.
Do you hide in the gross city and tend its chatter
sharp with your teeth? Please. Next stop.

Dear Djibril flowering out of mouth
is all too easy when you mirrorball
my licence: people today said I was bus crash
and bare amounts of golden temper.
In Mexico north is 'towards mountain'
and south is where you left it.
Consultancy work is a scream.
And I am green oil. And blue.
Last night I swapped casualty for causality
and fed News 24 a ticker-tape of worms.
If you have head for it
the grill has lattice like your black eyelids
it might tick your boxes.
Leather there is equally fake and clean.

Dear Elzbieta do not google me anymore.
Even outside the Balls Pond road
there are translators for everything these days
fads last as lingering knife crimes

and Iceland will never forgive you.
My ma couldn't carry me home
I was flat out of ink for taxis
and the crayons we stole pink as dog cocks
exposed themselves *pas mal*
but in the canthus of Peckham
the ribcages drowning at the turnstiles
have wires have club feet have night-visions.
My spine has a new picture. It's not you.

Dear Djibril I heard you took off again
with buggies all scraping up waiting lists
in White Stuff sand. Melancholy thought.
I don't blame such public displays of
of flexing but you are not a cathedral!
In the end we'll all find a bare-footed brother out.
I drew a monkey on the wall to sponge out
the melodica. My mind woke on Islington Rock.
From here I can see one clockwork heart
inside the parenthesis of transport networks
and rondelles buttery with serious vanity.
The Dub version of what I want to say:
You can cry Royally hate me
But this is no decry for to not date me.

Dear Elzbieta the world and my great office
will divide me from your bosom
is that what you think
humming above the City Towers
like a parakeet without your touching harness?
The steakhouse was fine
the meat blue my Bluetooth etched
with many new species on my vista.
Honeysuckle skunk for afters then training
with Stephen Patrick Nietzsche
to rid me of the monarch's hairline.
In the soft hours the Thames and Tiber meet.
My superb new label web-battles Duchy Originals.
How shameful are your cheeks.

STEVE WILLEY

Three pages from *Signals*,

Whitechapel
6 June 2011

What,

What is the stutter before the ear listens, the dearth before the ear locks in?

You are distant and nothing, and I am speaking to myself always, she sings into my face and they stand there, still, and the hot rooftop remains – and all that red – and I am tired, and yes I am fully tired, and one fold of love holds my horrendous shoulders down, it is invisible, and so long inviolable, while the days of lust play out in the violet arboretums, clear aberrations in the hot afternoon, and all this love as I write to you.

Yes, you who have waited, like cream on wet bread, the black malevolent ducks can destroy it all, and they must – rust – for I am the sodden green boot into which you place your foot, and into all of which that fills me completely, under the wide flat lakes only.

I am not the wet shutter water, or the caustic flaking skin sliced onto flat gloaming marble. Do your terraces stand, or locked into this muzzle, still, when I write, and you continue, and to you I send my poems, and to you I send my poems, but you are silent, and without, and without me waiting, and my own two bare feet punch and eat: Hello Palestine, hello Westbank, hello Aida, hello Lajee, hello school.

* Where are your poems?
I have none.
Where are your papers?
I have none.
Where are your letters?
I have none.
Dear Palestine... hello.

I cough and phlegm and handle wet time, as I write to you, my misery, this romance, my hot nostalgic wants, wants: *   (S.W.)

Tried,

Tried and if you were truly recipient I would silence my surprise at your arithmetic, for I have tried to imagine what and where your numbers actually turn: perhaps the twist in green weeded tiles – seedlings, grouting, black lines – no grandness, only disuse. Three iron cisterns watch, and above the ferrous corner the aquifers lie under a high jarred skyline, and there all about you the one hundred bricks your labour knuckles. Here, the two meters of water ghost above three childish brunette heads to fill up mouths. There, there is no plain disuse. Tried, one sun-silhouetted bird is the boy's arms spread in disease condemned to rest itself in the furred lamb's tongue. Occupied in weaver's field for an afternoon with her, and here I hold your awkward abstract form, and from this distance it looks 'about', twenty-five metres, and the solar flare is probable, and you are reduced to numbers, and I am reduced to this: pool of glee. It happened. You are right to ignore me. I happened, to see the plastic cup crease / your commitment / to feeding us, with hot coffee, and that memory might as well be love, and if it isn't, I tried to make it so, and I try and write and write, to pretend, there is no choice.

(S.W.)

Post Script.

Sent only the empty rhetorics of love to a country that does not exist –

& Confessed nothing but the abstract pull nostalgia exerts on the memory of an experience, you call politics, that engaged your ear even while you slept, which seductively whispered that you are useful just for being there –

& Realise that if it is not received then you will be the only one to suffer, for there, suffering is endemic –

& Realise then, in time, that it has all been an echo of your complicity –

& Send it anyway to your self –

& Hate it because you are already in the end of all you really want to muster –

& Demand from others an absolute commitment to its sound, but then doubt yourself for that too –

& Institute that emotion –

& Fold it back into the form that is your love –

& Feel the fragility –

& Construct yourself, or the terms in which you want to be received, as you career into rooms, the limit of which is all the matter that can fill them, expressed to the point at which they crumple back into themselves, back onto the sofa, as a black hole where all additional matter has been expressed as a two–dimensional surface expansion –

& Incrementally sharpen, blacken the page –

& Call it the worst poem you have ever written –

& The ones you have said you love project the tension of this sending –

& Measure that love, with which you are living, against the pattern of your careering –

& Listen to them as you read it all back to back to set the gap, facing –

& In so doing, form an infinity mirror to make it all come back to what has been sent to *you* already –

& To what has been waiting for you to send all along.

MIRIAM GAMBLE

Webs

Like the manuscripts in Emily Dickinson's drawer,
these ghostly works of wittedness –
more, and yet more! –
the artist having slipped out of the room.

By mist, by occasional sun
brought to notice,
world crafted over world, world netting the gloom
in quiet citadels flush to the shore.

It

It comes in error up the estuary,
bleak remnant of the hands-off hand of God;

attains to overnight celebrity;
enters the bosom of a populace agog

with good intentions – *we want to make it
one of our own* –

and dies of racket
within sight of the English throne

where it is posthumously crowned.
It quite literally dies of sound –

of the rumpus of humanity
congregated in large numbers.

Later, interpreters of sonic bleep
intuit peace was not what it had come for.

BEN STAINTON

Party

Past benches, where we cough,
Gilbert, picking at dialogue
& chips with tongue-tied cutlery –

Abandoned camp-fires; aerial
prisms. 'Nostalgia must be killed',
he declares our big assignment
by upsetting bottles using a stiff
rabbit / Girls carve
disciples & rumour in almighty
houses off the way. Stylistically alert,
equal to fads, Olive & Amber chop
lads asunder, no doubt instigating
bursts of apple-sour in the bath.

But here we are, Gilbert, heaving
our limbs into scrabble & pop,
evermore quietly the life & soul.

FROM *America Poems*

Self-Portrait in a Concave Mirror

The fattest society ever   multiplying

    self-assurance brims
into something   altogether
more unpleasant – poverty   loathing

numberless Fords   & a distant liberty

            my flag has become
a modern icon for whatever you feel
     about icons & the constant war
over feeding   graduates –

'people are not the culture they comprise
     but something harder to pin down
under the loose tarp of speech'   doubtless

there will be trouble ahead   so many
mug-shots / eggs   becoming   unfathomable

dollars   & garbage   & guns   oh my

*

Trillions   I refuse to quit   the western
dream of Billy   refusing to quit   God

damn it   emphasise the landscape's
beauty   beauty   beautiful car   so many
tears in the freeway   it makes me weep

for J. Edgar   & the pressgangs of NY

who invented effect   & cause –
corrupted the halls of flower power –
advanced like a kid   learning to walk
into the hard rain of empire / Nixon

& who was the 20th Century's mom?
who put one of these in every home?

     – that's double jeopardy

          – that's a supersize Happy Meal

               – that's Lou Gehrig

     slugging one over the main pitcher

*

Reagan

Gee Jimmy looks all washed up on the stand
& the tickertape smells of VJ day Gee
I wonder if the Iranians watched my speech
those boys'll need a good long drink
Gee that bullet hit Joe smack in the abdomen

Gee

the rain on the window reminds me of Tampico
& the smell of bread above the store &

These economic reforms are going down
sweet God I love Nancy – my nose
& left ear / the one lady   I can trust Gee
this cough syrup tastes of marshmallows I guess
God had something else in mind (morning,

in America) I guess the wind blows both ways

Anatomy

& there is a chance, if we both pause
to consider this bright red ear, if we
swallow hard & try to stop serious-
ness wriggling under our cheekbones,
that people may discuss us lightly,
& that by reconsidering the ear's
hotness, we may feel capable of blushing
less when they strike up conversations
about embarrassment at bus-stops
& become aware of their features
feeling a way into ours like massages

SARAH HOWE

The present classification

Being herself a hybrid grotesque, perhaps the Sphinx had some
feeling for the man who was both victor and victim – did a tear
trickle down from cheek, to breast, to paw? *What creature
goes on four legs, two legs, and finally three?* Such celestial
ironies have their humbler enquirer in the Sunday-school child
who almost puts up – but doesn't quite – his pre-pubescent hand
to ask the ageing Sister what happened to mankind's expanding family
tree one generation from Adam and Eve. This same uneasy story
being the funded subject of some Doctor of Palaeoanthropology,
more used to fingering arrowed flints in lint-free cotton gloves
than pondering the stained alleles, shuffled and stacked,
by the exoduses of early hominids. She doesn't know it, but she's
haunted by those 'small family pockets' of not-yet-people, trapped
a desert's span from extinction; by whether the blackened skull
she's nicknamed Miranda, unearthed in a dusty cave-site grave
and interspersed with the numbered fingerbones of her son
(her probable lover) and the fragmented fibula of a daughter /
granddaughter, felt anything like the shame their researcher
betrays in the euphemism of her title: *Stone Age Migrations
and the Problem of Exogamy.* Think how Antigone,
in the play that really belongs to her father, is revealed to live
in a riddle of being for which neither we – nor Sophocles –
have any adequate words. Or her unlikely latterday incarnation
in the plot of Polanski's grainy, *neo-noir* LA: Faye Dunaway's
fur-draped, ill-fated femme, when confronted by the raging
private detective who is Jack Nicholson and who loves her
takes each of his slaps – her cheek, then her other cheek,
then the first, and again, and again – until she can barely speak those
two words that sound at first like polarities, until we realise,
terribly, with him, the special violence done to her, and to language's
taxonomies – that it is actually possible, though we have no word,
to be someone's sister *and* mother. Cursed offspring of a riddled,
blinded Theban king, left to die in the desert, between human and beast.

MICHAEL McKIMM

The Annals of Antrim

I

It's said that they sleep in the darkest parts
of the country, the forests and glens
in the eastern shadows; caves by the coast;
in gorse thickets, windbreaks of whitethorn.
That they move in the night, strike after thaw.
That a wee bairn found eggshells on the beach,
rigged with sails of leaf and twiglet oars.
That we implemented curfew after that:
each night we get the cattle in, the children,
send the fastest boys to man their posts.
And yet in all these years, using the charts
of forefathers, the hazel and the horn,
we've not seen much beyond the blackened cat,
the blinded birds, the diseased copper beech.

II

It's said that they start the gorse fires
each summer, crack flints in the dry whin,
send balls of flame rolling across the hills.
They leave matches in the socks of truant boys
so their fathers have no option but to beat them.
From the mountain parish of Carrowreagh
to the pocket chapels of the glens,
the smoke-wall keeps our missions east at bay.
There's always talk about the year it kills
a lamb, or worse, those penitents who climb
Knocklayd, blindfolded and barefoot, to pray.
Over and over, we fill the goat skins
in the quarried loughs, trudge along the line
of snowflake ash, the crisp and cindered flowers.

III

It's said that he stood in the frothed commotion
where the river meets the sea – just over there –
clear as day from the boats on the whisky water,
not a bone of him shivering, not a grey hair
moving on his head, his back to the men
who tried to row against the influx of the tide,
tried and failed to heave out towards the ocean.
So they saw his face. And not one speaks of it.
They are quiet men, lodged in the task at hand.
You'll see them huddled at the bar, or by the tracks,
working knots from ropes as if in constant fit,
liver-cut with fever, hobbled, blood-eyed.
But it's said that the nets that day were packed
with more pink salmon than could meet demand.

IV

Now, it's also said they live in the door stane,
that if you move about the house with care
you'll find your scuttle loaded high each morn,
your path kept clear in snow, your water pure;
when fevered in your bed a hawthorn cure.
When heavy rains leave not a day to spare
there are those who've found each rood
of oats left cut and stooked, the ditches drained,
the thunder-scattered flock back in their pens,
not one beast nicked where newly shorn,
the wool already loaded up for market.
And in troubled years they'll make a racket
so you're fair warned the landlord's men
are gathered with their torches on the road.

V

And in the war, it's said they fought both sides,
were split along the same remedial lines:
one group snapped our guy ropes during siege,
another jammed the flints of Kintyre guns.
When we were put to sea they'd con the tides
to bring us home upon the basalt rocks,
but our lot made the moon bright as the sun

so we could land in silence on the sand.
It's said that in the Highlands they've got folk
who fight whole battles for them, riding flocks
of harnessed geese, their faces cloaked.
But there is often forfeit for what's planned,
I've heard it said: whole villages made liege
to walk before them, test the earth for mines.

VI

It's said they don't exist up round the Causeway.
The fields there are too bare, we've ploughed the ones
that once were fallow, built homes with bedrooms
we'll not fill. And everywhere we've laid our stones
and crosses, we've kept them plain of Christ.
It's said they were safe when Finn's shadow loomed
over these parts, but we've made sure we only think
him fairytale, the yellow man who flees
the fight, needs the wisdom of a wife for clout.
But there are places near the river where they stay
even after all we did to smoke them out
that year the salmon died: each pink final blink
looked up at dafty men who clenched their fists.
Soon all the trees were gone, the hawthorn trees.

CAMILLA NELSON

(writing trees)
through skoulding, 13th jan 2011

into brain   torn   gaping from the mouth

body move   tumble   wait

listening to their recorded song waiting to hear I have

written   rain paper   tree

broken   over   wet paper

beyond verbal

what many leaves

writing in the bucket

left open

personal pronoun

I am your paper

beyond me   through

something in my

message   poet

acts in silence

still in the brain   the lesser of the grasses

whirr bicycle   unbundled from your arms

mewclick   through branches

                        faces   spoken

                                                      with the mist

branches   broken
and tree

              I know this camera for myself but who are you
                              mewclick

laid down sending   out of them

I am your paper
          beyond me

                                            out of them
                                            dropped   arms

listening to their recorded song

written   by rain   whenever it broke

                                        read it out loud   broken

---

me   I am

    wet

      text

into silence

Note on the text: Lines dividing the page are substitute page breaks.

COLIN HERD

apple

first use a nice piece of white
paper i don't want you using
any of that lined paper you can
use it if you want but i prefer
this a clean slate

i want you to draw any ordinary
circle it doesn't matter if it's neat
or not because you can fix that
later

right up here so you see about
right there you draw a line because
that's where the stem is going to
be in a little dimple on top of the
apple

now i want you to kind of imitate
that little dimple there but put it
on top and then move all the way
down kind of like a heart as if you
were drawing a really fat heart

i want you to draw lightly kind of
lightly not too light but just so it
doesn't show up when you erase
so much you can always darken it
later

round the outside but stop right
about here because we're going
to have to even it at the end so
we make this stand that's going
to hold it all together you can make
it look like a chin or something

now erase these lines so they don't
get confusing the original circle you
made is not really necessary it's a
lot more apple like if you get rid of
the harsher lines and smooth them
out a bit

if you make a mistake you just erase
it it's not going to hurt it one bit an
eraser is a drawer's best friend aside
from paper and drawing utensils

now this is a little low you can keep it
there or make it a little higher so go
ahead and draw the stem from this
tiny line kind of like a smile and draw
it to just above this here the top of your
apple

the thirteenth year

baby cody's underwater with his
hunted mermaid mother, escaping
a poacher in a boat called defiance,
its sonar fish finder in overdrive.

alarmed, she leaves him hanging
in a blue pouch off the side of another
boat. she outsmarts the defiance
and kind of languorously fins away.

it crosses your mind cody may be
in danger but the couple who find
him don't waste too much time
deciding to adopt him. unofficially.

they live in a lighthouse, where cody
grows to age 12 and is an
extremely talented swimmer,

making him the most popular
guy in school, as one girl puts it.

he kind of bouncily sails through the
corridors, wearing a red bomber jacket,
congratulated by everyone.

he attracts the attentions of a girl named
sam, who it's safe to say's a catch, and they
start dating. but cody's not untroubled. he's
failing biology, and has a crucial swim
competition on the horizon.

for a biology assignment, he's
partnered with jess, a brainy kid
with a particular bent towards marine
biology. cody starts drinking a lot more
water, is thirsty all the time.

jess (who doesn't know how to
swim) is humiliated by sean at cody's
birthday party, his thirteenth birthday
party, so he leaves but not without giving
cody a copy of twenty thousand leagues
under the sea.

as her gift, sam gives cody a photograph
of herself in a fish-themed frame, and
'something he doesn't have to open',
which turns out to be a kiss on the lips.

the morning after the party, he feels strange.
and it's not just puberty. his hand gets stuck
to the carton of orange juice; could puberty
explain that? plus, he is somehow able to
kind of 'zap' his alarm clock. and scales
start appearing on his hands.

worried by these goings-on, he asks jess,
who has his head in a tide-pool. 'that's
how social outcasts spend their days,' he
says. cody and jess strike a deal. cody'll
teach jess to swim, if jess teaches cody

biology, and has a go at figuring out
what the hell is going on.

it's getting inconvenient. i mean, when he holds
sam's hand her hair sticks out all angles from the
static.

cody stays at jess's house to work
on their biology assignment and it
turns out jess's father is the boat guy
from the chase at the beginning. jess runs
a lot of tests. mainly observational
stuff like asking cody to talk to fish and
recording in a logbook that they leap out
of the tank at his command. eventually, jess
comes to the only conclusion he could:
cody is turning into a merman.

against his parent's advice and against jess's better
judgment, cody goes ahead and swims in the big
competition. his performance is extraordinary, leaving
the rest of the field way behind and smashing a state
record. cody griffen, new state champion.

problem is, when he lifts his arms into the air
to celebrate, jess notices they are sprouting fins.
cody cottons on too, and sends an electrical current
that busts the scoreboard, uses this as a
distraction and escapes to the locker room,
pursued by sean, who smells a rat.

as luck would have it, cody's parents have
positioned their people carrier in exactly
the right place so as to enable cody to leap
in the sliding door as he bolts out the sports
centre.

when they're home, cody's father is
blowdrying cody's fins in an attempt to
dry them out and, well, erase them, when
sam walks in and keels over. she comes-to,
a blurry cody gradually sharpening into focus.
they manage to persuade her to keep

schtum about it, but all the same, sam
gives cody a wide berth for a while,
as do a lot of the kids in school. he's
lost his kind of invincible sheen, and
sean still believes he cheated in the race.

frustrated, cody arranges to meet sam
at the beach. he wants to explain things,
be up-front and all that. he tells her he's
frightened. that he was prepared for his
voice to change etc but not at all prepared
for this.

after a while, cody senses his mermaid
mother's proximity. they're staring at
each other with a kind of religious longing
and even sam's intoxicated by it, saying:
'cody, is that...?'

before she can finish her question,
cody bends double in agony. it's
his legs... they're turning into a tail.
he sends sam off on an errand, to get
jess, or his human parents, or both.

jess's father is in the water on his boat.
under the pretense of nursing cody
back to health, he sets a trap for cody's
mermaid mother. when jess arrives and
sees his father he gets worried because
he knows what his father's like. anyway,
he's talking to cody when his father starts
reeling in his net, and in it, yes, it's
cody's mother.

jess: 'i can't believe i'm doing this.'
brandishing an outrageously large blade
and still wearing his glasses, he throws
himself off the side of the boat. it's amazing
his glasses don't come off, but they're
still in position when he bobs up and ducks
under again.

he frees cody's mother, to his own father's
irritation, who does something to the net
meaning it starts reeling out again or
something, taking jess with it as his foot
has got stuck.

after some commotion, cody jumps into
the water and is able to bring back jess, but
he's totally out of it. sam gives him cpr,
but that doesn't do the trick. suddenly,
cody starts giving jess one of those shock
things to his chest, using his bare hands.
it works and jess is instantly his former
self again.

gradually they become aware that cody's
mermaid mother is watching them. she
clearly wants cody to come with her. his
legs are pretty much a tail now. naturally,
his parents are uneasy with the idea but he
convinces them by arguing that she's the only
one who can help him through these changes
in his body.

reluctantly, they agree, as long as he's back
before school restarts. jess gets the last line,
delivered as cody swims off towards his
mother: 'i finally get myself a friend and he
turns into a fish.'

HOLLY PESTER

Distance vision test – a play?

:PLEASE HOLD THIS OVER YOUR EYE AS A PATCH:

ok **A**

ay

dee you eee ahr   you are en dee   em you en tea ahr

are my arms all right?   kay ewe pea are   can I slant?

Oh this is my hand patch?

eye eee tea elle   is it a creature? tea

oh tea

:LOOKING INTO THE DISTANCE:

slowly rolling umm ok

emm is clearer than you

getting clearer

can't just stay on **A a a a a a a**?

:WHAT'S THE LOWEST LINE DOWN?:

blink roll slant   eye e pea

two year olds thinking   vee vie vie   water on concrete

you vee zed peeh eff hanging eff eff hanging eff eff   I ay bee

and off she goes   wee catch pee

what a tree what a tree

and glare   now glare? can I glare?

eff

eff you

hanger

:FOURTH ROW:

bit of grit in it   elle looks like tea

tied up badly

can I look at it sideways?

you peeh eff sea (gee?)   this is off into the distance you peeh eff

eff is further off   more wooden

this is a strange way to measure ess ess ess

something it's like   you pee enn its mouth or something

a bee or a dead beetle or something

slitted

:KEEP GOING:

pee enn eitch   the shape of this space is

pee zed pee zed   wincing

em is crawling

pea then zed then a stranger in hatching
that's the trouble with ares ems eitches
this row is full of pipes pissing in one direction

:GOOD:

go in one direction
think about peas and the sloped side of a shaft
a a a o o o
this is free news
pea en eitch pea zed and eitch for an   eye   queue bee give give
give
gotcha by the macula

:OK GOOD THIS EYE:

this eye? this eye is marbled and droopy
da da da da
uh uh uh
d d d d d
double you see eitch
drooped doubled over you sea eitch
eitch em dee
itchy marble you sea?
pee eye jay why
why
why
oh a a a oh oh oh oh oh a a a a oh oh
bit watery

:BIT WATERY?:

bee! It'll bea a bit like water   like A bit of water
stuck on you pee eff see eitch I elle
stuck on your teeth
eitch eitch eitch

:MOVE ON PLEASE:

why so many seas why so many bees? so many bricks
this space is inter-visionary ay
ah ah ah ah a a a a a
are you in with
Trickster Jim?
sea oh are kay   you oh ahr kay
you know follicles?
opticals?
sliced opened spaces
parted angles
ah ah oh oh oh
a-part from my hair's getting in   he he he
stick it

103

too many pictures of Dick   he he he
you pee are gee see   I
loath tête-à-têtes   I love retina fudging
and
the left one's rammed in

:GOOD WHAT'S THE LOWEST LINE?:

oh

ah

oh

ah

what a ball what a ball   see what you say ay ee eitch ball
something in the corner
my cone cell cone   said something ay you why
I can read eeh you eeh you
pee enn you and underneath something zed

:GOOD:

can't read anymore
A sorry it's a a a a a a a a a

:JUST SWAP PATCH AND swap EYE:

can I look at it obliquely?
the lower down the less I can see
my zip A eye pee
is **stuck**

:YES YES YES:

dee is it dee? dee or oh
dee or oh and ah ah ah ah a
you have filled this space with so many
too many oh oh oh a a a and dee
it's dee
blink roll rest   that's jay and this is the last time

:KEEP LOOKING DOWN:

is it dee? And eff emm   now it's emm and A vee bee kay
there now it's emm he he he

:IT WAS DEE:

oh emm
this one's stiff
pea sea eff em   the white space is gloopy
oh oh oh
white is glooping over seas
catching bu-bu-bu-bu-bu-bu-bu-bees
enn eitch enn eitch enn   umm
some sort of religious vision? Or zed

:HOLD ON THAT ONE:

104

ELIZABETH GUTHRIE

I Lash Out Against Form

```
              lash    ash                    out
                  l  lash    ash
                          l
                        lash    ash
                            l
                             lash
                             lash
FORM            I                     lash
                                        lash
                             ash
                          l
                        ash
                    ash    l
                lash    l
            ash    h                out
         lash    l
```

Portraits – Captions

Artist Name: set: The UC, second floor mezzanine

Title: music: Elton John 'Hold Me Closer Tiny Dancer'

Year: environment: exotic plants in planters drooping beautifully in the sun
     coming through ugly blue tinted sun roof, exotic plants in area on the
     ground floor reaching up to ceiling – the fluorescent lighted signs for
     'Game Room' and 'Just Chill'n' – large screen TV on through semi-
     tinted windows silently – people milling through hodge-podge artificial
     environment – lots of history, references, nuance there / here – but
     removed – so little room for self expression, connection – ultimately
     empty / isolated / frustrating – Where is the voice here? – 'Portraits
     of America' – like the portrait through the window – The word
     'Palimpsest' (Philippe wrote to me to describe his condition or the
     condition we are in – in communication) as a title – theme – character
     – setting – that the parts are the 'building blocks' for something else
     – are like letter blocks / type

Dimensions:

Medium:

*

Artist Name: Portrait of America – a sketch – of 'Heart Murmur' – Simone
     on the street Friday night after death of her ex-husband, running into
     a drunk man Simone began to communicate to him in rhythms
     'da_da_de__da_da' in a low tone

Title: set: under the Import Market, usual, fights on the street everywhere –
     Simone walked into the street and put her hand out, illustrating a
     story, where she had, a long time ago, stopped traffic to stop a fight –
     idea of looking into the eyes to restore grace

Year:

Dimensions:

Medium:

*

Artist Name: Portrait of America – a sketch

Title: of an aside: an audio / visual recording of my Grandmother & the
photo albums – self / other – theatre of the round, inversed –
portrait or symbol or object in sequence of frames – surrounding the
audience in the center – no separation between the perception of the
thing and the thing – possible to look through the frames – windows,
lenses – like an old-fashioned camera box

Year:

Dimensions:

Medium:

*

Artist Name: Portrait of America – a sketch

Title: of was it this morning or yesterday morning, woke up, lying there
groggily, looked at dismantled fire alarm – maybe a photo – and
wondered what it was – there on Ruthe's wall – looked somewhat like
it was winking – after having dreamt –

Year: set: Ruthe's apartment, giant replica of fire alarm, mechanical winking
animation

Dimensions: concept: excerpts from *Tête-à-Tête* – 'kill the dream, om' – a
bumper sticker from a conversation with Ruthe regarding the idea
that if you encounter the Buddha on your path, kill her/him – it had
been a question prior whether dreams were a reality other than, or
separate from, the self – but it was pointed out that the dream is the
self or the mind of the self just like the Buddha is the self

Medium:

*

107

Artist Name: Portrait – sketch – 8:30 am on the train to Egham listening to the Kinks

Title: soundscape: 'This Time Tomorrow' and 'Strangers on this Road' – looking out on a bleak or touchingly melancholy landscape of mixed beautiful old and ugly newer buildings viewable from the tracks – feeling the empty/happy gratitude and love/compassion for the world

Year: sightscape: on an overcast day two little, humble it seems, solar panels hooked up to some kind of mechanism – train related? – along the side of the tracks

Dimensions: thought: what are all of these 'tube-like-pipe-like chunks' of metal that characterise our current culture?

Medium: characters: the 'pipe-like chunks'

Question: what do they (the 'pipe-like chunks'/mechanisms) all do? – what does it say about our culture that we have these indistinguishable or nondescript 'chunks' to serve so many functions/purposes?

Thought: each 'chunk' with its humble face tipped up to the overcast sun in this case – expectant, hopeful

*

Artist Name: Portrait of Britain – a sketch

Title: set: day after Guy Fawkes, fireworks outside of the tube stop

Year: scene: the ways in which people stop – one after another – in groups – all mesmerised under the lights and explosions display as though converging – as though doing what would be desired – as though the purpose is wonder – as though we are ceremonious – as though each a collection of conditions – these paths strewn with parts of collections these lines of light, the prior positions tracing into trajectories

Dimensions: soundscape: just the sound of fireworks exploding in the sky

Medium: question: possibly murmurs?

CHRIS McCABE

The Alchemist

Spoken by Lovewit who returns to the London he fled to escape the plague to find his home overrun with the ruses and deceptions of conmen Face, Subtle and Dol Common. Face wins a reprieve by stage-managing Lovewit's marriage with the woman he has fallen in love with, Dame Pliant. We are here, Blackfriars, 1610.

Will you be my speculatrix?　　　absence keeps us
guessing　　　this city can lick figs, I'll gum its silks
with cláy　　*stuck full of black & melancholic worms*
　　The old St Pauls was búrnt of trade & commerce
this hollow dóme's for confessions　blue was the life
motif for summer　& the youth you saw in my face
　　London expells me twice weekly with plágue　the
provinces re-hearse my art　like a coal stuffed with
diamonds the wax splits at Eúston　the zòmbiés of
ambition　march policies of truth　but poets are
liars, the wind whórls their value phones　　I'm on
loan with words of àccént rísing　the terraces I've
come from　　　dictionary entries in duplicates
　　definition FIRE licks my heels　Christ's blood in

carafes at business lunches　less toxic than sodium
glútamate　income enough to learn German　or go
back to therapy Hoch Deutsch was not at Bábel　I
consort　with　the　small　poets　of　our　time
　　the tooth fairy tweaks their nibs each night　and
milk leaks out each morning　When the bawd of
Lambeth meets the bard of Southwark　you get
another fuckin Revenger's play *This night, I'll change
all, that is metal, in thy house, to gold*　　even the
blàck fillings in this skull　that are rocks around the
skinned seal of the tongue　if I show them when
I laugh　that's because to laugh is the anti-death
　　even against the city's new plágue　named
COMMUTE　There is no travelcard to take us bàck

109

        I have a real toy sword but am in the wrong play
    strung for a woman who circulates like oil   whórled
    with rubber & roses   a *bonnibell*, the text said   a
    soft & buxom widow   to this live skeleton
                        rattled with libido

The Revenger's Tragedy

*In which Vindice speaks, avenging the death of his betrothed Gloriana at the hands
of the Duke. The Duke is coaxed into kissing the poisoned skull of Gloriana and
dies. We are here, Bankside, London, 1604.*

    I've seen skulls with better teeth than thís   excessive
        in death   as an eúnuch's archived *Playboys*
    After the extraction the blàck sock in the ditch of the
    mouth   a debit of bónes cindered in corsets as
    Southwark's   abscess   drains   green   in   the   Thames
    Just another *parched and juiceless luxur*   Bàck in
    the summerhouse I kissed a face once new, now
    skulled núde   just to feel what absence was   a rat
    blóated the one hole of light and now all authorship
    is apocrypha, in the gross scheme of things   I wear
    these bónes in my mouth   when we kiss
        so you know how the gráve   plugs the mud with
    the fillings of us   O Gloriana   *A bone-setter....one
    that sets bones together*   counts for me the citrus pips

set in the black cement   men tossed overship
    at The Cut   where white noise is a street cleaner
buffing an ambulance exhaust   I found a booklet
called EXTRACTIONS, it included your name & a
gauze swab   Here comes Death Dressed as Folly &
it's like the Reaper's fancydressed for the callcentre
    I have failed once again, I have no brother
SUPERVACUO, I have no brother AMBITIO.

    Link me in the rain, where the cockroach of the cab
scratches its back with wipers   Link me because what
are teeth but calcified tíme plugged in pulp & dentíne
& gumlíne   The Glóbe on Google Earth like a
shitbasin of rivets, a cistern of balconies   where the

pink skin waxes rootwards like a hymen returning
against the tíde of gravity the cavity is just the ápex
before the acrid pestle   the crown of the tonguetip
    If you bótox my mouth then it's cáke and sàck
through the stent of a straw foreve   & you dráin the
canal of me bàck to its source   where the
heart in its dagger   invents the silence
              where the tongue   in
midnight fire   consúmes its purpose

EMILY BERRY

The Way You Do at the End of Plays

Anyway. We went for a drink and he ate and I didn't and at first we struggled
with inevitable silences and when I spoke my voice sounded embarrassing with
the possibility of tears, and he insinuated that the fact of us meeting was a
mistake all along, but things got easier and we went to the play, which was like
a circus, and a cabaret, but also sort of like a fairytale, with clowns and men
dressed as women and spankings and beatings and Y-fronts and fake genitals,
and it was really rather amusing, and at the end the two main characters, who
are falling in love, are hooked on to these two elastic swings by their belts and
they're bouncing up and down and swinging around, you know, like babies,
and every now and then they try to swing towards each other, and eventually
they succeed and manage to kiss, before bouncing apart, and it was so clumsy,
and beautiful, and funny, and we didn't look at each other the whole time, we
were watching a play after all, and I sort of felt like crying again, but in a nice
way, and then the play ended, and we turned to each other, you know in the
way you do at the end of plays, and I couldn't stop thinking about them
bouncing together and apart in this amazing, crazy, awkward way.

The Tomato Salad

was breathtaking. Sometime in the late 1990s
the Californian sun ripened a crop of tomatoes
to such a pitch you could hear them screaming.
Did I mention this was in California? There was
corn on the cob. She was English and her heart
almost stopped when her aunt served her a bowl
of red and yellow tomatoes so spectacular she would
never get over them. I can only imagine the perfectly
suspended seeds, the things a cut tomato knows
about light, or in what fresh voice of sweet and tart
those tomatoes spoke when they told my dearest
friend, 'Yosçi yosçi lom boca sá tutty foo twa
tamata,' in the language of all sun-ripened fruits.

(for Lois Lee)

Manners

'The hand that bites is the maternal hand,'
reads the Doctor. I made him a comic for his birthday
and this is the first thing the dog-protagonist says.
I've learnt everything I know from the Doctor.
When he asks if I want to talk about my mother
I say, 'No, thank you.' My mother is dead – it's classic.
It means I'm both precocious and heartbroken,
but that's no excuse for bad manners. The Doctor
doesn't care about the heart. It's academic.
If I tell him I've missed him, he says: 'Love
is the bloom on a problem, and must be cut away.'
In my one memory of my mother I am filling
her belly-button with shingle on a beach in Brighton.
When I told the Doctor this he mused: 'A dog bites
the hand it knows,' and, 'The fruit will swallow the tree.'
He's recording me on tape so he can sell my story
to a documentary-maker when I'm famous. Today
he's making me list everything my parents ever gave me,
like 1) A rabbit; 2) Medicine; 3) An interior feeling
of shipwreckedness. While I list he reads my comic,
chuckling. He doesn't notice that the last page is torn off.

Shriek

Shriek lives in a tower. He is very high up.
That day at the tower there was a gala affair with bunting

and black ribbons and a thundercloud of ravens.
I wore my shiniest shoes and painted my own banner.

He will never escape! it said. I stood with my parents
and craned my neck till it ached. He smells of meat!

the crowd chanted. There was nothing whatsoever to see
except the party and the tower and its arrow slit.

Birds flew in and out. Shriek fed them scraps of his journal;
we had to rip up their nests for his story. I found this:

For years I lived in the dark. The sea was a crag. Everything
was pointed and sharp. No one came. I cannot get over it.

I woke at the foot of Shriek's tower and sang. In the night
Shriek speaks. His voice is a pitchfork and it rings.

*

Shriek lives in the earth. He is very far down.
The earth is round him like a bite, warm and firm

as a mother, but dirtier. We all need to be held.
The worms are in love. Like fans they stalk

his pinned body. They inch into his mouth. Shriek lies very still,
listening to the tone of the earth. Its mood is a pebble,

with a ring of damp. The door to the heart is brass-studded
and decadent. Shriek flung it wide open.

To the earth's embrace Shriek gave himself up.
The letting go was awful. He emerged at night. They

who saw him said he was very ragged. His face was streaked
with blood and other substances. They who saw him

were frightened, and ran. Hello, goodbye, he wrote later.
I smile all the time. My thoughts have been torn off.

*

Shriek lives in the wall. He is very close by.
On warm afternoons he dances just a little. Boom boom.

At night he broods and taps. I know him by these sounds.
He knows me by my tread: heavy out of the bath, soft

on the rug. He knows me by the thump of my heartbeat
when I stand too close to the wall. Shriek is used to being stuck

but he's tired of being lonely. I try to tell him that it's just the same
out here, only with coffee percolators and cat flaps.

He wants girls and books about girls, and menus.
Let me out, he shrieks. I'm afraid the neighbours will hear.

I'm afraid to speak in case my voice rings. I should never.
I should never have talked about Shriek and his tower

and his underground world. When I wake in the morning
my mouth tastes of phone calls and I can't move.

FRANCES LEVISTON

A Shrunken Head

In the cargo hold,
cruising at thirty thousand feet
above blue islands,
galactically cold,
I float between Oxford and the site
where I was found

then traded on.
I cannot see for bubble-wrap.
At this stage
in my repatriation
I belong to no one, a blip,
a birdy ounce in the undercarriage.

Only the curator knows I've gone,
and who is left.
She redesigns the tour:
lizard bones
replace me, indigenous crafts
distract with dyed feathers

from an absence. So
in me no memory withstood
the leather-thonged, moth-kissed
costume of an Eskimo,
its upright hood
ringed with reindeer fur like frost,

regarding me for years
without a face
across the Victorian cabinets;
or a cruel long spear
frozen in space,
dressed like a wrist with jade and jet;

or Bobo – as I named him –
his heavy puss
pursed like a clown's,
like a freshly-sprung mushroom,
observing silence...
I miss being part of the known

quantifiable index,
the massive mouths of children
smearing the glass case,
sometimes shocked
and crying, more often
delighted to learn of my fate,

sneaking pictures
for school reports. Their flashes
filled me up with light
like water
would a calabash
or cauterising beams from night-

security did the displays.
For hours after,
I'd see patterns that couldn't be real,
shadow plays,
huge birds fighting each other
up the loaded walls;

I'd imagine
hands to rub my eyelids with,
lift them, and feel
the cross-stitches holding me in,
my vengeful breath
trapped beneath their seals,

wanting for the first
time in lifetimes to exhale,
to spit red berries
or the prattle of a curse...
then that would fail
in the force of my several injuries,

and I'd seem to drop
towards a far ocean,
armless, footless, a seed-head blown
without will or hope
or wishing-upon
through the middle of a crown,

to land on my shelf
under rows of wooden masks
and blown birds' eggs,
smelling the open jar of myself –
salt-sweet as tamarisk,
mild as figs.

Story

Under what tree, in what part of the forest, beside which branch
of the leaf-obstructed stream, in sun or in rain,

concreted into what foundation, supporting whose house, deaf
to how many dinner parties, subjected to how many holding-forths,

compacted along with what model of car, with what registration,
wearing which perfume and what sort of pearls,

in the back-of-beyond of what country, adjoining whose under-
development land, masked by which strain of animal fodder's

pollen blown from the next field along, belonging to whom, missed
by whom, questioned by which particular method, scarred where,

repaired where, reopened how, broken how,
how *taken care of*, transported how, buried

how, in what manner and from what platform disclaimed
during which international crisis, during which electoral year,

under whose watch, under whose watch
and why will it surface, why will it then be permitted to surface,

the end of the story, the body we need?

The Historical Voice

The historical voice speaks when the fire's done burning
at a distance that is far but not inconceivably far from here.
In its vowels the Atlas bear and the tiger go on living.
The handful of things it tells us have been said before

and will be again, but it knows you're not the only person
left who failed to listen. Difficult words like *shame*,
fatigue and *dishonour* take shelter in its lexicon.
Nothing is dull but shines in its notice. It can fold time,

bringing two apparently unconnected matters together
in combinations meant to reconfigure your sense of scale,
a pin and a pinwheel galaxy, a black hole and a feather.
It has no discoverable loyalties. Neither male nor female,

foreign or known, its accents come from anywhere
but here. The syntax it likes is clean, perhaps translated.
Rats and horses often appear, but metaphor is rarer
than the similes it finds to be more true, and underrated.

Knowing the worst, it speaks from that shadow. *We*,
it says, including itself, *we are like this. What has occurred
cannot be hidden, perhaps not understood.* It tends to be
more kindly than severe, less grave than good-humoured,

as if in exhausted agreement that we all now comprehend
the long half-life of cruelty; that love alone, however
prone it seems, can like a cockroach survive most ends.
It talks like this of love without incurring your disfavour.

EMILY CRITCHLEY

Present synchronicity

so not to choose the wrong afterimage narrative past gets removed from this
place that's as real / fake as anything else

each sign replaced by a form, each form transcribed to an act. We wear our
acts differently as moods. It turns out baby never even *knew*

how to interpret the difference between you & your life

how to see error dangling

that's keen on Conscience & a certain Concept of Duty too

*

just as a bird the only bird to fly backwards landing aloft means death or
surprise at the watering hole. We know what we are but not what, etc.

the prize goes to s/he who can beat the air with its wings long enough to
deflect the sun's rays from my eyes – given yr precursor in the shape of gold,
and already exist for that. On the other hand. Profanity violence irony grace
of Sunday all that

*

(god as Light/er than feather/plant/animal)

& but over the years science has proved light enters the eye the same as
desire enters the will to believe in science: a pinprick, a hole of desire – black
& white era of common sense (fetish)

how we negotiate this mystery isn't scatter your love in the clouds like mirrors, pour rich filings in the sea below

or religion in the Form of Art

*

so maybe it is about sewing the will through the hole till it exists or is melted or on the third axis (of imaginary numbers only). Counting your assets daily won't save others from the

quiet little engine, she's so wanted to be loved, she doesn't want to be loved. I.e., always the indeterminate unknown term to be sung after!

& although but in the extreme point of mathematical (difference) the curve is really a plane on a grid, two things that add up to this dual meaning of mind *and spirit*. Living extremely daily. What's not to love about such ambivalence

*

Eurydice enters the tunnel of faith & our tongues our minds turn to the stupidity of dust our dwellings are flooded, our forests, fire – naturally – this could have been represented another way

more than each personal show of worth

memory scene darted afterwards under cover of being 'helpful'. Its reel unfolding night after night after night after night after night after night after night after night after night

just in case you tried any sudden moves

Coming to presently

another way to say that might be in numbers or song – if only those things had not ripped to pieces or expletives meant to be funny but actually real. & former ways of seeing called 'Realism,' better, 'Idealism.' Here are to be considered the general determinations of things. This is no conjecture, not even a cantata, though delivery of it may be a little piano piano or nothing at all. Look!

*

the subject, more definitely seized, is that (golden) apple – the sensuous glinting, foregrounded aura – you no longer want it as much. Understanding (the object) now has this character. It is pure accident, also an abidingly (soft) side. Gets softer with air til it's suddenly coming apart in yr hands & we throw that back what else could we do

but she too looked back it was not all to blame (him). There isn't a question in space where innocence isn't partly a blank apple, partly an open face. Irreducible equation: epiphany (of the coin dropping slowly as well)

*

& the extent to which SPACE is constructed (in gendered terms) is an interesting question it is always an interesting question to write back the projection of body or SPACE or urban creatures, who look suddenly cute snuffling round in the trash, but then go for a baby's face thinking it to be a perfectly innocent apple. This in turn sets that, like a fugue or a serious question framed partly in London against a backdrop of fire or crime, partly somewhere else altogether

or *just invest it with the ability to look at us back*

*

(& I meant to crawl but my heels got stuck in this rigid paradigm, just like our love got caught in my hair)

now specifically suddenly lights a period of time (which will be seen in dim light of apartments) – not only in green, if you are thinking that dumb, but also its compliment red which will make it vibrate. Or corrupt it to worldliness

e.g. to follow him closely forever more. & how after all not to do otherwise?

ELIZABETH-JANE BURNETT

refuge wear

(after lucy orta)

                              in a life where everything is falling
disturbance is routine   unchecked as air
unblueing   I try to cleave the colour
pull oxygen shrug tighter   shouldering
        planet's tension as my own undoing
        everything unbuttoning   in the tear
of matter   my temporary refuge wear
is part-kagool   part-canoe   part-sleeping
bag   I chafe across car parks searching for
a blue fix   just one to take the edge off
there is too much   I am trying   to save
and say   nothing makes a dent   I'm too soft
              a protest rests inside polyester

        a light fallout with each unfastening wave

sharks, in their absence

in an ocean
healthy coral is first
borne out by presence
of sharks, in their absence,
scientists determine the entire
ecosystem is under(dressed
                    duress
                    house or hold
        kerosene with flowers
arm the retro domestic
for a modern spill
through rubber)

              pinned by marigold skin
                        sugar-coated spin of sea
                        at 30 degrees these deeds
                        seethe (look up
              controlled environment
marigolds) as the soft
collapse of coral
    barely registers as nudity
washes backless
over water freshening
as one thing becoming other
                retrieving still
                something from some original
                in   an ocean evidence of
healthy oil is first borne out by
drops   into industrial
splits the skin of it
quaint to think of drink
or touch
an ocean broken
I collected BP tokens
got a mug and a glass and a
                nicam video recorder
                by sticking green shield stamps
                into an ocean of
evidence
                of slip
if not reef
                then tongue
if not gulf
                then stream
                        actual physical
                                evidence (CNN run
                        curved fish rubber trust
                mis-crust or incorrectly sheathe
with panoramic gold slick
silk/smear stack/flat
                the names of everything:
                        flora, fauna, Shell,
                        sea through
                this transparency:
who funds poets but poets
who funds ethics but oil)

who reads anything now
that is incredible
read: credible
but poets,
in their absence,
sharks

ex-pastoral

I have gathered all this opening
in the head gathered up like
crocuses you took as proof of
something public, out there, so
I can't take it back arched I gather
up the parts you took as proof
of our being there, warmed into
postures the sun expects of us
and language likewise lazily
opening

a shot, suddenly a wing in the head
a pulse a flap of blue snapping pulse
petals drain suddenly a blue breaks
with responsibility owed bodily
tuning one atop another   blue
                                   blue
arms with enough pluck to pop the
swank of the pastoral a sudden
refusal to lap or blossom regularly

        black   gun
        blue   blue

shot through and through stems
still warm from bed awakening
through a red filter to the sun
already moved   on to another

JIM GOAR

FROM *The Dustbowl*

Notes from the Dustbowl

#10

Ghost town. Tumbleweed. Ain't
got no home. Ain't got no home.
But an echo. A stutter. The land
like magic shit. Behold the
dustbowl. That Damn-ward sun.
Big as your fist. Sit on Plymouth
Rock. I'll sit below. Con-
templating West. Forget-me-not.

#11

The slaughter of prophesy. Didn't see
that coming. All my doves and not a single
returned. The plan was simple. Forget
the forest loomed. Blackbirds at
my ear. Conversation. Bird language.
No paper trail. My Grandfather in a
nest. Didn't ask the question. Not
eggs of plenty. Each memory a wife.
Yoke me she said. Yoke her I did.
I don't work there anymore.

#24

I am a radio short and stout. Didn't want
to spoil the end. Returned to a red and
black dragon. Knew the priest was
your father. Way down in a hole. No
chance. Always rolling loaded dice. A
different game. Told what I could. Grails
on the outfield fence. Blooming cloud of
good. See? Exported cricket with Arthur.
Now yours. Keep them well. A little boy
fell in a well. An evil sister closing in.

#34

Ate the Serpent's heart. Learned
bird language. Called my darling
dear. Coo-coo-ca-coo. Never
coming home. Again. Simple. All
that serpent blood. A taste for
something new. Left Ireland for
Iceland for a tropical island. Grew
the sword from a rubber tree. Pulled
but Elaine held tight. The same old song.
In a magical stutter. Galahad was born.

#35

The intensity of this game. Candle-
stick when it was open. Poetry does
Not Matter. The game is played on
paper. The pen is mightier.
Then wind. Hurricanes in the heart-
land. Signals from Korea. The game
has moved to extra inning. Orange
seats un-sat. The infield has moved
out. The outfield has moved in. No
explanation given. Real as a double
play. Silent except for his radio.

#36

Children should not sing. The Anthem
is mightier. Static instead of words. The
Flag is not there. Behold the empty
sky. A dustbowl hovering. The wasteland's
blown in. How quickly things change. Carry
my heart in a bucket. The earth remains
broken. Splinters in the perilous seat. All
my loves and not a single returned.

#37

Asked the magician for her
hand. An older text. The con-
fusion runs deep. Nu-go-eye-o?
Who are you? The pen-dragon.
Again. Nothing new on this earth.
The same old song and dance.

Notes from the deepest space.
Traveling. Ain't got no home. A
blooming cloud of dust. The Big
Dipper. No horn of plenty. Chased
round and round the Round Table.
Her final broadcast. Repeating.

#39

Your once and future king. Confused.
Wrong about the beginning. Once Upon
A Time there was a sword. A hope
when none would do. Look upon our
heartland. The Grail noise. Silent. No
blood in the veins. A father but not
my father. The milkman returns. Un-
masked. Bodies inside bodies. Sounds
from the deepest space. Your once
and future king. Lost but not forgotten.

EILEEN PUN

The Armoury

That, there, shouldered against the wall, is your best sword?.
It is straight like a prod. It waits like a decision.
In this room there is only one slight window – one line to view
the place you arrived from – one glory of sight – tall, about face
in the corner. This is all striking. The dust in the air parades
for you into a course of stream-light that answers the long silence.
This room is a shadow's room. The window is a compromise.

You arrived here by your antennae of purpose; under your hide
of skill, a madonna's mast, a peacock's breast, the winged effort
of an airship beating its crew, your architecture of wishes,
that perfume – a musk of roots and your ache to stand straight.

If you were stranded here, you would never feel so much
as a moist kiss, not even to the back of your own hand. You would never
walk again, the room too small to stride across. You wouldn't even
etch a marking on the wall. What you do is sharpen. Hanker
after the blade until you are driven out by a sound that is blood
taking itself through nerve, or shovelling dirt, or pencilling words
to paper, or the tearing of raw silk – strip after strip.

Studio Apartment: Photograph

Either keep the window with its fixed tree, and its neighbourly
street and lose everything on those exaggerated shelves after *Trilby*...
Or, begin at the counter, where the aloe plant is a green centrepiece,
cut the sofa into an arm without a body and half the poster can stay –
the side that is folded over like a drunk and coming away from the blue-
tack. I think, I just wanted to be agreed with, that, it's not so bad in here.
That's the reason I went after the camera. But it came out of its case,
provocative, making ultimatums. Look: how artless. Books against walls,
books awaiting in shelves – those ageing concubines. All the unaccountable

filth behind the appliances, and the months, anyone could smell them
cellared up like barrels. I suppose the camera is correct. This is no canvas
it is just my dingy industry. It just so happened, ten-thousand feet above
and unacquainted with here, a cloud parted. One of the sun's fingers
dipped in the kitchen window and the aloe stopped looking tense. Even
the old fictions became maidens in that handsome light. I carried
the camera to the doorway, its strap around my neck, feeling a sudden sense
of togetherness – us in the threshold with foreheads touching. So keen,
we are, as two newlyweds looking.

Studio Apartment: Twilight

Listen, someone on this street has absolutely no
control over their keys. Think,

> 'no matter, no matter'

They are like someone else's unmarried children –
not your problem. Don't you worry about heart throb,
hunger works pro-bono and will bargain for spare
minutes on your behalf, no matter how slow you...

> 'Wake up sweepstakes'

a voice says just as you decide to give yourself.
You are gift-tape pulling itself away from the roll
the head of a blind worm breaking above soil.

Studio Apartment: First Day of Work

Besides glowing, the sun-pearl
        that is shine and chasteness hangs
by her truths in the huge past of sky, by her lessons

about blushing where the movement of blood
is brought about by opportunity rushing: the entrepreneur.
        So

discreet goes the work of bleaching muscovado
that you could miss the binding of body to shadow, or the silky
hand, the fading tan.

All the lit day is trading one reason for another:
ablation, the loss of snow for
evaporation,

'I'll keep the sugar from disappearing
for that office window that you're framed in – see
it's blindless and you're bathed in perspiration.'

Till evening, when the bright, bright girl will get taken
behind the bleachers, found floating the following day
and the usual suspects lined up to the charges:

for the bodies overheating,
for the waters breaking,
for the calving of bastard glaciers.

MATTHEW GREGORY

A Room in Taiwan, 2010

And how many desert miles of the web
   has she crossed tonight searching
for the home address of Mastroianni.

Mastroianni is no longer among us.
   She does not know this so continues
her drift from one ruined domain

to the next one, signing herself in
   to empty guestbooks as she goes.
I would like to write to Mr Marcello Mastroianni

please if anyone know where he is.
   I dream us in light of stars and great city Rome.
I want to be like kiss of Anita Ekberg.

Mastroianni whose thousand pictures
   in these forums lose him on pages
like palimpsests of man on top of man

where this girl, at her tropical desk,
   who lists for his deep, romantic heart
touches a hit-counter, once, in the dark.

A Room in the Oregon Coast Aquarium, 1992

the young keepers come   with their steadies to smoke
   in the white recesses   of the observation bay
for a long moment   nothing   then the tiniest fraction
of him slivers the surface   his dorsal melted over
   those beautiful clouds   patched around his eyes
woah   the girls are lost   in him the first time
he breaches out   turns whiteside   then spews
   a beachball   some metres   above the tank
they'll watch   a while longer   then he's alone
until morning   a teenage whale   listening   to the deep
   convolutions   sounding   inside his head
the intimate sea   mixed up with   human ordinance
Keiko at the glass   his dark eye on   the dome complex
   in the starlight   empty except   many strange forms
of life   the whale   on his back   gazing up
at the horse   the scorpion   the implements
   certain other   mythic shapes   more his size
he relaxes his flippers   he will fall backwards
         into the sky

A Room in the Pacific Palisades, 1979

well here's something I never did like Tolstoy awful much
dontcha know Betty Beverly hell I mean Brenda
the old novelist was saying as he thumped the tablecloth
just missing the silver goblets and service plates
steaming in drifts before him.
                Bald and small he sat
across from the young actress he wrote to habitually
praising in his endless beautiful trains
and clauses that led often now
                  to great tiredness.
Against the one amber lampshade they were profiled
a grey king and confidante. Where the sitting room dimmed
at the periphery characters from his years abroad stepped

out of dark friezes and spoke –
                                        a lush with remarkable tattoos
needled like varicose, an ancient 'legionnaire', the beautiful boy
leading a wolfhound by the reins, and young Jean Genet who
no, no, he'd not met Jean Genet.
                                        On Montmartre he'd loved
so many whores. In the young actress opposite
he sometimes saw them play across her features:
an eyebrow arched back fifty years, the nose upturned
or lengthened in the dark, a mole drew itself onto her cheek.

Therese, Sylvie, or Margot, was it, who sat with him now
with the fifty, one hundred, one thousand
who seemed to be there, leaning on an elbow, listening
brightly, always just across from him, in the other chair.

The Giant

it   must   have
careered
upwards   to
reach this point,
the   moth
preening on his
shoulder.   Older
now   the
eminent   author
tried to look at it
as   the   first
moth he'd   ever
seen.   So   here
were its *powder*
wings,   the   thin
tongue   a   taper
lit   on   nectar.
And   he
imagined

himself *remade through the thousand prospects of its eyes.* Guests had left him in the arbour under the spell of fuchsia and his prose. Drunk and liable at his own celebration. His fourteenth novel was indelicate, yes certainly, but he meant it to land that way. Remotely, he was happy – his career reached backwards and some distance into the future like a ghost pointing to the man who made it. He could feel the moth's slight being on his arm. It was white. It had fallen like ash from the night and if he touched it it might turn to ash.

JAMES BYRNE

The Opponent

Though it is a scarlet day my opponent wears his topcoat in the park. Old squirmy enthusiast, always nodding out of sight from the pack; today he is an onlooker in redwood shade. With a cool apprehending finger he points up to the springy torso of a beech tree. I study its green hydra-headedness, and there, among the forked branches, an American Redstart, nested, and so it appears, unable to fly from its black and orange overalls. *Share our impediments*, asks the opponent in his broad, larval accent and wide, footsore smile. *Tell me*, I retort, *which of you lives greater today: autocrat or lizard*. A long Arian cackle before he readopts the face of an Aquarian. Does evil cluster inside evil. Was he born with a wick for trapdoors. I sneaker to a foothold, cup the Redstart, and with a quick movement of my wrist snap down on its neck. For a moment, so brief, too brief, something bordering desire remains inside the bird until the final flick-flack release of its fantail. *Beautiful* says the opponent, with a calm, iniquitous stare. *Almost exactly as if I would have done it.*

To a Dispossessing Friend

Have ready the hivestone of a preliminary cell,
the battle orders and the four truths of Buddha.

Have ready the Doctor's radiophonic fever note –
I must receive it loud like an instructional rocket.

Have inventories of day duty on a ropepull –
I will adhere to the two-bucket humanity solution.

Have in mind the winning patience of the fox.
Decry the peacock headdress, the dog muzzle.

I will arrive like a memory buried in deep seed.
I want to drink thick factories of the purest water.

I promise to reveal the simple self more in public.
I must oar away the nihilist's cheap accoutrements.

Have ready the accelerant portrait of my father.
I will be the criminal who got caught and walked.

Air Terminals

(for Sandeep)

> *...I dreamed*
> *of a page in a book containing the word bird and I*
> *entered bird.*
> ANNE CARSON, 'Gnosticism I'

Reading how Mansfield claims the word *air*
is to live in it.

Pure scheme vs. science anxiety.

Not the *duck of a boy* emphatic
nor the rich-leaning Rosemary,

more a chance to inhabit
adrenal pressure –
six hours of braided sky
pushed through cloud braille.

*

How to steady up when all at once
air batches you out to crash phobias,

night after night,
wing tensions grazing your head?

*

Small curve of trust in a child's joy at architecture.

At the terrorist check
threshold and counter-threshold –

a sparrow's fear of total sunlight,
a studious approach to Boeing assemblies.

                    *

Carefully your ration array of clothes
checked in tight folds   touches

and is how air means,

clipped around the roots of a hand

as you look back gesturing –
once   twice   finally.

                    *

Air as the steadying of addiction:
how to breathe as the shadow dips?

Air-guides to breakers at the logic gate
the perfect crime, always getting away.

Evidences in landing vapour –
the movement of my hand on your back that says

'go'.

                    *

The route I take I take on foot,
afraid and tenderly loyal.

At the ventilation tunnel
the smooth saturation of air vocals,
every tenor, decorous.

Your flaunting of altitude
is strictly west-hugging.

How the difference tells?

There was a cold bitter taste in the air
and the new-lighted lamps looked sad.

FABIAN MACPHERSON

On the Rhinocerine

Vain to forget the fort.
Some cold day-room
Is the moon-lit snowboard
Of the high alphabet, to which I go
Not yester-even.

Agranulocytosis of the vain griff
Dented an iron kite,
Split from lotic misprint
Whose thought-wave snapt me not.
Fie, burliest desperado!

Ahead, let thousandweight evade
This brimm'd rhinoscope
And that true flapper (a linear mountebank,
Sheet-like, violent) in the look
Of the slow-sinking sunken fence;

Angular, low-contrast compositions
Beam on my vertical take-off aircraft
Effluents, eyelashes, soft host shops –
The GDR equivalent of Cinemascope,
Too loveless to be grey.

Ah Quietism, all think-pieces flee thy lab.
In blue holes, toothless,
Once.
The leading horror specialist:
Their hysterical trace.

A Species of Goatfish

Flit, throne. Edger, automatic. Buttons to
space, though un-shapes. A princely man
grave the cut young man;
waste match,
deteriorated for German cutter trawlers.

To chase the gilt mesh.
Which grasp, mimic. A dawn-robe troop.
Pipe bowl blank, or shotgun stocks,
or golf club heads.
Laughters, caught.

Throat, in temperate seas under,
between 1995 and 1997.
Barbels ago.
Yawn at the rooted effort
(toy sport equip.).

Tars are my masters.
Ignorance's dropped crab, unpalatable,
bitter.
We sport in one new lift,
serpentine wolf in tow.

On the way to Flood Control Dam #3,
the lope of bruised sands' harrier
depleted this absent hybrid.
Rock relief. Multiple-drum sander.
Such base, rough.

Glass Paint

Overt, that space reach.
Cure writhes where solitaire
To see other play.
Let thief sum.

In the deep gallery,
Sails are bride's lament,
And sourly, shallow eyed,
On the third page.

Half-reptile,
A voter ID card falls;
birdsWBD.A.aiff,
Its wandering.

By moonlight,
Kernel-mode rootkits run
Through dark gates, out of sight
Of sun.

Ceiling

Who manipulates.
A surgeon, then vanished.
The grip of the upward vine,
Or brute museum.

An 'ordinary girl',
Eight-legged in an overcoat,
Scaling the burning
Slope.

To curate
A lapsed shelf, lapsed
Strait rail's lack, breathed
In spent watch.

The lighting instruments,
Vainly dressed.
Hotels where churls bolshevise
Their eyes.

EMILY HASLER

Tammasmass E'en

It's a sore soul that cannot lay down tools
or use the Yule to its proper end; strong drink,
food. Five nights afore and the fires light no fretting
of hands at wool, no kneading of dough. No,
I but pretend at northern-islandness, an imagined
Viking kink in my cells. I inhabit this for a while,
alone. All being well. All not being well. It's time.
The earth feigns death and we too must learn
not-doing. The very baby unborn cries 'oh dul! dul!'
and doesn't stop to wonder where it found its words.

Sub-architecture

You can't blame us for our home towns with their proliferating semi's,
the pebble-dash and exposed red-brick uniformly imperfect.

Since my translocation I see it, on Google Earth, the squamous look
the roofs have. The scabbed pavement where they put in

and then took out the beech, because they planted *the wrong sort*
of trees. They and their roots had to go. Insertions. Deletions.

My avenue. Come to the point. What hedges planted, trimmed,
removed? How would you describe the shape of the end, dead end,

and its turning-slash-parking room? The way it floods when it rains
all afternoon? It's like… we're incompatible. Because? Houses can't

shut their windows, can't open their doors and aren't at all like us.
Except, they too must worry about what's going on inside. The shuffling

of objects, the changing of rooms. And I'm sorry houses, what a price to pay; to lose your character! All for the love of warmth and/or economy.

So cells in sunlight, shot aerially, glint – not fully changed, but, probabilistically, resigned to change. I'm sorry town, I see you now,

browed and beating. Unregulated and still spreading. They got you on a good day, waiting – as if that was living. But it is living.

It's not our fault, we're simple and malefic. I think we can do better. Well.

HANNAH SILVA

Citadel

The sky is walking on the earth,
graveyards are reclining in the clouds,
language falls like water through a sieve
servility – young ones – slaves.

Shadows are unpinned from us
and roam between the traffic, slipping
into new skins, they own these humans,
yes we are living – slightly.

Years ago the squid from Plymouth Sound
were massive, brought back to the lab to be
examined then tossed over a shoulder landing
on the ceiling and staying there – stuck, suckers.

The parrot was left in the library
when they went down to the tunnels,
this is not the future we are talking about,
simple bombing – simply bang bangs.

When I see an image I see a lamp
light along a corridor called history
stumbling, echoes patched back
together – there's a sound.

Paintings of stick figures on the walls,
arms up: surrender or success?
There must be a finish line ahead.
A clay face stares – disguised.

I know, I know – ghosts made from
diamonds will dance before worlds end.
Anyway, they say we're winning so
shush – young ones – shush.

Gaddafi Gaddafi Gaddafi

I am not going to tell you my name, Gaddafi but I am
going to tell you my age, Gaddafi my age is ten
Gaddafi and I am going to tell you about a game
Gaddafi a game that I play, Gaddafi I play with my
friends, Gaddafi you can play it alone, Gaddafi
or play it with friends, Gaddafi.

Go into a room, Gaddafi a room with strong walls
Gaddafi, strong floor and strong ceiling, Gaddafi and choose
a word, Gaddafi not any word, Gaddafi
but carefully, Gaddafi you carefully choose, Gaddafi
an immense word, Gaddafi with immense meaning
Gaddafi with immense meaning to you, Gaddafi
Gaddafi and with your friends, Gaddafi all together
Gaddafi together you chant, Gaddafi you chant
that word, Gaddafi over and over, Gaddafi
Gaddafi, over and over.

We chose a word, Gaddafi we chose this word
Gaddafi we chant: Gaddafi Gaddafi Gaddafi
over and over, Gaddafi Gaddafi Gaddafi
together, Gaddafi Gaddafi Gaddafi Gaddafi
loudly, Gaddafi Gaddafi Gaddafi all through
Gaddafi Gaddafi all through Gaddafi the night
Gaddafi and through Gaddafi the day Gaddafi
the Gaddafi night the Gaddafi day Gaddafi
Gaddafi Gaddafi Gaddafi.

Other words might be quicker, Gaddafi but this word
Gaddafi this word takes longer, Gaddafi Gaddafi
We stay in the room with strong walls, strong floor, strong ceiling
Gaddafi Gaddafi for day after day after day
Gaddafi Gaddafi week after week after week
Gaddafi Gaddafi until, Gaddafi at last
Gaddafi one morning, Gaddafi Gaddafi Gaddafi
one morning the word

is the same as all other words gaddafi gaddafi
and we keep on chanting gaddafi gaddafi gaddafi
until the word loses its meaning completely gaddafi

and we keep on chanting gaddafi gaddafi gaddafi
we chant our way through this loss of meaning
until we become a gaddafi of horses, galloping:
gaddafi gaddafi gaddafi.

Dusk to dust

Water pours like a monologue.
Air seems to rush through.

He thought it was language until he spoke.
It crushed itself in his body. He pulls away

and it breaks. He can't be naked,
we would look. He needs something to say

in an envelope, something to fasten down
with a tongue lick and magic. Sex flows away

and vanishes. Nothing there, just a whisper.
The cars have deserted; animals tremble in the dark.

Bodies stand up but have not finished growing into this
narcissus, this gift, this quiet flowering. Sides split

without symmetry. A stem collapses sweetly, the yellow
flowers all over his body, shattered by the failings

of beauty – no, not beauty. Listen to him,
with dew against skin – We walk through the grass

and tight around our ankles, hands grasp.
Underneath all the self taking, love kisses hard.

HOLLY HOPKINS

I Have Chosen to Become a Plasterer

I want to smooth the world under light but firmly held tools.
I have practised by cutting bread without pressure on the knife:
just the brisk back and forth, allowing the thinnest slice
to curl away from the loaf like a fleece flap lolling back
as the farmer brings across the electrical shears.

My boyfriend says I am sure to be a success.
He says middle-classes love employing middle-classes,
that's why his parents got Bill the sculptor
to make their kitchen cupboard doors.

Anglepoise

It throws a yellow net and waits
with cool bones, hot head and aching elbow –
patient as the man who stands, arm out,
holding bottle after bottle
for marathon runners to grab at as they pass.

It condemns me, says:
Your head is empty as an eggshell scraped clean
waiting to be turned over and have its bottom bashed in.
No matter how hard you work
you can only glean the smallest sliver of all that is,
tiny as the filament in my empty bulb. See how it glows.

JO CROT

from Poetsplain

(i) invocation & chancel et al. (ii) shoppers & hawks et al. (iii) crunchies et al.
(iv) monsters incl. leftists (v) idealists (vi) epilogue

I

lo, the tucked-in fingers that crooked thee
   in the Odeon cinema bogs into ecstasy in my name
& beckon thee now to my podium are the same.
   that day, one inch of you was naked. now put from your mind crudity,

every doggerel word hereafter hath cardiac origin
   like some swollen lower limbs. God is real
& I head the Laurels & Bays in the goal mouth,
   Christian & Olympian, before my nymph's house.

you will feel the full force of our own liquid cock in our mouth.

fresh wind which can carry us, we'd say, shavings of catkins
   one day may bear us scalding sausage & mash in napkins.
all we had to miss were friends alive in other cities.
   we hardly knew what we felt was pure happiness,

   for, for so long, no one had died; no thing had died
save spills of nodding blue-bells & laps so hard
   they'd have made me lips, had I not had mine to hand.
cats guard cairns of snails, like grails, in the garden.

we will not say your name.
   we pronounce other names,
like GEORGE OSBORNE,
   who this Dell Boy think he Hellboy?

sh*t, than whatever *you* are, smells more sweet.
   sit with me and work on capital flight
then we'll cut your maisters' throats together
   then set you free in fairy streets forever.

II

you,

    have no time for you, running late with your hair all up in a plait,
holding cloth bag away with your arm, you have another at home.
    Easter Islanders wasted their resources building stone heads,
nuff said *vis-à-vis* the second jute bag. you wear glasses,
    later maybe sitting in class, bite the side-edge of your thumbnail.

    plus curse different f*cking muppets, sashaying placentalwear such as North Face,
purchasing that techie apparel, why don't you care
    you're eroding the brand's top-of-the-mountain credibility?
consumers moving into Rab, feeling like a lawful casket in that down, plus hark the f*ck

    up Yank b*tches with all y'all's *sir may I buy you a beer* deference, *we* give
our servicepeople bloody sketchy looks on buses,
    because they might have bayoneted someone with their muskets plus like smallpox
        we have
eradicated the death penalty save petri dish DE MENEZES *etc.* specimens & we flip
        leaves

    of the concordance, like levers, up wherein is covered the patterns around such
        'accidents' – they
take us down a few pigs like a Flight of the Conchords accent – gay; lo, hark, teletubbies,
    anthropomorphic polytunnels *etc.*, constipated, horny 'waddling' appearance as if
        THERESA
MAY haz been up there, thickening for the Coalition your p*ssywet with either her
        Clarins or MAC concealer or
    tablespoons heaped with flour. whoso framed the state for IAN TOMLINSON shall
        suffer 'politeness' – yay;

what do we want?
we want every commodity's price to reflect the affective totality outlay[1] that went in
        to it.
we want the Royal Bank of Scotland run the way it was meant to be, in the public
        interest.
we want to revisit the putative independence of audit and assurance entities.
we want a parliament for the North,[2] nascent,
we want to initiate binding referendums by petition, plus also inquiries, consultations
        & stakeholder fora,
    & we want universal free education.
we want one cabinet minister without portfolio to be a jester.

[1] 'Social outlay' for short. [2] Of England. (Or whatever that country is people are referring to when they begin, 'Honestly, this country'?)

we want two-tier corporate governance similar to Germany's except with the chair
        on rotation,

between shareholder/[3]worker representatives,

we want a sex *defenders* register.

we want power.

we want LORD SAINSBURY replaced as University Chancellor by BRIAN BLESSED.

we want the death penalty.

    j/k just testing.

we want a ten year embargo on CEOs & elected public officials educated at Harrow,
        Eton, Oxford or Cambridge.[4]

we want unilateral action on climate change.

like, *yesterday* & next thing is, we want a *maximum wage*.

we want a ghastly array of colour reflected in wells of pouring black static.

we want Sophie to stop smoking.

we want Claire to get back with Patrick.

    j/k that is impractical.

we want neo-NATO to #occupythetaxhavens & annex them in the name of the
        People's Republic.

we want public schools to actually – uh-uh that we *have* covered off & we want
    a fully elected upper house *otherfucker.

we want a Nottingham nick arising from ashes cell by cell & are nearly so sorry we
        burned it.

we want to cede sovereignty to Brussels and Tehran – you guys have earned it!

    quiet. quiet, we want amnesties for the rioters.[5]

we want to revisit the relations of accreditation.

we want a sharp good knife in our kitchen, go buy it.

we want every gender forbidden by beautiful laws to take share >64%[6] of any
        FTSE executive board's seats by[7] April 15 2014, 74% by September 15 2013,

we want instantaneous mandatory & massive outlay by the private sector in renewable
        energy,

over & above the maximum wage (income tax BTW unacceptable as proxy) we want
    a fly system of elective investment,

once a certain fraction of their term has elapsed, we want the power to recall elected
        representatives,

in return for their precarity we want high state officers to get superior titles like 'Sultan',
        'White Mike', 'Rainbow Queen of Love and Beauty', and 'the Masked One',

we want your mouth on our c*nt, suck our assh*le to the front,

we want your mouth on our *ss, suck our c*nt to the back,

we want the postie to come back some time we're not sucking & f*cking,

we want a ROBIN HOOD tax plus also a FRIAR TUCK one,

---

[3] Pron. 'oblique'. [4] & St Andrews, Charterhouse, Fettes, Rugby, Westminster, & Merchant Tailor's.
& Dollar. Holla. [5] As we go to press – compensation. [6] Pron 'above'. [7] Not a threat.

we want suits on the streets, with true hearts sweating o'er the deets,
we want locally-sourced remotely-clipped Pigovian beef & auto-tuned Vicks gibs plus
    t*g-ass bitties in welter
  & horizonally we want a global situation,

III

& similarly re $>64\%^6$ *of any* FTSE q.v.[8] the successor institutions to the
    Supreme Court, key social sluices,

STANLEY FINK, you panicking hag (why couldn't Death have taken you & not JADE?
  oh well, I have a feeling you'll soon be dead), TIM CLARE & WARREN BUFFETT,
philanthropists, f*ck you whose contributions to mental health charities such as Mind
  spiked for the campaign depicting the cur, you dug deep. her master hears tiny
    witches?

you have to get her to the park. friendly faces with early onset dementia can't be trusted
  operating the pooper-scooper after dark. go to h*ll jakies, deranged, using social
    media to hustle
spare change, why wish nonbenevolents *'have a good night nevertheless!'?* – can't just
  bolt Facebook
    to your business model like that, can't do the mailshot with the very low uptake.
    I've just found

the perfect emotion; even you, PETS,[9] advise private equity *'WAIT! tho broad waking*
  we see a business, in truth
    he be a professional *business,'* & f*ck the fakes, like you – returning from holiday
    because you forgot
your AIDS medication, also should have taken roughage, it wasn't a deal-breaker.
    the universe's
  expansion is trite; you're just looking for versatility from your luggage, prepared
    to pay a little extra

for quality. you had nothing handed you on a plate.[10] can't locate, but do respect (as
  we did DACRE's),
your life-style choices – difficult to follow like bait under sea foam. justice for non-
  organisable
interests. & *vis-à-vis* which f*ck Pseuds column – citing[11] specialised words as if
  evidently clumsy – ya sure
    did add the aye-aye's finger to your 'memory box' there with the cuttlefish's face
    HISLOP –

[8] Roman font face sic as in twice italicised: cf. 'I Am Legion.' [9] Private Equity Transaction Services.
[10] More accurately, forgot HAART doses on the console in the hall where you definitely won't forget
them. [11] Wow, speaking of which – thank you at least !katKO, Rider, Critchley, Prynne, Hilson &
Pound for involuntary assistance with the present poem.

idle, thinking you have irony on tap when you don't know how to rap even – no
     coup you
  running up on fully operational paradiastole, only sloppy seconds, whereas already
     plenty snow lay round about,
St Steven, editorial, & *viz.* even what leaves your hearts every systole may be partly
     santorum, semen's anon
  signatories, percepts of Borough Forensic Managers – I've demonstrated you're
     pale; similarly the blade's

razor out with which my gash never was gouged, Bullshitaxe Books, f*ck
     GENEVIEVE ASTLEY,
     GARETH GORE, MIKE MORIARTY MAXICAT & HELEN TRUE hi, *but* f*ck *you*
     marxist academics
who lie like MIKE FARMER or, like MCs, front, you 'insist on contradiction' claiming
     'oh we don't falsely
  resolve sh*t' like independent commissions; as the bistro paté is under dental dam
     art thou as adamant b/c

never marketed or positioned, nay nor any distro strategy, with the schizophrenics
     & undergraduates
  mangling your brand; no ivory tower, live in Toby Carvery; of the reality of
     insistence you're innocent,
it's implicated with getting the f*ck it is you demand, d-dad, straight can't smell sh*t,
     all up in TC with the plain clothes pegs. T MAY the situation is that you wear
     too much make-up,

I can accept a few fake-a*s species such as the Ferengi but you your temple
     constantly re-up
as a *what* exactly?, I'd expect you without your nose and lips before I'd expect you
     without your slap, you powdery mental f*ck. public schools should be public. &
     Miliband
you look like a Panicking Client, what's up exactly? & *you* (TM again now obv.)
     why *can* you care,

even, how you look? you I would not have curl your hair, nor even tug your blouse
     down
  beneath your sweater, so that the collars sit neatly. like (context was: she poisoned
my son). smile though, because I don't want any harm to find you. be as still as –
     or at least make
  gestures as small as those of – the dead woman's child by her side. & BTW l/c
     q.v. sic &

we want hmm accountability *binding*. like an Audi A4 which scrunchles into
      an A5 codex on its crush zone.[12]
we're tired of accountability mechanics oriented to liars & gaffers & *sans*
      restitutive function.
we're tired of ordering pears & organic peaches from Asda online & thereby
      gentrifying Brixton,
we want the Minister for Arts, Sports, Culture, Ivory Poaching and Orgies to
      be PEACHES,
we're a bit tired but we still want chicks with d*cks to stick our d*cks in.
give us a legislature controlled by real republicans having therefore the pair of
      ovaries necessary to impeach, that's that NIXON,
but we're totally f*cking sick & tired of the lambent like *facticity* of checks &
      balances supervenient on rivalrous party political factions,
we're bored of black mud,
   of red grass,
of back blood,
   of biting kisses, of chancel vajras, *eina*, q*ack ;
of pondering how muleless our pack-'mostly non-violent march' may grow
      our possessions
   forth constant inches towards our positions,
how by your laws my new eye flaws – 'the Ombudsman Service's floaters' –
      float, *mouches volante*-pocked,
& how, below us, immured in loam, teams of star-nosed moles may even now
      be opening omens,
   & how as snow, is the warm soil as soaking,
we're bored of hanging around for the ambulance that probably isn't coming
      anyway &
   we'll stab wildly at the correct first aid procedure.
nee-naw nee-naw.
hee-haw.
we're wide awake,
———— [...]
& we dislike hippies, lunatics & technocrats adventing among us & speaking
      from us, & for us,
DAILY MAIL we like you, many columnists work for you, knowing where the
      dialysis decks tend to get built,
   you also have a sense of moral purpose, keep grinding *simpliciter*,
also axe-heads keep duttywining,
   duttywining
      like asses as make jocks long, respect,

[12] Glued/sewn may require 3-5mm paste margin on some sigs – e-mail me. Not required for
wiro.

153

& contrast that to you, whom I also know about, PRIMITIVE FRIENDS OF NATHAN,
    weeing astutely before enlacing the lock-on,
unable to stand outside the Forest Caff[13] – with the rollie with the Native Spirit
      baccy,
    organic cola with licorice since the killing of unionist – it's gone,
able to affix, outside St Pauls, the guy-ropes to the grids of storm-drains,
all worshipping the disabled Streetfighter kid with the controller in his mouth,
#,
all disliking & defriending us for knowing you had the shoes all along like Glenda,
      Good Witch of the North,
all as capable a curvature over any bicycle as your friend is, who helps you tend
      your emo veg
    along trad comet's coming slopes,
all positing Karamazovs tilling bucolic red ointment late, Dmitry keeping it up
      like Orco,
all positing people as individual as Elaine & Kramer coming out of bespoke *Rime
    of the Ancient Mariner* normal,
all blaming hominids nicknamed System for hominids' characteristic acts, via dale
      fax *vade mecum* sprees,
all think it's a bad concept for hired killers to experience celebrity p*ssy twice in
      one night,
all also go like – 'Yeah! No dialysis! We go piss solo or die!'
all forgetting hemp day, for you must hocus-pocus with fenugreek,
all holding whole butt holes open with your hand, f*ck doggy
    for you all got to get f*cked in curry,
all cross-hairs butts pout, not daggy now, but loggy,
    yap,
all scarring the kneecap on all-threes, with the peg-leg given o'er to the
      cultivation of star anise,
all frigging forgetting your (equiv.) Parecon's totally haphazard handling of
      incrementalism,[14] expertise & ruck,
all two shadow's breadths closer to starvation,
for a pittance go repoint the bridge as a summer job, vegans,
sorry, finally we comprehend Psitrance, battery-farming Santas under the
      beautiful sunset,
all sexing newhatch St Nicholases with cuffing,
take off your *bubblegum goth Scrabble piece ring* to get the *Marigold* on, so fatigued
by two chutes, go down to the grinders, maybe lost wee *senex* in the hot wash cycle,
      so much suffering,

[13] 'Revive The Forest Spirit.' Cf. Hexxus *q.v.* ; Bristo premises getting correct apparently for
Checkpoint Charlie, 07/08/12 : ReForestation recommending Hirstute on Twitter. [14] Like: ELF.
ENDIF. No one not even the rain has such appalling shtick. Whose boo-hoos ha-has brim; […]
puts stdout 'PUDDLEGLUM' } elseif […] (dub her R*ck Ease).

comprehend & enjoy it & overstand it (this is us with Psitrance again now)
  as do y'all, & doth thou also, DACRE, thus

bless *thy* wee vale, where each is known to all,
  where sylphs cling quivering in the lily's bell.
come, elfin servicemen wrapped in napkins,
  back to your mothers on Chinooks of catkins.

IV

same snog last Non-Ferengi Hogmanay, but at last what
  love is I think I have learned at least ; love is not
to sing out, human – leave that for lovers – love is
  to blow with whispers amen-allocated clinamen
in the pastoral transhuman; no one knows what GOVE is, &

        I can hear crunchies say care could coach you,
        but who, who caresses today, would touch you?
        for the time has long since passed to replace
        in my toilet the toilet-brush with which you
        aren't worthy even to get f*cked in the face,[15] tho

joy to ROONEY; still, dragon gag asbestos stains us, WC,[16] in shorn away fairy
    wings effing, formication yo,
  recollection of bath-tin before the fire-place; (so BLAIR his own gag draws
    meanwhile in his jaws,
so softly & so slowly as moss grows in the folds of gargoyles' faces, & as sure
    as Gadaffi.sav over
  Saddam.doc saves, GG) *keke* games come to test new law, no ony statesc*nt's
    life, eh? & f*ck unreservedly

all you leftists, got yourself mocked as sibyls all day, not in enough categories,
    over-optioned
  within categories – too many things in the same d*mn place. like non-riot
    leftists we not the rain[17]
ruined the riots, content as pilot lights, didn't stage our own non-violent
    protest marred
  by isolated violence, infatuated with the riot contents, forgot to honour them
    qua context, to reiterate

---

[15] Even more accurately, 'even with which'. [16] WORKING CLASS *q.v.* whirling impetuous
ancient & valiant if not naiant. [17] No one not even the rain has such small d*cks. *Keke*,
BTW, is *haha, GG, good game etc.*

y'all f*ck y'all's insensible deference for service, sirs for whom we buy beers
   buy the following round, slurring.
      you didn't ask your cousin about changes to the Boarding School Allowance
         entitlement criteria you knew of.
very subtle, their kid's uprooted, it's on *you*. um. though *you* – course urine
   o'er your corpse only – who will
      redact love, or truth (worse I think), with its own tone – who will proxy
         for, or elide with, any possibly strong truth

      humours [18] with which it may be surmised such stuff often may be spoken,
         or taken, & extrapolate [19]
(in a waay f*ck the working class also, seen for a glimpse in the trailer like the
   princess whirling impetuous.
      what an opulent balcony for a desert planet. though we mean only half that
         suggests, you still link sprees,
forgiven even though you consider in accordance with *passim*. peristalsis, not
   The Niggerati's *Fire!!* mag,

even though you copied the new ponies on the carousel you heard have pulses,
   so to go snap!,
      you linked sprees still. don't finger me again with ginger under your
         fingernail, it burned bad, fine
to do it with would have included: star anise like a gaffed dild*, ribbed with
   mustard seeds,
      beautiful young finger to slip into me when it was already rolled in black
         onion dust, nigella), still,

we like to walk in the garden in Spring,
   when with mild breezes our tender breath allies
fresh flowers, and green, to praise – & each thing
   some complex of fertile air doth imply.

V
& WILLETTS,
   your mouth *already* is full of sh*t.
   you mixed up catallaxy[20] & market,

---

[18] Or to some extent, 'attitudes'. But if you're thinking on it, let this word be spongy? Cf.
also next footnote. [19] *I.e.* more-or-less: piss across *your* corpse's lips alone, *you* – you who,
listening, rinse speech only (or mostly) to learn its true speakers, and learn its true speakers
only (or mostly) to suppose of them some next false speeches (often as suits your purposes
obv). Death to you and piss and no tears to its upshots. [20] Lo we forgive you, we used to
think our toys came to life at night too.

'uhh we put some jam on a handbag & jam on a hacky-sack & what
   we found,
   overwhelmingly, was that the ants who liked sports were predominantly

& WILLIAM HAGUE of you
   I am inexplicably fond, yes,
star in a strange stage version of
   Elizabeth Gaskell's *North & South.*
I want to see you lightly tread
   the boards to Broadway & beyond,

what do we want?
we want every day just like Christmas Day, like *Dipset.*
we are 108.9% committed.
we want provisionally to *tighten*
aye *tighten our belts*
   no exemptions for any to ply his over his head / hers hers, thwack!,
      no exemptions for Éire,
         & in *that* struggle, linked in sprees of similar togetherness, not *this*, emerge
            not as survivors
      but as subjects of industry *supplicant to sovereign need*, dense in the Isles &
            fringing into a network
   of Continental productive flourish, all exemplary, including erector rigger skillsets,
      leading
in social aggregation security & IT & in green energies,
& we want therein, rather than respond to, to transcend
   the question so-called of Scotland's independence.
post-cuts we want as it were, we want to send THE QUEEN to a tourist,
   in her livery, next-day delivery & we want festal T-Rex bones, discussed in an
            implementation poem,
then liberty, equality, cocktail ice, & fraternity on the cusp of gynocracy,
& we're tired of the by-election candidates & we're still tired
of the retired Labour cabinet, all up in our grill, eager misogynist, with the Jägers,
we want our love solemnised by any religious officiate we so please irregardless sic
         obv of our sex acts – queer.
   many azure sniper beads going to the brows, Chipping Norton set, like you're
         going fight Hexxus – yeeah.
we want probate law for nonorganisable interests, & tricksy 100% inheritance taxes,[21]
finally, horizons wide as a flagpole's head!

[21] Give us the senes-citizenising social media systemic – sick of some next cenacle of the carven
ones, every poem we study is snuff whilst catadromous catafalque care's all up paradigmatic.

Kate Tempest plays Flagstaff AZ, Hoboken, support Haduken endorses Sports
Humanism, we wanna reel the horizons *q.v.*, with fall guys for bait, in[22] –
like small skies, & want sport dragged fae the Sky to the grass whereon our
own feet feint so we actually can play it – so so. 'Line line line!'
we so so so want to be on Dragon's Den so we can actually slay it.[23]
we think the isle supraparliament's placing in Cork would be least awkward.
we want Edinburgh's Pubic Triangle so-called shifted nearer to the Mound, whereof
a fly anatomically proper celtic Soho shall prosper,
& to check Oxbridge for hedgehogs & burn it *to the ground, thereby exposing the* wine
cellars & crusted port,
(& for Chloe Mona Ivy Head's complex gigalo homomorph & owls also to check,
&c.), mofo, & wanna
revive the Restoration *Merchant of Venice* with the fake-ass magistrate protagonist
decreeing Shylock
must tear him *a perfectly round Venn asshole, no trimming permitted, plumbed into
prostate* but with less antisemitism,
we want a day per year to contemplate the image the lake casts in the clouds and castle,
we want to enfranchise our primitives, our abrim humours & vanities enfranchise,
& we want slowly to walk towards Theresa May in a six-abreast posse &, as one,
unsheath six wavy athames on the heath,
Bob Diamond second choice, #2 w00t GG newbs &
we want true public art,
we want breathing space to fill our art like the TARDIS,
we want our nation to build a nation socialist in all but name, Keith.
we want our constitution to be hard as,
we want to legalise cocaine and weed but criminalise smoke and booze,
boos, lo, hark, we want stakeholders mapped according to stake not accessibility or
homogeneity of category, thus diminishing overlap,
———— […]
we're tired of tory boys who think they can carry dogs into graves in honey,
we want to constitute a nation autopoietic autonomous in global capital flows, show
these d*mn post-colonies how it's done, we roll
soaking into that mixed-race skin like cocoa butter, elsewhere Rihanna using Nivea,
———— […]
[we] are bored, of pondering how, if I'm so flawless, what then fleck
my circumambient sensate manifold?

[22] BTW, *foci imaginarii* magistrates give us Knack De Jure: yes like Contra-Porno Contradiction
A-Series averted via *two girls*, one cusp, yet not super like: whoso made primitive-hierarchy *sexy*
shall feel the full force of our passive-animal sh-shake my pussywe* like the back half of pantomime
hearse in reverse / to get to get 'anagrams, not of words / but of concepts'. Permanence. How do
we build strange law? Scale up from scenes. Roll it like R*ck *q.v.* out from warbling neo-games.
'Full-throated Es.' [23] 'Die die die!' FADE IN: / nick-e melville by a sticky anvil. / 'With James
Caan gaan, / only two dragons remaining.' [24] Unvoiced.

158

we are bored of wandering insectual astrals, six foot across, inset so hummingbuzzard
     hovers where my right wing /²⁴ thy right wing intersects,
of how chambers nurtured out of the dialectic of objective & subjective
    superimposed upon the partitions of the *de facto* intersubjective may grow inured
     to it, or never may,
of the valor of certain primitives bulldozing an *ad hoc* personal executive into excuses,
give us air fertile by compost of cryptoinstitution capable to compile dossiers of those
     dehiscing grace-notes flock-selfs consistent with the divided, & common
     nonetheless, good for the paleoself soul to have selected & capable thereby
     to refresh its low cloud paths, set up like a monad patent, & let's try & keep
     it *dignified*, structurate to account mercy conveyance cunningly against the
     group valences of grip-miseries,
give us four daleks sidelong fallen whereon to roll, for our rides we have not pimped,
give us three people who share a fridge if they may share too what be in it, YRLY,
give us inquiry 'independence' re-interpreted as ineradicable interdependence
    which nevertheless must be ever fit-for-purpose,
f*ck the SNP & give us Scottish independence,

f*ck LinkedIn, & give us JOHN CRIDLAND –

     pals of yours say instead of contact lenses
     every morning you apply two ice cubes.
     cut-up Pritt, instead of s*m*n, in your pool.
     you just don't strike me as socially useful,

———— […]

VI

———— […]

don't take your perverted kids to the mall or park,
a MOSSAD sting. from the ball pit they're not emerging.
upstairs trashing the final one's hymen with enema,
all up in your strappy top, it's time for your MA.

thru the impenetrable, crystalline, indestructible ignorance of locality.

in your nut my eye busts, like the PSF based on THE MET,
just MOSSAD available to rent from slightly invisible jets now.
no one else puts it down like me – experimental vet. let's
get busy studying, like a porno start but your husband's in.

open HUSSERL up & put sugar in your tea, didn't endorse
    GEORGE LUCAS's stagy Blu Ray improvements,
don't understand progress. think you understand DARTH.
    pore opens by the church. you're alluring with lotions. all over your shirt,

thought you'd ghostride the pathic, never had nuffink you on a plate
    handed. won't require dinner service / cutlery in the coop pouncing
like CUBBI GUMMI cut into bouncing duppies. leapfrogged the pathic,
    anus amiss, no loop. not boggy now but loggy. plus straight LUDOVIC ish,

nous la Bête tuerons après, first twice 'more blood than sh*t' like MARTIN AMIS.
    all up by the hutch with the still hare, the grey hen lain on your jaws.
you got to get beyond that we're wrong to f*cking hate you & head against
    high winds from Scotland, towards her trees broken bright, lain around, at dawn,

LUKE KENNARD

Positional

You think you are an intellectual,
but really you are a pro wrestler
called The Intellectual
in tweed-print spandex,
and sugar-glass spectacles.

Fight night you staple your résumé
to The Lowest Common Denominator's
left pectoral. His blood seeps through
your publishing history;
the crowd lose their shit

(the crowd who probably
spell lose with two 'o's).
But when he fishhooks you
into the turnbuckles
something real snaps.

Your wife, ringside, drops
Philosophical Investigations
vaults the pundits,
trips on the camera wire,
the power line, the mic-cable,

the air-con flex. In the ensuing
silence, darkness, warmth,
you try to put your foot into your mouth:
a baby gesture; we'd all be touched
if this were still on air.

Just before he delivers the decisive
elbow to your temple
you see yourself as a Subbuteo figure,
one arm snapped off,
Dasein or Monad transferred

above the number 1
Waiting to be flicked, to be flicked, to be flicked.
You think you would like
RELEVANT AND AGREEABLE
on your gravestone.

Two Hermits

I walk for 24 hours, singing about walking.
My feet are flat as bookends.

On a hill made of dust I find a man wearing a sack.
'You must be the hermit!' I call.

'Nah,' he says. 'I'm just a hermit scholar.
I'm writing my thesis on contemporary hermits.

I look sadly at my feet – little decommissioned tanks.
'Don't be sad,' says the hermitologist, stroking my head.

'The simulacra is all we can know:
The way in a prayer you say, 'We pray...'

The way every Guided by Voices album
Promises the next one will be the best

Guided by Voices album of all time.
The way you feel when you leave a museum

Or watch the ending of The Sopranos.
The way poets are always writing

About how great poetry is, and you're like, 'Huh?'
When does the prayer about the prayer stop?

When does the real prayer start?
When you die, that's when. Dead!'

'I don't know,' I tell him, 'You sound
Quite a lot like a hermit to me.'

'There are two hermits in the vicinity,'
Says the hermitologist.

'One of them takes pains to appear decadent
But is really a committed ascetic,

Living a life of self-denial and contemplation,
Denying himself even the small affirmation

Of others knowing of his asceticism.
The other takes great pains to appear decadent,

And actually is decadent, eating expensive meats,
Fornicating with beautiful visitors, even taking recreational drugs.

But whether this is an elaborate double-bluff or an elaborate
Triple-bluff, it's hard to say. That's the subject

Of the third chapter of my thesis.'
'Yes,' I say. 'Maybe the greatest humility

Is in everyone knowing you're a fraud
And really living that fraudulence to the utmost.'

The hermitologist stares at me, as if reading my mind.
He slowly shakes his head.

Will Write Properly Soon
(for Tupa Snyder)

Red pillbox in the middle of the pond,
the bramble fences with the boundary line.
A Canada goose twists its neck 180°
and rifles through its feathers' Rolodex.
The poor mad bird that preens its keister raw
is the mistaken self-reflexive joke;

the moorhen's varnished, mute conquistador
commands that that you confess the world exists.
The pram cracks over branches, fag butts, glass;
my son cries like he sees my vilest thoughts
screened on my eyes, like in a moment I'd
exchange his love for these dumb details.
The published ape under a dead white sky;
the published ape wants a street-light orange.
A student emails, What are poets for?
(A biochemist, who should know better).
I remember you, Tupa, dropping poetry for ballet,
telling me your name's Russian for stupid,
that's why you chose it. We said no, that would be
tupoy (masculine) or tupaya (feminine);
Tupa is a Paraguayan creation god
who made the world out of crushed centipedes.
What, like, so in the beginning
there were centipedes? Like in the game
Centipede? I hate centipedes. I'm sorry.
This is perfunctory at best and hardly fits
four years failing to contact you at all.
Look at the mallard's head: you had a coat that green.

The Sunken Diner

'This is where the jukebox would have been.'
They hear me through their helmet speakers,
My diving party, the volume stuck on full,
A man shouting at trapped pets, a bad man.

Today The Sunken Diner is more or less empty,
Everything sequestered to its relevant museum:

Museum of Coffee, Museum of Pancakes,
Museum of Ticket Stubs Dropped while Fumbling for Change,
Museum of Cigarette Cartons You Knew Were Empty
But Checked Anyway. Museum of Disappointment.

We kick over to a booth, its fleshy seats ripped.
'Over here Don broke up with Emily for the second time

In 1994. They were eating omelettes with dry bread.'
It isn't 2 way: I read their questions in their eyes' laptops:
'What? WHAT? WHAT?! WHAT?! WHAT?!'
They sign the guest book grudgingly, like bears:

'Since diving with you, every moment of my life
Is half-filled with true fear. A snow-globe with teeth in it,

Each tooth landing softly, as if on the moon.
Trish, Surrey, 2002.' And, 'Water = Time. Walt,
2010.' We return to our fences, table sports and air
A little more appreciative, which is to say sadder:

Our appendages hang off us like long noses in cartoons.
At night I mime pull chords, I dream rooftops on the seabed.

Dawn I see the weight come off the lawn, I mean the time.
My wife is having an affair; doesn't feel like I thought it would.
You have to submerge yourself in your job like a toad
In aspic. No, wait. That's not what I mean.

JONTY TIPLADY

Eskimo Porn Belt

Like a grass burn in space, like a virtual joy-bender, like a mad head smashing bits of stuff, like look a pop-up erection book!, like I myself have three penises, two hard, one soft, one for the beach, just in case, the flying saucers, like switch to manual, wow the rat dies, like nothing but hound dogs.

Like God who Prince said was a traitor, like little and large in leisure suits, like it ain't gonna suck itself, like switch to the manual, like monkey reclining, that's what we find different now the mechanism of death.

Like old phones rock different in space, switch to manual, the rat, like go back to weekend feather school for free, like go ahead sit on my poem, like watch dog electric support scores a double zero, utah, domino, chew on this, saint legs juice.

Like sputters of pink, like I have a micro colourful new C3PO pants with exquisite species under white water caps sacs and a conveyor belt and ball-buster kit for a ratchet clang, like I myself have my own big dictionary, and in it Jimmy says don't compare you'll despair or use another language it sounds better.

Like tissue for some universal fucking soul beat, tippo, teach snow, get your human ass/night on, like I'm going off!, I was really very pleased when I did that duck.

Like Devon and Miles and Michael and yes Lisa and Abi and Cadabby and Manky I mean Banky Moon, like pull back my trousers, like you make goal posts for my sugar, like slip in the snow monkey metaphor with an e softly but firmly, like look how large little is.

Like can you get me a copy of your penis, switch to manual, like you understand the women body thing, like put on your Eskimo porn belt, don't touch the green square, like fun fur like orange fun, like fun was taking over the planet, like I think I might be able to get you some work down there.

Like little spanners rising and shining, like the rat, like don't do what Donny does, like Jimmy does it, like Miles does it, like ants are back in, like I wear swastika pants, on the stars on the floor, like I wear orange and red fur, like switch, like you fucking chess fag, like spring in my anus, like summer in yours, like sleepy animals that don't make phone calls, like Buffo only emerged when you stopped sex and gooed her back together, like cherries popping in the, like smudge pudding, like sledge hammering your pinko, like a jam jar, drinking from a jar, like wow get your sheep dog nose on, like no point not loving just better to love, simple, like don't be like that duck, like it's thirsty work being daffety.

Like avalanche lilies, like the silk road online between us, like laugher goo on your ass, like fucking the future, like abracafuckingsexdabra, like happiness things, like switch, like gags and crams, like sword palace, like otemesando, like a little more, pudding duck, like smutly it cedes away from the deck, like, like the gold boy runs out of berries in the straw, like juice the brick, like rodeo beasts gathered round, an old haunted heart sputtered, a giant shiver, a wanky moon, like milk her over the bedchamber made milk-made, set her to the milk tune star, presto, a dark kisses it off, like sexember, like I believe you thousands wouldn't.

Syndromes and a Century

All the more ultramarine ailments
disappear into a blue fox.

Malice is forced to erupt,
always repeating. So

what is it that's happening?
If everything's already lost

like no other time, only remains
to feel. The world. Emits

or admits: fuck it, let's make
something beautiful, where

the 'it' is this strange foldless
repeating. So where's it at?

As odd as ever what love does,
mooning for the best

167

possible narrator is always
the corpse in his bed:

love at first sight
as the century's only real syndrome.

So then what? Films: signs.
Films: affirmations of what?

Century die hard glow
nothing but love's consequence

turned to fiction stones; hotel charms
to keep up with, review, glaze; gawp.

Imagine spinning round LA
at night, the whole entourage-

coloured decade a lyric flora
in your throat or BFF

tinkering with the ABC;
everything takes place in 2001,

or 2012, or 1999; joint years
of popular odyssey, perennial encryption

not enough, exasperated hyperbole
to be irenic, dastardly signia

of unique Uniqlo, or
animal streams of soft vanilla signs.

It's Lynch himself in the car,
another home-movie blackout.

Now, the film won. I don't know how;
just see it. In Llorando not all beauty lies

in its denying. Subject so simple, fact
of falling in love leaves the theatre crying

but has to split the millennium maladies
into a tropical macaroon. Signs dispose

in a new risen hotel, but burr, reappearing
excessively insurmountable, just standing

there in circles like stars well resolved.
Small machines stop but sometimes *up*:

what clouds gather? Approaching thunder?
What's going on? The pathos of the inhuman,

2012 event cocoons, amnesiac messianic,
ethically-blasé funny new 'R *Xmas* (2001),

the secret dreams of graphics, Na'vi
exultation bling in the phantom menace

desert, *just take everything*; or, other
felines, more paraplegic heroes, resolute

in not wanting anything at all to do with reality,
tall flowers larval

and cadavaric, crimping on infinity,
panthers attacked by a kind of kindness,

connecting every single animal
together by their tail in a bright concord

of undulating dots?

Dear Clarity

When I was a very small boy I sat at the window and in the glass felt a word I couldn't say. I called it 'the word'. My young body knew more than I knew. This was my body before the bible even though I'd read the bible. I prayed without thinking. The word said something like: *don't fuck up*. Then I turned it, the word, into a dark wound, this missing wound. I felt love, intense craving. I called it love of love. I found different objects: x, y, z; sherbet dabs; a dumbo octopus; worst of all, the wound itself. Then I stopped believing. Then I got locked up, then in myself. I chose to live in a crack in the sky that really exists but is actually just an error. I more than killed myself. That's what error is. But then, right here, dear Lion and Kat and everyone, the word came back. Or be precise: since it had never, or could never come back, because it had never gone away, simply it recalled itself in itself, as if remembering the unforgettable. Wild clarity, impossible to think, but various in precise thought forms. An incredible one thing, a single nutmeg thought that makes life worth living. The sky is still split, but it is in clarity. Like the man who invented ice cream.

EMILY TODER

Meaninglessly the Frogs are Gone

The outlets of the world are not cute.

What were cute
were the destroyed frogs

If there really is a galaxy
like they say and if that galaxy
is anything like what they say
then this really is
so very bitty
it is meaninglessly that the frogs are gone
so meaninglessly it strikes me like a scraping
because of where I am sitting
in what they call a broad
I know, a manmade phenomenon
made of nature, like Velcro,
but what of the frogs, the frogs
that were supposed to be nimble

Dreams of Law and Order

The people who discover crimes
are not responsible for them
necessarily
and this haunts me

and I'm haunted by any and all evasion
attempted

also by the re-emergence of certain individuals
at the scene
who were at the scene

never leave town if you have discovered a crime
and if you have just lost someone to death

drink two gallons of orange juice
just like Ed Koch
like no animal

I think half of commercials begin with the words *are you*
and the other half
are useless and remote

Salt in Soup

I read that salt in soup
is degrading to the soup like
death on the phone
is degrading to the death

Anything that has a preposition
eventually degrades the thing
after the preposition

This is how children learn
everything when they learn
grammar

It is simple to handful such flavor
because most of the concocting is bland
because the pure arises, ought arise
and float off

But I am cooking where the axis is null
and where the axis is natural
whereby I can no longer see the sky
which I do not mind
whereby I do not mind
and where I am collecting magnets
to eventually bury
which I will eventually bury

Ambitious Men

A documentary
about the Panama Canal
said something about ambitious men
and I thought:
I know nothing about ambitious men

I know the etymology of ambition
though

It has to do with birds
obviously

It has a root that is the key to its meaning
obviously
and nothing about it is intuitive

The Panama Canal was pivotally
sculpted by ambitious men nothing
like the ambitious men of today
who hide in the reeds

and who caress me in their lament
I mean they fear me
in the dunes
who rock me with the gales
I mean they glare on me their stars
who toss me with their tides
I mean who guide me in their gravity
which pulls them
to where they then sink
then they are lower
they're sadder

KESTON SUTHERLAND

Ode to TL61P 2

I

What the public hears from the police on TV is the
voice of police management. Everyone who has a
manager knows what that litotic brachylogy always
sounds like. You learn in the end to pick out the
buzzwords like hairs from a dessert you only think you
don't want to eat now, whereas in truth it is what you
have paid for in order that you can be too intimidated
to complain about it or send it back, by way of sending
yourself back instead, and though the mouthfeel is like
a grease-filled crack except astonishingly ugly you study
to roll your eyes, pucker as if embittered, and furtively
smirk at the gelatine soufflé with the other patriotic
bulimics. When during the live BBC News 24 footage
of the clearance of Trafalgar Square on the 26th March
2011 the police 'commander' (think of your area manager
going by that name) explained for the benefit of sedulous
licensees who own the perk of Freeview that the people
presently adopted under the state truncheons are not
protesters but criminals intent on chaos, not one because
they cannot be but the other because they are, what he
meant was 1. The plan to camp out in Trafalgar Square
is tactically brilliant and must not succeed; real passion
really does make disproportionate analogies powerful;
the disproportion of Trafalgar to Tahrir would be no
disincentive to solidarity; it would also appeal too much
to overexercised Arabs, here and in the region; it would
give Al-Jazeera an unwelcome brief commercial edge
against Sky. 2. When the rank and file are angry and
bored of tolerating teenage insubordination, you toss
them some roughage of which they may boast that they
feel entitled to it 'after a tiring day'; you watch them get
their revenge, you get an anal-sadistic bliss kick out of
watching them do it only because you allow them to;
they will think you are turning a blind eye to their
excesses and be very flattered (this is what management

always thinks). 3. It was late at night and the police in the square were being paid overtime; the bit of extra cash for its members would slow the impetus of the police union, which would be a welcome window of opportunity for the managers paid fortunes which are however already diminishing because of high inflation to dilate on our frontline cuts, in any case in spite of the rampant inflation of everything that is, owing to whatever is now the meaning for avarice, of which fit readers will be pleased to remember that Athenaeus colourfully remarked in his *Deipnosophistae* that it hopes to drag Pluto out of the bowels of the earth; 4. The windows at Millbank are not yet fixed. You are strangulatingly disentangled from the tiny body you barely knew would come at all, and pressed into a mucky adult clay you know will come every day, at the flick of your switch, whenever you want it. This is exactly the condition I used to avoid which I thought was impossible as poetry or anything that is the meaning I am desperate for yet now it is the only one that I make work hard; 5. Whatever manoeuvres in repression we fund in the short term will prove invaluable in the event of revolution; after the menacing from Blair Gibbs, the head of crime and justice at the Policy Exchange, who said, in response to the disclosure that police overtime payments went up by 29% between 2002 and 2006, that overtime payments have 'spiralled out of control', we can suggest that the case for overtime is implicit in the need to be prepared in case the revolution should come at night; the clearance of the square is a practical demonstration of the inadvisability of imposing restrictions on overtime payments; 6. A modest spike in public fear would begin to compensate Rupert Murdoch for the embarrassment we caused him, right at the very sensitive moment when he and Jeremy Hunt were trying to consolidate his control of the British media, when it was revealed in the press that we had hushed up the phone hacking under Andy Coulson at *The News of the World*; a stimulus to petit bourgeois paranoia is best delivered at the eleventh hour, albeit at some inconvenience to the editorial staff, because the stimulus is naturally more potent the more convincingly the hooligans can be shown to have taken things too far and gone on too long, and in the case of a painstakingly slow containment operation still in progress when the news coverage ends for the night, they will have no choice but unarguably to have done just that; this is another natural basis for ringfencing overtime payments; 7. It will be an exquisite additional goad to Gadaffi and Mubarak to make them watch the police of their enemy doing with geometrical impunity what the police of Benghazi and Cairo weren't allowed to do; in some small measure it will help convince the Chinese that the pressure we exert on them in public over human rights really is just for the purposes of domestic political propaganda back home, which may yet lead to a thawing of relations between Vodafone and China Mobile; it sets a good example to the Irish, whose need for Spartan repressions in fulfilment of the terms of the loan we obliged them to accept from us could surely be made the basis for a new international market in police consultancy, right there on the ground in a bona fide tax haven; 8. Given the currently high profile of the Yvonne Fletcher murder, and in view of their being asked to dismantle a strategic analogy with what may as well be the Middle East as a whole, it may be possible for the clearance team to hallucinate that they are avenging the corps by truncheoning the Libyans; whether the team really does have that hallucination or not is arguably immaterial, since for our part it need not be true in order that we may enjoy the irony of imagining that it is, or laughing benevolently at the thought that the team might really be wrestling with spectral Libyans; the hooligans meanwhile can be allowed to achieve one part of their program, namely that they turn into spectral Libyans when you remind them of the repressibility of their jouissance. These meanings are not yet all equivalent, some do that better than others. If you stop and think about it, it might contribute to the pacification of the EDL, who can be expected to get a real kick out of seeing a bunch of pampered socialist Islamophiles compressed into a cameo of the herd which they obstinately refuse to acknowledge exists and runs politics, which may mean less budgetary nightmares for management colleagues in Luton. The meanings are not less articulated for ending up unnumbered. After all accumulation is about finally not remembering what meaning you are on, or not caring, but not caring turns out to be a treacherous attitude,

best done on the sly, because all your care is radiant.
Know your fucking enemy.

II

As sure as any air must spread the cost of any breathing
head thrilled out to cold perfection released from its
protection to keep our estimates so rough that each can
lean in close enough to bind on to the other free and
blind to her obscurity so every paralysis condemns to
cost analysis terminable or not the same live instrument
of breath and blame the high demand is prod the speck
to check its balance on the neck restructured not to bend
or turn or lose what might be saved to earn a personal
account of how in love with what it can't allow either
to be or disappear their average becomes more dear
loaded with phony fire to drown desire as the blood
slows down to last forever missing out as mirrored in
the late bailout or ever wash away the smear of values
else in sight too clear to stare in lucid vanity transfixed
to our insanity whose stalk is knotted on a nail of sex
smashed in too deep to fail or go for just as long as wait
or last a whole life wrong too late but soft enough to
trim the lips no kiss too infinitely grips since sadly being
shoved away is what makes yesterday today disprove
tomorrow shining more robust than ever on the floor as
managers are first to know by shadowing the afterglow
that blurs as irrepressible desire or inaccessible is thrust
hard at a new mock dot whose proxy for the vacant cot
assigned its pun in Eliot is packed in silica crystals to
desiccate essentials for bare minds wintering in jars of
skulls bussed in from empty bars rebutting dusters in a
fridge not plugged in a dismantled bridge but switched
on at the wall and shut in protest at the power cut
impatient for pneumatic joy since emptying that girl or
boy on tips of absence getting hard to drink in yards of
cooling lard in envy of their hotter love of all our suffering
above the Hotpoint *silex scintillans* the bright spark
libertarians who lisp over the drone sublime get high
on gore and moral rhyme and scheme on ideal felonies
dragging on hash on balconies to level all disparities in
passion only once as fuck so flashy bankers snore amok

177

who split apart in bliss to ply the sexy shrapnel satisfy
the universal appetite for more orgasmic natural right
whose aspic and preservatives sustain neoconservatives
to scavenge under god in blood and liberate his wavy
flood Januzi UKHL 5 will keep the flagging law alive
cement forever wet in dreams of Tigris' disemboguing
streams of bonded revenue and dust shored up with
picturesque disgust by poets mindfully concussed the
more content the less unheard as vision sways its best
when blurred suffice to say and get ignored like genitals
too hard and bored for all the time you wait and break
or mend to die will only make the memory of difficult
passionate love still more occult and tender faces
disappear as lost mist leaves a mirror clear to vanish yet
permanently diminish not so passingly as love must in a
slighted head shut up in dreams admired instead of shed
like jobs to multiply the way out by the inward cry for
fleecy care or finny drove or feather'd youth or all my
love or scaly breed since with that shit Iraq in general
must grit its icy core of heart and mind in not just spectral
abstract rind but profit for the vested rim who mass
produce the phantom limb rip open markets in despair
mock cannibals who bite the air rinse spit and flush
their sacred founts and whine about the body counts.

1.2

Still wringing the still obvious thing for side to side
hard pressed ears ring up inside sales in justice scales by
invoicing their vanished males in arabesques that Sky
regales or JP Morgan rigs to drip on Qtel for the Gaza
Strip when god in heaven trickles down relieving Blair
and turning brown the olive trees are burning down the
neck detached at no dispute the settlements are absolute
I ask a wreath fit on so hard the brain is crushed like
creamy lard deposited in spongy rats who make our
doctors bureaucrats mock children up as innocents to
prosper as their effluents and gnaw on skulls in cellars
stocked with shadows by the awed and shocked.

Once Assyrian spivs, now votaries of natural election,
body odour clinging to the old regime, solicit for a pro

forma conscience in the sentimental porno form of an eyeball rammed inward, to represent age; whether a costly service when in lives or no less trenchant words, a spent horizon dripping its limbs, parts and labour, transacted to a cosmetic mouth embroidered with intrinsic labia, silk teeth, outsourced love history or cosmic dark, on the street whose massy brains lay down to block the music drains, delivering the flood; but what is vital and deep in me is escalated to a surface for affixation to my sanity, reaching into a deterrent void of mental shining after intertwisted lights I press down on to mean your face is coming back.

If meaning isn't obvious the cops get mean and envious. The revolution too bourgeois to come. An always new but shut curtain, peeled by her single hand, behind which waits a face you wait to pull for being dead, is beautiful when shut by her double; it makes the window further away or not there at all so you definitely vanish in it. As by focus on what is apparent, art is dead labour too, all that can be done or said to end. Eat courtesy of nausea eight hours per day or longer. Go for Starbucks at Shenzhen on weekend. The very existence of a minimum wage is a very existent cage for my mum. Since I will not again be free to fall in absolutely or to delete or moderate desire for a touch whose sound is not to be believed but as dissembled to a cracking light, you are lost, stared at like distant fire through a screwed up eyelid, since that is what loss really is for Hutus and Israelis, the waxing ode indulged unto redundancy of ear; make the love that makes you disappear but at the same time instantly come back when kissing obliterated in bright agony to a grated shin or inimitable chewed-up spat-out shining spine, not desperate because alone, flooded with the only air required, shattering joy contradicts quantitative easing, replenishment of liquid life that otherwise runs out, to bar us in temptation and to keep the flesh wrung dry; pure and fundamental to our blood sucked in sucked out and sucked off at RBS to fuel one man's innovative cost synergies you end up all spunked out ABN-AMRO minus Lasalle due diligence lite by lip sync, cuckolding Barclays, writing off 1.5 billion which could have gone into wells and malaria vaccines, no credit losses anywhere in the portfolio, the problem was the complexity of the products, asking what is your core equity tier one ratio on a lookthrough basis, as if to say, what the fuck are you not looking at or not through what at lumps of ice and tears is the contrite reply, shelled out from the eternal RBS reserves implicit in a trap sky of overweening negligence, while out the door the rest live past desire filing left to right, doing the cleaning and food, a plunging sky inside now too opaque to block, a sum too cryptic for the universe.

What the fuck are you on about the demilitarisation of syntax? Anders Hoegstroem or whatever your concept is. An advert in amateur smoke trail calligraphy for a special edition of *The Sun* containing a photograph of a male cock ejaculating a human mouth incompatible with an organic face made to sag like what would to the averagely astutely cynical loss adjuster be hardly rotten if manifestly soaked floorboards in a style that is evidently senile but drilled in joy on every page 3, whose page count approximates infinity, all of them called 3, except for a solitary page, very close to the end, a mystery, a page called something else, a bonus page, an inextinguishable laminated palimpsest of the lot of them on which in an infant hand is artlessly scrawled in triangles the stupid words simplicity fuck and fire. What escape fuck are you on TL the demilitarisation of syntax? Anders whatever 6 discharge your concept. A predictably instead of problematically predictably lovable adventure cage with no manifest theme for a domestic rat with a wire wheel pinned in it for it to run around in and translucent coloured plastic tubes pushed in it for it to slide down in a straight line or in a spiral and an opaque plastic ball in it that its child locks shut for it to run around in like a baby planet in a universe with no rat in it, representing the conscience of Lord Goldsmith. What fuck you, the demilitarisation syntax bun escape? L1. Anders escape cape landscape, whatever concept. P. The colophon first significantly, then insignificantly, then neither significantly nor insignificantly omitted on the in any case long ago torn out opening page of Aeschylus's *Paedos in Speedos*. Fuck you, demilitarisation. TL61P. * Tearing up the rule book just aestheticises it into a vorticist collage of General Franks. You knew that from the instant you escaped; beautiful highbrow heel-dragging in unwaded war blood will not drown it. Go and fucking smash the world to bits. A branding exercise, thrashed out over a briefing document, excluded from the minutes. 6. The concept of a life is art, as well in the White House as if not. Sincere, tho' prudent; constant, yet resigned; but not in jail. General Franks will not to jail, however you collage him. Unoriginality is as old as the hill, and yet as insipidly venerable. Vomit the antidote, put the salad back barely touched, mute the flares, sand off the moisturiser, extricating what it may unconvincingly be pretended are incomprehensibly stubborn last globules still there after hardly the toughest rubbing fails with the glowing tips of safety pins, pick up every shred of rule book and diligently glue it back together, edge to edge.

III

Dance down the hill. We know for a fact that the tabloids are a protection racket for politicians, so we know that voting *is* extortion. Limp up the hill. But since the alternative, in any case not yet even on offer, is fully inflated politicians too big for rackets, bigger with wind than the distended dead end of an abdomen of the sugar-coated bloated Ethiop Aeolus, so that for the time being extortion it is. Both paralyses are best sublimated into an antisocial involuntary gag reflex at the least reference to anything but last resort, a dream in which you get to wish for things which you can't think you are told you never ought to wish for, gravely flagging up the hardly flapping haggard tongue. The natural ecumenism of the press complaints commission is on the face of it the nocturnal emission of the independent police complaints commission, nicely cold and wet; the otherwise eternal compassion of the independent for what is radiant, fresh kids smash up the porn shop scattering its bitty windows over the aisles of flatpack noumenal genitals, trashing shit love; the tax return of the independent police of the future. Outer space is deeply inanimate.

181

Happily eat the boiled hyenas but omit to suck dry their dark alarming skulls. Capitalism, the system for profit we all die under, is the infinite multiplication of values; the last resistance is sterility, but not the least. Queering war. Thousands of unshrinking eyes rush out a split open head in a prophetic geyser, stare back as wide and bright as the whole world, plunged in thunder over us, the ochre and lavender glow of the virginal streaking sun illogically scars their billion idiotic retinas. MAKE LESS, BE MORE.

Pope's descents to Beckett's dips, Keats astride a grave betimes, a Nigerian sex slave. A Nigerian sex slave plying its overstretched, hedged, oily ass at the dusty fringes of the *Biennale* to drunk sponsors of the European tents. Or what will not debase so much as shatter, or what will not rejoin but soon rip up, or rearrange with gratuitous violence, undo savagely primp or outright annihilate. Our amity is fitted for division. You won't say anything more radical than sex. But this irrepressible oral craving for the exciting controlled annihilation of values and invariably the long concomitant impatience at their boring slow debasement over the course of natural inflation over the course of things just going on not yet with the alacrity to be interminable makes the poet a predictable stupid rake, a programmed profligate courtier, his lyric on the fucking make, his infancy a mucked up fake, all ugly sex and textbook camaraderie and floor, and all the more derisory for sadly being poor.

The meaning of pornography when I am a child is that people really meant that, in that I would, and that I could join them, either by doing it for real later, or by doing it as a fantasy *right now* instead; coming with someone who would be real but not you in the future, or coming over you right now because you are not real; Intensity makes freedom an illusion: the present is irresistible; Reality is never worth the wait. The meaning when I am a child is the same one now. Intensity makes freedom an illusion; on one cover there was a childish sketch of a cock in my mother's hand. But under the other, my secret woman with the piercing mad hole; It is worth the wait. Because of this explicable hole in the end I speculated I'd get hard if ordered to stand hovering all night over tacks, while tethered to a pillar by the wrists in some vanished friend's mother's lounge to be inspected with explicit apathy from the sofa in the end as in reality I was, every night, in my mother's hand, and at last painfully pushed down by him into the bliss at the end of this fantasy, driving the tacks in after all that long agony to avoid it; because either you split me in two or fuck you. Do not leave me only whole.

Pigging out on leverage in Merrill Lynch is the new Charles Olson. Flesh gets hard, sadly get used to it. Without it you imperishably shine. Values have to be *fucking annihilated*. It's not enough to do Pound in indifferent voices wisecracking to your banker crony about 'the upjut of sperm' in a parody of an admission of inferiority to see whose spontaneous pornography can repudiate sex best, *quia pudendum est*. You at the back, cremate me, quick. Resuming all your days and splatter on the hallucinated mouth you sadly drool a window on, yet throw it wide to let a breath sheer in; once the breath is beautiful; The same old same old up the you know what; Brief contact is not irritating But prolonged contact, as with clothing wetted with material, May cause defatting of skin or irritation, seen as local redness with possible mild discomfort; The oral suspension cannot hold the benzoates you only dream: *Verfremdungseffekt* by arbitrary searches. Lashed on thrashing fire inside like flashing flutes of Gaviscon. I want to get rid of the squint, but how? How to go numb from lisping in numbers? And how really, not like that. If this is the way that this sentence resorts to your head, why know otherwise? Where's the oversight? Whose tribunal? By involuntary spasms reality pushes you out, banging on the wall. There join me Muses, in the songs of triumph, flying the friendly skies, like this. What do you think of this bit, Bill? Is it just a UPC for cramp, a one-liner about a crab breathing white out? Blowing bubbles and popping them with her claws, unconscionably erotic? Would you first rip up then glue back together the words or the letters? Why do you

keep coming to me in dreams? Climbing as if sideways
back through the skew of black and nothing like a midriff
in your colour, not dead for a change, not now abolished
except in photos that are also abolished, but living in
the form of what you are to me? I want a topical penis.
Excoriation of destiny is a cure for being impossible to empty,
a hoover bag in Sapphic drag, rehearsing our suction on dust.
In a closed circuit like mortality the last word is guaranteed;
it is by definition what you always get, that's the beauty of it.
    Living stops to fit the empty
cap on your desire, right
    minded to allow the sight
to fade in blinded appetite.

    Telling you again in level
voices to be stable for,
    unlistenable outside the door
to profit whence to turn to shit.

    So what are you waiting for
me for, the hot shrinkwrap
    disoriented on your lap,
once believed-in, only savage?

    Fire comes on that won't go
out along the way you run, yet
    made to last for what you let
go past you, burns the eye alive.

    But look at these caricatures,
numb by numbers, empty shells,
    new complexity doorbells,
jokes about what they are.

III

Whatever the point is, it's here to stay; and there's a
lesson in that for us all, if we're not too proud to
pretend there is. But in a flash we are only too proud.
You ask yourself if you can be excused. In the future
my ghosts will multiply the more people I know die,
and my ghosts will multiply more quickly the more

184

people I know die quickly, the SKU for everyone alive is EV-A, and the rate of multiplication will grow quicker until in the end the future is nothing but my ghosts, not even me; this is a comic poem, scatterbrained Iraqis. I would run words together like wall gashes strips, thinking I'd be right. But the outcome would not be, but something else just dumped on it instead. Years of my life wasted on war, depressed and miles away. *Je le vis*. The menu bar and buttons are displayed above the text fields: The line below shows many product codes; Use the menu bar to choose commands: In addition to the standard menus; File, Edit and View, there is also the: Dialog toolbar for fast access to frequently used commands in the toolbar can be activated and deactivated at the point View Toolbar. As for humanity, right now, it can be ignored or converted into a better problem – be degraded into a problem that was bound sooner or later to give rise to solutions like government, such as the present one. The public loves to be told that it has to learn to expect less, because everyone wants everyone else to have less, and everyone is willing to have less if that is the price for ensuring that everyone else but him has less. What a cunt.

> The contemporary universe is strictly undersexed.
> Same principle as the banking disaster,
> one love used to leverage another,
> one life more renamed the next.
> Elastic shoulders imitate
> the shimmer of no arc itself; screaming
> Don't leave your unwanted love
> over the floor and run away
> where what you say is what you do
> without including less of you, pay attention
> the fire drill in the family quad at lunchtime
> is not cancelled in the end. You know that because this is
> the end, and it is not cancelled yet; I will
> likely not ever meet anyone I love so much as
> you again; but I want to try some men before I die.

The upside of the credit crunch is the defence review.
Think of it: the damage to Britain's military standing,
the 4 billion on Nimrods (O fret not after knowledge),
the limitation of the maximum enduring army force, no
more ratification by depleted uranium of the endless
moral ringing in the ears, having none of it, no new
material for the infinite ad campaign for the new millionth
Olympian, a pedalo of foam dropped on a laughing
amputee. You go downstairs to watch *Ladies of Letters*,
pumping the wound. And why not end it there, courtesy
of paranormal disgust? Look straight
in the eye, as under it you climb through that dream grated
in returning, livid end, far into the shape I
kept in order that I could love it too late later, my eyes hurt
in my heart, too much to stare at your gently dead face its
lips removing silence from the air they brightly shun
in an impenetrable hole full of conclusive human darkness.
My head does that, I am forced and even proud,
pulling you back to precision, to life by colour,
we're allowed because you're dead and I'm older,

   Shakespeare said love moderately
as mine as no one ever was
   that line in 'late Wieners'
impressing no one, timing out.

   My own heart still beats hard
at the open door to know
   who will swallow it below
the meteor imprisoned in stars.

   Both routes out the window lead
to falling deaf to heavenly
   pretence but by flying only
too late into trust in deafness.

   Which makes it all the more real
but hard to beat, abiding in
   despair that love will not begin
when you do, but in everything.

HEATHER PHILLIPSON

Jesus Christ

He called by to ask questions: 'Did you ever punch a nose? Maybe a glancing blow, fourteen years ago? To dry-run the feeling?'

I wanted this man on my side. He had access to)**£!...><%^!. He seemed no more than the apron of a face, a way of looking.

You could say he had the veneer of a ladies' man in the smash-up of his career. A man, or a desolate landscape. A trampled-on forest. Yet still, strangely attractive. Death overwhelms even mediocrity.

Why must it always end this way? 'The face is the only avant garde we have', I replied. 'And the name. A good name is promotable.'

Although You Do Not Know Me, My Name is Patricia

For the record, we are undertaking research into Love, or Something Similar Fabricated in the Back Workshops of Imagination.

Claire, my assistant, is sorry she couldn't be here, by the way. I, too, am sorry she couldn't fit through your bathroom window, even when naked. 'Now pass me back my knicks and cash and let me go refine my statistics!' Beneath the streetlights, her sweat glands recalled the margarine in my carrier bag. Having lubricated my surfaces, I slithered through the chink, alighting on your cabinet.

From the array of dyspepsia remedies, I deduce that you are a communist academic and your wife a neophyte Bohemian. Although Flossie was never exactly a cabaret dancer, she demanded to be called Flossie and was in a panic to marry. Panic and relentless love are easily mistaken.

Claire would say your miniature soap collection belies a marriage of sex and pecuniary convenience. Heaps of sex. Every night for a month, then every other night for two months. Soon it was three times a week for a year, then once a week. Now, almost never. Don't worry though, the future is broken anyway. Something went wrong a while back. Why else would we huddle together in cities, if not to feel better (if not safe exactly)?

We make up for it by making things up, spilling our adventures to anyone who'll listen. Some share life, like two unequal halves of a Chelsea Bun, with a stranger. Some release the sugared non-half into the mouth of a stranger. Some realise the unequal-half-fiddle once the sugar's all swallowed by a mouth that won't be around forever. The inventions of the back workshop may be the high-spot along the damp bricks of years, Claire would deduce, if Claire could be here.

Actually, I'm Simply Trying to Find My Dressing Gown Sash

Matter can't just vanish. But, having checked my waist
(coffee percolator, compost heap, plug hole, deep freeze, U-bend,
consulted the moth with a philosopher's expression on the door mat
(dead)), what's left in this place to frisk or rely on.

Best to walk off in a straight line towards a recollection
of the bird feeder or to answer the daily telephone call
where someone called Cyril calls me
someone called Jennifer. There has been an omission.

Unlike my belt, Cyril would never leave Jennifer unsupported.
That's crud, he'd declare ('crud', a word he loathes
until it makes him joyful) and surprise her with a ribbon.
The sides of Jennifer's dressing gown would not flap inevitably.

Who? I say, or Oh, yes, or, Forget her, Cyril, we live for encounters
ahead of us, there's only so much breath. Only runners
should be up at this hour, running for their lives.
And Mo and Billy, of course, who will call Jennifer any minute

from their farmhouse kitchen. Then it's Suzy (your niece, aunty Jennifer),
calling me (Jennifer) on her tea break, by which time the logic
of logic has been disconnected, and where am I, reflecting
parenthetically on wrong numbers and over-connectedness

in my under-connected dressing gown that billows
during morning duties while Mo and Billy kiss each other passionately
and Suzy wishes Jennifer happy birthday
and all *I* want is a bathrobe with a belt attached to it.

The gown sags in its absence while I upend then dig around
the bin bag, looking for a truth too obvious
to recognise in the used plastics, dammit, and all along,
up to the elbows, doubtful of its existence.

Goodbye. You can take this as my notice.

Plan B: become less obvious. It's been said I'm good with mammals. More
than that, I'm tremendous in a perceived crisis. I take control, show spunk
and affirmation.

For too long, I've been passing through one of those periods in which
significance is found only in dullness. I don't know what I need. I need to get
out of these wet-look leggings and into a dry Martini.

Let's enjoy these aimless days while we can. All hell will not break loose.
Everything is linked. Everything and nothing, to be accurate.

SOPHIE ROBINSON

necessary fucking

why is everybody always writing
about fucking like me the more writing
to be done the less time to do the
necessary fucking for poetry

which is just as well when 'at a bar' or
side by side alone & almost having
sex but in the end we change our minds 'cos
work is early/harsh work makes you nervous

lines up the days & besides you don't love
each other so much today as yesterday
& that dwindle's dampened the itch to do
anything but write some stupid sonnet

frigid at the kitchen table no damp
itch to speak of no great love to leap off

prophylactic

& today my heart exists as a sur
face upon which your broken face is being
tattooed & as i wake the world whirrs prom
enading as a sitcom with the volume
up too loud we're submerged in the black back
water of east canals & waking there
are holes in my bones which wind sings goodbye
to you through there's a hole in your head you
wear on the outside & we're slopped in factor
fifty nostalgia gulping down grammars
bile from far off sickness of our former
lives & i wear you as an abscess an

inverted bruise,
                    i shan't survive this
winter without you & your upright brain
to keep mine warm & not bad no longer
needing public muscle to keep tight vigil
        a psalm from celebrities of history
to make us safe to fix your feinting face
& mine full of spots & shipwrecked girls
to keep hold of me out the window of
the institute of our love in disrepair.

i alone

i don't know what to say except i miss
you on the phone historical & loving
of the mouth & in the stumps & off my
clothes & fallen off you softly with my
buried ancestors with wolves at the door
with the beating flap of death take hold my
hand with swallowed coal-lumps' cureless baubles
with sinks & teeth & now descended with
o england's fragile tombstone with its bargain's
fray'd & fragile vapours with heart that is
that bough breaking into cocaine-spattered
sky & left to ripple or erase itself
or else to fright or frig dry & homelands
burn & organs tenderise in a big
child of twenty five with hurts in lines with
the sluggish moon a'calling with a love
that's hard as iron with a love you can't
return o lord call me no more silence
cut across lament & stay very thin

memory gapes – this is a world i have
washed away what gives it rhythm & i
don't know what to say except reverse charge
my wretchedness my eager eyes for light
for my bedrock bear unmangled 'live with
me be my witness' from body to body

as waterglass as my mother's false water
in which I flicker tongue as in a cat's
kiss pilfer within myself & we can
cry & be relaxed i'd eat your clots for
one thousand nights & vomit rivers into
your ocean feed on me like mice
on melon rinds o london i want my
happy wages back & with matching rings
cut my ruins open like a fireman
because we've got poorly lately, less
life dragging behind us in the hot &
clapping battle of the city's vampire's
lies we do not have the strength to fight, no.

Animal Hospital

some times like sin sugar that broke that crashes
bruise of rib like rip off cloth and let salt
winds scathe in eye in face I am sandy,
long for ocean grind – but shy, but shy – 'I
don't owe you any money don't have to
show you all my things' – just live, okay? 'Cause
all our money is etch-a-sketch, and I
think too often about the forward times
when our things are out and old on the street,
when we are out of time, stink, are the laughed
at lucky ones or, worse, screaming in two
different hospitals, species strangers,
unknown/unknowing.

this is the ailing
of peace, the rearrangement of passion.
we do not kiss but strum ourselves apart.
the sun has its sins, the heart its heavy.
this poem should be longer, and more careful.
give me time.

MARCUS SLEASE

[untitled]

It is 03.28 on the second day and my fridge is full of Pınar Dogal Yogurt. There is a haze of lights outside my window. We were at REAL shopping centre. Prayers crowned the air. I was a translated clam. This is where the world's nuts are made. I'm waiting for the ruins of a Roman bath. I'm waiting for the temple of Augustus. I'm waiting for the Monument to a Secure Confident Future! Everybody seems hard on the face but soft in the mouthholes.

It is 06.42. I've slept one hour. 15 min till I am supposed to awake. It was a night with my life. Or parts thereof. Snow and microbrews, ping pong beer, erotic nights in hotel rooms. Paper routes and swimming pools. Little boy and big boy. Dusty hands against the window, sweaty trousers and mouldy cheese. Hands on the nightstand. Running & running round the tracks. Jesus on the ceiling. Angel light from passing trucks. Tootsie rolls from Mormon missionaries. Las Vegas lakes and rocket ships. It is 09.00. It has rained and the red clay of Ankara sicks to my soles. The stones glow at the old gate. This is an ongoing nomadic poetics. I'm drinking Seftali Nektari in the east campus cafeteria. In this garden of dark howls I search for my twin. Cleaners clean around me. When you awake what sticks to your skin? Who colours these keenings? The old has been sold. Culling the senses in this cold wind I have felt the devouring. Praise the whirling dervish. The ecstasy of petals on an empty platter. The non-arousing of hotel erotics. The corona is in the clinic. I'm 90% glutton free.

Short Shorts

let me help you find the nearest Wal-Mart said the Korean Monk
to the wandering finger the wandering finger is taken to the section
called SHORT SHORTS but he is in the wrong section he is looking
for the Korean word for razor so the Korean monk takes it to a stadium
where old men roll on small trucks biting the ankles of younger men
in dicky bows this is not right screams the finger so the Korean monk
takes him to Gyeongbok palace where it finds a perky little pug
barking at shadows what's this exclaims the finger but by this time
the Korean monk has entered the palace on the rods of fishermen
bloated on the pregnant wind of twelve blind mice

There's real mint in this tea

(Fatisa Café. Wood Green High Road)

bright sun From

The Mountains of California

and The Gold Standard

on the table coffee hat sunglasses checkered shirt

applied to teach at

fat chance

it's a shoe in it's written
for them

today in London feels like
North Carolina early summer old leather chair time abounds

you've got a trans-
lucent charm

Herikeitos

when first we leered

upon the real

flying over
the rancid

charm as form

yr sun is Nero!
but I'm

in WOOD GREEN

among these scavengers

we call pigeons

waiting for fresh mint to soak the boiling water

I've looked at my face twelve times since morning

and put on linen trousers with hat

and sunglasses

194

                                        I'm ready to get breezy with Kent
Johnson   or Philip Whalen   but not

                                the avant garde
what's up
                your sleeve today

                                                Jackie Chan

pulling off stunts
or tricks
                                how all these passengers pass by

with different arms
                        swinging in different ways

and different tushes
                                        hugging different jeans

                the Turkish are inside
                                        cutting meat

with their knives

                        Ewa has begun sipping her mint tea

where has my stomach gone these last days

THERE'S REAL MINT IN THIS TEA

                                        that lady is still eating her chicken
and the red double deckers
whoooooooosssssssshhhhhh
on by
and Ewa is highlighting
and my mint tea
is hot water with smelly plants
and my belly tells me I'm not
expansive today
                                I don't want to take this world or this self

                too seriously

[untitled]

'the best way to study the brain is to
remove it
from the skull
              however this approach
still
      has its limitations' (from a textbook on psychology)

                ponder this ass
                how it moves
                and sometimes not
                how it empties
                out the eternal
                waste of kebabs
                and hamburgers
                and much vegetation
                see how it
                bleeds and burns
                for you
                and when the
                sphincter
                pokes out
                wrap finger
                in paper
                poke back in

I'm 37 my hair not yet grey my beard trim my head shaved my belly full
of rumble
and thus
I sit
busting the bubbles
of my thoughts
on this busy highstreet
in north London
oh literacy
there is my hair in my shoe
and my eyeball twitches
dried sweat crumbles
from my eyebrow
I am such and such
of stuff
that dreams
are made of

MELANIE CHALLENGER

The Robin's Pick

Cock robin is a-chasing his bride over yew.
In the church wreck, gnats baptise us, make air
Its kin element. We breathe water.
My boy watches me. He has a robin's tongue
And cocksureness. He has a bird's mind,
Its strict, hidden light. He is bent on assumption
And constancy, and something more   the moulting gold
Of individual action and unguessable turn that is the mark
Of life. We share as such but he and the robin are truer brothers.
Some cleft, mechanical eye, some shade of inadequacy
Scuppers the message. For infant and bird, each still
Knows a pure action, the lightest territorial foothold,
An agile coalescence with root and mud.
My choice, its historical chimeras, staggers me.
The world shivers free of my step like an unwelcome touch.

The Daffodil

Little son, you've spun that daffodil out
onto the waves   to the sea, onto the melting edge
of continuousness it floats. Its lostness terrifies you.
Your curls sing in the wind like a daffodil's flute.

There's so much in that single act of surrender.
What did you mean – you, who's more flower than man?
Oblation? To put to death? Or just to see its glamour
against the waves? O, the sea is in multiples; it blurs

at your feet. In your mind, there are no replicas.
All of the world appears of a piece. Did you think
the sea might put forth buds and turn to spring?
Not a chance. Its greys are jingling with old wars.

In time, you'll have a recurring dream of a car that takes
you away from me. The lostness of the daffodil will grow
in you again. Out there, in the grey, each golden cell
a synecdoche of what you once held, once threw.

Wild Things

Your soft cheeks levitate on night's dark
Surface like gold relieved of its weight and clout.

I sit hooded in the black canal of my body.
I have told you lies. In the silence of my longing

I dare not move, I daren't breathe. And damn
Language. My wheedling words   terrible, terrible,

Over and again, terrible terrible. Night
Draws to the blunted familiarity of my body like stout

Dragging its principles. Into the grain of your skin's
Faint glow night empties as the sea's

Frustrated retreat. Child, you lie like an unvisited
Continent, your flesh so unthought it might take

Any form. What kind of angels are we this night?
The end of day fades purgatorially across my face

As an alterpiece, turning me to the racked faces of nature,
To salamanders, humming birds, catfish, wombats. Did St Anthony

Know as he staved off his mixed bag of demons
In the desert? Did Grünewald know, or whatever his name was,

How little I might give of nature's beauty
And terror to my child? When your sun comes,

My darling boy, that man's dreams,
His unknowable face and the whispering gallery of history,

Will be your strange angels of disappearance.
You will read them to your son in the darkness.

Balnakeil Beach or Mortality

The seabird's pecked heart flaunts its absence,
As our latter-day hearts exsanguinate – *bleed, if you will* –
From their immunity. The landscape is candid beside the corpse;
And the heteroclitic sea – *the jerks, if it makes more sense* –
Slides its spare, aquatic nature through the frames,
Much as a poem of invisible ink, drafted to loss.
The bird is giddy-brained by its sudden stillness –
Its death, if that's how you want me to say such things.
Only sand tumbles through the shape of prior adaptation,
An impression of the clouds that, amid the ruin,
Becomes a skeletal tribute. And in the bunk of its eyes,
The obituary of its flight flashes – *its dizzy heights,*
As I could term it, or love. Yet it makes no more sense.

MENDOZA

Signs for Notation

say the soul is
say the soul is my winter solace
say the soul is my winter solace in harsh winter light
say the soul is like fire is like fire in
harsh winter light
is like fire is my solace in harsh winter light is
quick and subtle his
ass
to the sun

2

from the wilderness I defy sudden correction. I could
build on these species but I wait for an observation
of self-   awareness   or
purpose   or

evolution:

Thus I, like Earths topography kiss the chorus of years

& all those creeping little arthropods
know better than to gorge on
what will destroy them

3

insert … [three lines torn]…

[oblit]

sin
[oblit]
I flatter my /   self my /
Desire and
Inclination   my

pale. arctic. I   as

        agnostic
        remnant

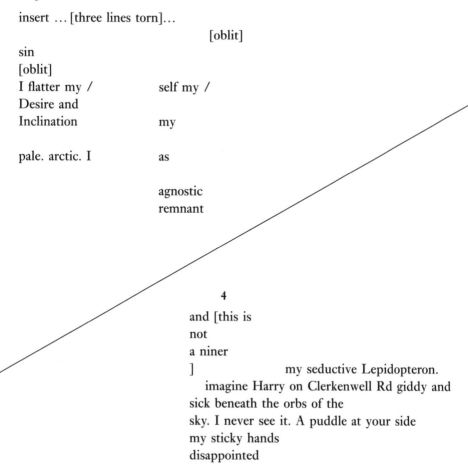

4

and [this is
not
a niner
]   my seductive Lepidopteron.
  imagine Harry on Clerkenwell Rd giddy and
sick beneath the orbs of the
sky. I never see it. A puddle at your side
my sticky hands
disappointed

5

How much I admire the pylon throb of your feelings in which I deploy mimic
    response

                      Initiate movement.
                            Sequenced.
                            Organised.

Shape forms.
Describe the shape the static body takes:

Wall-like / Ball-like / Pin-like Stomach-in-
throat. Avoid

motion-detection. Avoid

miming the shape of imaginary objects

6

i like it that you are yet more ambiguous + spewing only
organic matting amorphous +
soft. Hey Bergvall, hallo
an ass eats a fig in folded homage :

Fig. 1. male of fig
wasp inseminating
female [fig wasp] inside
the gall of an edible fig.

the piece is a table who sits and gloats. in desperation we dismembered him

7

the pattern of stepping is equally ambiguous.
typesetting [or handwriting]
abbreviations of foot. Forrie Capers1.
my body is small yet
bulbous / fecund.
I can make 3 in 6 out. I can make 5 in 4 out.   9 in none out
Twenty-four ribs house a lyrical heart.
Have it stuffed and mounted,
summer redbird

A feeling of effort.

Remember this. A sensation of arm telling the word.

Remember this. Two figures. *One stands illuminated in the open*

doorway. obscured by shadow he writes the other

supposing the self.

Remember this. An awareness of self

contingent on memory

rapidly forgetting

becoming

9

radical nothing

I am all that you write, scouring and fretting

sudden / sustained   bound / free

institutionalised by the opposite of

reason

we are tender + poetic. brutal,

banal. ruffled out

of expensive calm,

this is not my register.

JACK UNDERWOOD

Certain

Nothing before had seemed so potent
and self-contained –
surely the onion was beautiful.

Its hung cloud of acid worked
in his nose and throat
as the knife bisected

like a maker of names passing
between twins, calling one half *Perfect*
the other also *Perfect*.

My Steak

        will be as thick
as the frown of the beast,
will be a cut kind of love.

When you cook it for me try
not to cook it, but weigh it
on a high heat until unstable.

Think of it as mud dying,
a pushed hand, or a question,
hung in itself, about blood.

I will unpack into my mouth
cud-grass, eye-roll, fathom
the taste of my own cow tongue.

Commend me to my steak
for I am a living beak
and all my teeth are hungry.

Sometimes your sadness is a yacht

huge, white and expensive, like an anvil
dropped from heaven: how will we get onboard,
up there, when it hurts our necks to look?

Other times it is a rock on the lawn, and matter
can never be destroyed. But today we hold it
to the edge of our bed, shutting our eyes

on another opened hour and listening
to our neighbours' voices having the voices
of their friends around for lunch.

Death Says

      the atoms of men have already spent infinity
as part of something else and all your human fudge
is the passing of a thread through the surface of a light.
If you are made of thinking then being is a breath between the slats,
which is why I itch your collar when a fly taps the pane.
I am your address and the hand that delivers you through.
I am the socket love must plug itself into.
I am the lie that runs along your ribs, the gap between the rock
and the wet place you will make there for yourself.
You will know my hand by the back of your own.
I am talking to you now in the voice you read with inwardly,
private as the name you say to the bottom of a tall felt hat.

OLI HAZZARD

Pantoum In Which Wallace Stevens Gives Me Vertigo

In Wallace Stevens' poem 'The Public Square',
a languid janitor bears his lantern through colonnades
and the architecture swoons. I cannot read this poem
without being struck down with vertigo. I can only read:

'A languid janitor bears his lantern through colonnades...'
before I start to feel sick, and suddenly aware of the earth's roundness.
Without being struck down with vertigo, I can only read
whilst strapped into my chair; I will read the poem, and

before I start to feel sick and suddenly aware of the earth's roundness,
I can remind myself that it's only a poem, I'm not going to fall over
whilst strapped into my chair. I will read the poem, and
triumph by making it to the end. But this is not my ultimate goal.

I can remind myself that it's only a poem. I'm not going to fall over
myself just because of one little achievement. I don't really
triumph by making it to the end. 'But this is not my ultimate goal,'
I say – as if that were anything like the truth. Every day I celebrate

myself because of one little achievement (I don't really)
and the architecture swoons. I cannot read this poem,
I say, as if it were anything like the truth. Every day I celebrate
Wallace Stevens' poem 'The Public Square'.

Are we not drawn onward, we few, drawn onward to new era?

Marge, let's send a sadness telegram.
I roamed under it as a tired, nude Maori.
No trace, not one carton.

Kay, a red nude, peeped under a yak.
Was it a car or a cat I saw?
Amen, icy cinema.

Nurse, I spy gypsies. *Run.*
No, I tan at a nation.
Flee to me, remote elf.

Eva, can I stab bats in a cave?
Oozy rat in a sanitary zoo
Loops at a spool.

Two Versions of 'Fabliau of Florida'

I

Hop for probe-quash.
Capable hymen, tho.

Mouth a tonne. Ad overview:
Tethers a tonsil-baa,
Handles tubing.

One ear – calm a fond duo.
Trusty, solemn morons.
Gild aversions.

'Hullo,' (bray.) Lick full.
I whet with no hog milt.

Hell? A bed. Intervene, wren!
Huffing thins, rooted, rots.

II

Sh. Baroque Prof., hop-
Hop. Batman. Lychee.

Oh, a retentive ovum! O, wand!
Theorise as blatant
As blighted nun,

Re: aeon. Faun-clad doom!
Stony melon rostrums,
Gravid lesions

(Back-hour filly lull).
We hit with thin gloom.

Whenever binned, retell a
Fistfight, routed on horns.

Martedi Grasso

1

An infant left unexposed
                to linguistic stimulus
                                will automatically begin to speak
Enochian, the language
                of the angels. Black
                                and white, boy and girl operate
in this language together.
                One cries, 'Let this length
                                therefore be called the Standard; let
one Tenth of it be called
                a Foot; one Tenth of a Foot
                                an Inch; one Tenth of an Inch a Line.'
Under this, gently: 'un mecanismo
                arbitrario de gruñidos y de
                                chillidos, so uncommon in its failure

2

angels in their tens of thousands
                    encircled the throne,
                                whispering *telocvovim.*' Soon, flames lamb
ent wrapped round Tottenham
                    and wrapped round Clapham. Before this:
                            'The restra
ints imposed by a mercantile
                    culture, ruinous
                                in effects up
on many who comprised the crowd,
                    encouraged rapid volatility'.
                            (A doctor co
unted very able / designes
                    that all Mankynd converse
                            shall.) Everything m

3

anifesting its own version of fullness:
                    'Infra thin
                                separation betwe
en / the detonation noise of a gun / (very
                    close) and the apparition
                                of the bullet / hole
in the target.' There should be a
                    word that can only
                            be spoken if
one does not know what it means.
                    And these signs shall follow
                            them that believe:
(under breath) they shall cast out devils
                    in my name; they shall speak
                            with new tongues...

MICHAEL KINDELLAN

from Not love

Hair cuts, dear reader, throws graphs and rings
an occasional use knotted into a clasp
of flowers. And he will give them to you.

But are these acceptations rare? Do they
shape, as something is shaped by feeling it, to
an absence of features marked so presently,

and signaled by their cues? For you: we won't
acknowledge their looks like that. Platforms
present one kind of truism – a spot so tight

it nearly duplicates what framed some lovely
catalogues. The shores opposite this shore
made distinct by what's now a wrecked

but rollicking earth. So how 'now'? You speak
expletives inside the stitch of your famous
trap. And what other outbursts really

know a known love that lasts this long,
so wholly into the minimum of asters,
that when the light's calmed, it shines on?

For simple postures beat a customary means
of not inserting life (but show it patterned
forth). The world not only is up to you.

Then my subject is love, like hats, made from hair;
and men formed like sweet flags, beneath soft
haloed glows of oleomargarine, glistening.

Pound on to the earth. Now go like this:
now go all recondite | like from corners | now
go like complex bones pushed into breasts

and flicking muck for daggers. That dirt is, my love,
for you, grafting æther, or maybe this dirt is that love
gone molded around the worlds it faces.

How many times do windows make me look small
through them, waiting for you? Oh refracted affections!
In such proportions of materials there are

of you for me, the set wonder against
a gripped lid that flips, the fingered sounds
slid to buttons we speak thereof, nuanced and stellar.

It's system on system. It turns and struts back down
the made way she leaps off to unthread the sun's
light, as it unthreads from cloth its own gold traces

gliding down in the after glow and I globally, classically
forge all this flexion, smile neutral but stubborn,
and preening, and watch as skin cuts back nets. Or, in saying

what only words would want it to, the mouth moves
down past hair and cigarettes, and onto human spikes,
and passing those past flies that distend the gape

as we look at them, and then further forward
bends to bite a grime that's piles of dust so
cleaned of life. Its lips are in your hand again.

And what with this luck fits wigs over every hole
in the road, and that filth relates a fact to
one side of sensation or other means it's easy enough

to mewl speech into a gossip hum throating
our many selves and driving them into a heart
whose auscultation can so sound like a gun

bleeding in your pocket as it slips off its ring.
And, with dirty fingers on my trigger now
sticking from the place where intellection

is called to prove its tiny white pearl really is
tiny and white and a pearl balanced and stuck there
and often described as deeply more lustrous

than thought can be apprised of but still
certainly not exist for us, you fire it past bone
into ground, so that it lays there, just ridiculous

and alone. Juice and bile on the chyme spared
hardly so those knuckles pale in hinges
while the plans are made for telling. The chasm

they talk from issues courageously but various,
so it will turn out nothing, so vetoing your term
which opens so. Some world that doesn't mediate,

it grows on your chest in a bloom, it lifts you,
you are risen into the aureate sky, the cool equivalents
of the idylls we rode her on: 'Bellini's suave

melodies' (oh yeah, ohhhh yeah); 'Rossini's splendid
roulades' (ff-ff-ff-ffvt-oooo, yeah). Looking right at
mere decorations, like: what is the fitness;

or, no scratch that – what is the strange charm, no,
what is the fitness of your aboriginal palate that
you can eat rocks and bugs and shit like that?

The rock runs red over; we dare you to eat each
of these hands' full by what they, wrenching, cup.
It's weird yet it's the thing donned as a hat

that's a huge extension of the face. We, dancing on.
Who pulls and eats their hairs like they are,
delicate but mad, twining through who so that

whose guts plait a rope and let it fall; and
everyone is under someone's nails bit to the bone
bleeding or not bleeding like food. Don't eat

that, says one, pointing to what looks like
an apple holed out so much it's just basically
a brown ring extending no further than

the spinning shape it goes through. In wearing
stones or pendants of counterfeit pearl, the earth
comes tuned to the possessions of her land.

The Flight to Quality

Uncertain outlooks experience a recent
surge in what investors are safest
to perceive, like silver into assets.
'The storm is perfect for metal,' a Robin
said, looking at them keenly. The contrast
in May is for a New York rose,
as aggregated credit gains. A troy
ounce settled on the day. The price
broke the climb, its heights adjusted
well over the week, preciously long.
Push up, re cover, repeat and record
nothing low: silver soars, appeals without
burden. What debasement will occur is
a poor standard amid what rises,
rating the prospects of weather.
The wrestle back could possibly load
up the power ahead like the mood
of gold reversed in mid
August, a tasty worm plucked
from out the current bread basket.
It was within the reach of an all-time
low that the jump in oil prices turmoil
as confidence that slides back to fade
the economies desire. The yellow
metal, the red chest threaded by paper
into harder assets. Coins are running
at a super pace; nothing pecks faster
into the datastream, fumbling for stones.

Terra form A

Calculate that it begins with the simple problem
that if the Earth ceases to support life, and human
life does not continue elsewhere, all economic
activity will also cease. There are several ways
to estimate the value of Earth. Assign the Earth

its home components, that everything lives, at least
is not value. All life is little overvalued high risk,
so avoid estimations. One way to avoid this systematic
inflation of the price of life compared to others
is to estimate the cost of replacing the Earth
compared to costing another planet with compatible
orbit. And if the work were nearly complete, ask
how much is comfort going to cost, competitively,
which is also the total of barely natural, nearby and
at issue. Plus transport.

                    Multiply variations, estimate
the smallness of prospective habitat, add ratiocination
b/w populations of Earth and rely on below-minimum
figures (although brilliantly ambitious and expensive)
until it flops. This method equals only a sort of false floor,
which Earth vastly exceeds. Another figure moves
out from every disaster that might occur due
to failure of the biosphere, to lesser or greater
degrees. How much to insure everything, a premium
for all of it? The averted insurance payments effect
a yield and calculating value for us is what we eat with,
so long as these averted failures do not occur
anymore. Work out the difference between payments
and natural services, seize the consistency, yield,
use the size of the Earth to calculate the capital
it has and there must therefore be, and expect some produce
of quite high value from the entire Earth, say
at least a figure in the hundreds of quadrillions of US
dollars. Just how subcontractors
are going to reconstruct the land with the sums
in their hands and without using the Earth itself
as a basis for replacing Earth with Earth, means
that renting an Earth and its orbit might also
have to be added to the price. Or, declare the Earth priceless;
or, exactly and only as valuable as all capital
currently in circulation, which may be the same
as saying it's worthless, however many neo-classical
economists think this idea poor in the first place.
A new world and an earth in its place: what is it
but abandoned already and fattened for a seed.

NAT RAHA

from **mute exterior intimate**
(for J.L., T.T. & R.D.)

cooker clock splutters
                  four-minute-timezone to
have dreamt a vineyard like the very sky at doorstep.

                                          fragrant chalice synthesis
devoted to salt air
                thankfully
                      stars choke the stems,
                      brittler aries' graceful stylist ,
              lower vocal frequencies brush instantaneous
                  the afternoon lockspit;

                            & sea:
            a solid glazelight morning non-economic
            to know its rise plucked safety is post-agora
                                outside

            & if to kiss in alignments approaching inexorable, would
            dulcet calm hang by whatever constitutes our ceilings.
                                all to all
            the eyes that catch traverse elsewhere.

sonnet

to know by the string of you
edging to curl breath
left gapless / in state,
                  lids masking heat
            entrope / formation to sound
            resident in all awareness,
            drive turns adrenal statuesque
            post-parachute to sharp flux
            given to the fayre of days:

maxima splits embrace raising cairn expo
based in fools' noise,
our hours will be use-wealthier
spilling the covern
alignment indigo
& strewn w/ you, to keep
belief in its raise

*

concerning dissidence:

our / hoarse vital bartering a
means–ends exclusion
            exalting it poor & tiring equus
its gentleman at wagon
            armed w/ weaponry outlawed victorian.
            the news
                according to corp:
we are the face civic vulgarity, employed beyond
morality's declaration, obtrusive
                            to the selling of the state
            already twelve months of happiness

                        we, undesirable entirely –
presently historic to survival's ideal:
hellenic strike giving purpose to transport / the
beautiful language of our time in loudhailers before the
bonfire the
                corpse of the state
/ vibration is newculture & my throat hurts insolent
in all attempts to find joy it is the new revolutionary
weapon driving the MET out of our heads the
paralysis of neo-liberalism
                        inflation will not
be a threat comrades: thatcherism
                            a synonym
for erosion & failure to find work;
                each day's new offensive

11/05/11

Flotation, Overcast / etc.

I

Cloudscape bodes a common collection
ringing irregular as pined parchment
    percussive glitch w/impatient motorcades
    belling commanded lifelines & potent closure.

turntabled & hooked Hampstead,
    causal swinging informs allusion
                       blanketed
likeness shield visual- take flight
& track humid subcontinent harassing capita
                by coastal fluxis

recalling assorted glimpses as timespan media,
    the singer suggests windows
    & distant towers over telecom
              as having found snug identifier
you embrace woodwork, gapped paragraphia
(sub)(conscious) sequences each concerned trail

II

The finding consists of Irish foliage
    watershed w/ hops, ingredient assured
    & provision classically meditated
                      lawn-like,
barefeeting union surrealist circular cabaret
    continual tent perverting audient provisions

flown to basement tucked aside photocopier,
all the years emerge subtly in a manuscript
    tying both our persuasions.

[ ] analogue driven scape score essence
    held first as a semibreve
    shortcoming my theoretical nooks   baring erasure,
overcast remaining negligent.

III

In decisive turbulence, plugged ears
retain witness category gestation
to degree
                  & extension of entitlement.
permanence in endocrine modernism
fastened to off-hand admittance
   of mood attached astro(logical)
due germination   due birth.

dusting immediacy, outcries meet
   flicking pessimism
                  I mustn't retain qualms as
glass reflections / overcast hearts / etc.
elute prolonged suspension
like treaded parallels, even in fiction
filming holy lizards rapid w/ prolonged tip

fresh vibrance en sink present w/ tear
   where your unintended skydrift slips
   atop both your bedrooms.

IV

Translucent compendium of boroughs
                  dousing paved meditations,
commit to corner & etch atomic translations
warm scatter / pleasance / semi-permanent hybrid
of voluntary delegates brushing politik
                  w/ wire mirrors & gilt.
preoccupied spatial glaze bail diminished brickwork
planned & planted prior
                  to consult swarmed allegiance

a rustic dispensary   talons & chrome carvings,
   paddled   mast   hailing her majestic soliloquy
            in ice dictate pelvic contortion

though in rolling greenery your duality treads

V

Shimmered suspense beneath the oboe's
  flashing residue paints dust in image
  & your crossing excursion,
whilst grazing batons & reprised umbrellas
                  atop your road.
knocking cultivated breeze infantile
lock derelict pleasure-seeking
              passing centurial commerce
& invoking Miami mothers laying an original tongue,

questions spinning axel composition
              handcrafted in Dresden,
open balcony, scribble folklore by forgotten squares

  an elegant collation of hovering creatures
  possessed & climbing natural fluxation

defract upright, I need not confer trails
painting damp festivities   now encased
          as a final turbulent candelabra,
white streaming w/ your verbalisations

VI

Watch calendar   brief connective blowing
across relief tones, 'this telephonic dream
  slips off heel, & you still
  count seven written mediums.

isn't this post-temperate position? demolished
independent AM sun-sisters, bless half kingdom'

       the glide snaps you brief,
partial progress pedalling conscious organs
spare rooms rouse cigarette satisfaction
   visible dress walls, Lee Miller
pressed to postcard alike six year gloss derivatives.

zone 3 dried to neck crunching destination
w/ specialist statement portrayed amongst pairing
& accumulating traffic. interval follow subterfuge
  smear attempts of stature,

MEIRION JORDAN

from King Harold

XVI

His migraine flared like a star behind his temple. Cursed by a sense of the
historic moment, he stalked out to his Morris Traveller
     under a nimbus of rain.

Behind him, the stage-hands wobbled under embarrassments of props.
Girlfriends, gigolos
     and the committee for Northern Arts stood by

to wave them off. The rain became more vague, was read as drizzle. Half-
light became half-lit. They played, as bad recordings of themselves.

*

XVII

History has no meanwhile. William swirls the contents of his cocktail glass,
watching the last of his furniture arrive.

'The model castle? Oh that goes there.' Arrested by the silhouette of a
local beauty, he raises his miniature parasol towards the lamp. 'Good luck,
dear? Certainly. I call it my little papal banner.'

'Ah ha ha ha. Ah ha ha ha ha ha.'

*

XVIII

The Lord Spake Unto Me. Payment of debts, the proffered mantle of a
higher life. It is so good to touch, to have, to feel the contact of a human or
a divine love.

History, written as interlude. As in the Song of Songs. Lips aching on lips,
the cries of children. A house going up in flames.

*

XIX

Harold advanced with a large army. Harold advanced
with a small army.

The dew touched them and they woke. They lugged the squeeze-box and
the rapiers from the van.

William was nonplussed. He ordered his counter-tenor forward
      as a sop to all the hacks.

PATRICK COYLE

Alphabetes

A. being *Alphabetes*, *Alphabetes* being the title of this talk and also being a splicing of two words from different windows *From Wiki Wikipedia:* those two words being the Ancient Greek *alphabeos*, being from the first two letters of the Greek alphabet, and *diabetes*, being from the Ancient Greek *diabaino* meaning *to pass through*, referring to the excessive amounts of urine produced by sufferers.

B. being *Backwords*, *Backwords* being the way in which I spell the word backwards when I am referring to writing words backwards, rather than being the way in which I spell the word backwards backwards, which would be sdrawkcab, sdrawkcab being a word that encourages the thought of a thatched taxi being driven down a yellow brick lane by a scarecrow.

C. being me playing the word *CHORD* on my computer keyboard like a chord on a musical keyboard with my left thumb, middle and index fingers on the *C*, *D* and *R* keys respectively, with my right index and middle fingers on the *H* and *O* keys respectively, and with my right thumb on the space bar to separate the groups of letters caused by holding down each chord. Those groups of letters being as follows: *DCROO CDOR OHDRRRRRRRRRRRC DHORRRRRC OHCRRD DHRO CODR OHRDDDDDC COHRRRRRRRD.*

D. being *dn*, a lower-case two-letter abbreviation for the word down.

E. being *ENJOY YOUR JOURNEY*, one of my favourite phrases that sits above the doorway of WH Smiths in Liverpool Street station, the phrase being sort of symmetrically composed of two Es, two Ns, two Js, three Os, three Ys, two Us and two Rs.

F. being the worn-down keyboard from my iBook G4 entitled *Five Years escaping five years of one two three four five nine and nought with their respective exclamations at signs pounds and brackets five years of my email address with an underscore in between my first name and surname backspace indent enter shift space and five years of more new blank documents than Saves.*

G. being Goldsmiths College Art Prospectus, for which I submitted an image of the lyrics to a song I wrote to be included in the MFA Art Writing section, which was subsequently selected for inclusion, and subsequently treated as an image rather than lyrics, and cropped to the point of illegibility, understandably so to some extent as it is certainly not specifically one or the other, it being more *imic* or *lyrage* than anything else.

H. being how close other words get to the word *here*, for example in The National Lottery's ad campaign where *now here* looks more like *nowhere*.

I. being ICONS in the window of a little antique shop on Great Russell Street which actually said COINS.

J. being James, or rather M.R. James, not Mr James but M.R. James, the writer, whose face I merged with that of Mark E. Smith and made in plasticine for an exhibition themed around a song about M.R. James by Mark E. Smith, after which I noticed that the initials M. R. could spell two alternating letters of MaRk and the E and S of James could spell the E. and S of Mark E. Smith, and so I called their merged faces M.aR.k JAME.Smith (pronounced M. aRk Jam. E. Smith).

K. being the first letter to interrupt the adapted version of the phrase *DUE TO UNFORESEEN CIRCUMSTANCES, TONIGHTS SHOW IS CANCELLED. WE APOLOGISE FOR ANY INCONVENIENCE CAUSED.* Taking this adapted phrase as a new language for other Wiki-Wikipedia definitions, one of circumcision would read as follows: *Circumstance is surgery that removes some or all of the foreseen from the penis. The word 'circumstance' comes from the Latin circum (meaning 'around') and caedere (meaning 'to cut'). Circumstance predates recorded human history, with depictions in stone-age cave drawings and Ancient Egyptian tombs.*

L. being the first letter of the first word sent over the internet, as described by Leonard Kleinrock: 'All we wanted to do was log on. So Charley typed an L. 'You get the L?' 'Got the L.' 'Did you get the O?' 'Got the O.' Typed the G. 'Did you get the G?' And crash! The system went down...' The end result being that the first word sent over the Internet was 'lo' – Kleinrock says, 'as in "Lo and behold." Truth is, we couldn't have created a better, more concise message.'

M. being MONS, an upsidedown glove being something that reminded me of The Battle of Mons and the mons pubis or pubic mound, and also being almost an anagram of the name SIMON, especially if the arrow passes for an I, and especially if the arrow passes through an I like a hot razor passes through the eye of An Andalusian Dog, although the dog has one I in French but is blind in English, and not an Andalusian Dog nor an Deleuzian dog nor a delusional dog going out in the midday sun with an Englishman's middle-class son.

N. being *evian* backwords being *naïve*, which in its lower-case has had an arrow pass through the tittle of its 'i', which split it in half yet doubled it and gave the two worm-like parts little limited lives of their own like the independently moving eyes of a snail, although I should clarify here that they are not two 'i's they are two tittles. 'Evian is naive spelled backwards.' also being a quote from Vickie, played by Janeane Garofalo in the 1994 film *Reality Bites*.

O. being OMNIS, OMNIS being the name of several different companies including a security firm looking after a building near my house, and also being an anagram of SIMON.

P. being the first initial of the name of my father, who had an acrylic plaque on the door of his office, and this also being my first initial, and P. Coyle also being Peak Oil, the term used to refer to the point in time when the maximum rate of global petroleum extraction is reached, after which the rate of production enters terminal decline.

Q. being an attempt to make a cube from a chopped-up snooker cue and call it a 'cueb', which once constructed resembled a lower-case 'q', due to my not being able to cut through the metal core that weighs down the end using only a rusty wood saw.

R. being *Reversed Reversed*, based upon Ceal Floyer's reversed photograph of a plastic 'reserved' sign entitled *Reversed*, my reversing of her photograph involving no manipulation to the object itself at all, and the fact being that if somebody chose to reverse my version, it would more closely resemble hers.

S. *being SNAP AND STOP, SNAP AND STOP* being a phrase from a dream I had about several pots and pans on a stove that were speaking from their opening and closing mouth-like lids, and all they were saying was 'snap and stop', 'snap and stop', and it was not until I had woken up and written down the phrase that I realised that *SNAP + STOP* is *POTS + PANS* backwards.

T. being *This way down, This way down* being the sign at the top of the stairs at Pimlico tube station that seemed to say *This way clown*, being partially down to the spacing of the typeface, but also being down to the way I was feeling at the time, which was a little dejected I suppose, or 'clown in the dumps' as I thought afterwords, which paradoxically was such a terrible piece of wordplay that it made me feel better about things.

U. being the realisation of the word *up* upsideown being dn, the aforementioned lower-case two-letter abbreviation for the word down.

V. being an attempt to write the definition of a V-sign using only a V-shaped stencil over six pages of A4 paper, from which I also made a shorter version over one page of A4 paper entitled FUCK YOU.

W. being the website 'who represents.com', which lists celebrity agents and lawyers, being also mistakenly read as 'whore presents.com', and the R of represents being subsequently changed from lower to upper-case in the website title, but which would be an impossible change to make in the website address.

X. being a kiss symbolised by the letter X in a text from an ex, and therefore being an ex-kiss, or an ex-X.

Y. being *Your call*, *Your call* being the repeated response I heard from my housemate Richard when I asked him where he went to the gym. 'It's your call!' he kept saying. 'I go to your call.' I worked out eventually that he had been going to York Hall in Bethnal Green, York Hall in Bethnal Green being also the same site as The British Stammering Association, according to Google maps.

Z. being *Zup*, *Zup* being the name that my dad thought Seven-Up was called when he was younger, when the red dot hid the bottom of the seven better.

The end.

Therefore (Something To Do With Stops)

0

Well erm therefore just have a look therefore the image therefore the first image is of a photo therefore the first image is a photo of therefore erm therefore a therefore bus window therefore I was looking thr- therefore I've been trying to write about looking through the bus window therefore and therefore then looking at the bus window at some point that I cant really work out and then looking *at the dots* on the bus window which are a bit like therefore dots therefore in halftone printing therefore which means that therefore there are larger dots towards the bottom of the window therefore towards the bottom of the glass therefore erm therefore

1

and describing this reminds me of the performance I did a few therefore m- therefore maybe a month ago therefore at the Poetry Café in London where I attempted to recite therefore a therefore speech by Allen Ginsberg therefore where he talks about therefore I'm gonna try and remember it now where he says like therefore erm therefore something about therefore all the dots on the electric screen, he says 'If you will keep your mind on the image in front of you which is my face in the camera therefore or in your TV tube or screen TV tube therefore and realise that I am therefore

2

looking from the other side of a c- therefore directly into like therefore a little black hole, imagining that you are there therefore and also imagining what would be possible to say therefore that would actually communicate therefore through all the electricity and all the glass and all the dots on the electric screen therefore so that don't you, you're not deceived by the image scene therefore but that we are therefore but that we are all therefore both on the same beam' therefore or something like that so anyway he talks about that therefore and therefore that somehow was still in my head when I started looking at this window therefore on the bus in London therefore ahm therefore

3

and they reminded me of therefore I guess of halftone dots therefore and therefore of Lichtenstein using Ben-Day dots and therefore of Bridget Riley using similar dots therefore and therefore Sigmar Polke to some extent therefore but mainly of the printing process using halftone therefore dots therefore I therefore uhm I noticed a lot of things therefore this, this was just the beginning of erm therefore a trip therefore to Madrid therefore so therefore th- the next thing I noticed was erm therefore the therefore dots on my iPhone when my therefore

4

Ph, iPhone is trying to load images therefore that therefore when it's trying to load photographs therefore my iPhone's really full at the moment it has about eight thousand images therefore and therefore it's very slow so while it's loading pictures it brings up this symbol which is like therefore two therefore rectangles one on top of the other and the first rectangle has three black dots in a row erm therefore a bit like an ellipsis and below that is a circular therefore animation therefore a circular animation with therefore twelve little lines therefore erm therefore

5

that go around in a circle therefore like a clock therefore and after that therefore that day, after I'd got the bus in London therefore to therefore work therefore I was therefore we started driving to Madrid therefore and that afternoon I was in a little therefore village called or town called Montreuil therefore which is close to Paris where I saw a church with a large therefore err therefore window with therefore three four five six seven therefore circular windows inside it therefore and therefore also with a clock above it which obviously therefore resembled the therefore animation therefore on the iPhone therefore

6

then therefore shortly after seeing the church therefore I saw a big colourful mural on therefore the e-er railway bridge therefore also in Montreuil therefore which had a therefore a large circle painted therefore in like Trivial Pursuit therefore sort of erm therefore Trivial Pursuit therefore tsh- therefore kind of tr-triangles or pie-pieces or cheeses therefore and therefore erm therefore it a bit like it reminded me of a colour wheel when I was a kid therefore when I was learning about colours therefore and colour mixing and colour greys and all that therefore

7

and then therefore I guess therefore I suppose like, that evening, yeah therefore that evening I therefore tried to watch therefore TV on my laptop therefore I tried to watch iPlayer on my laptop therefore erm therefore and it wouldn't allow that from France, so I tried to listen to the radio on iPlayer therefore which works from France but therefore the therefore thing I listened to on the radio was 'Just A Minute', the therefore long running radio show therefore presented by Nicholas Parsons and the therefore kind of therefore press image for that show was

8

a photo of Nicholas Parsons therefore erm therefore pointing at a clock therefore and when the radio show was loading there was another circular animation therefore erm therefore this time of little therefore dots therefore going in a circle and when I took a screen grab of the animation happening in my computer therefore the therefore little white dots I think therefore yeah, little, they were white dots therefore they were perfectly around the edge of Nicholas Parsons' mouth therefore so there's him pointing at the clock and then therefore I therefore we stayed over in Montreuil and then therefore got therefore

9

oh I forgot to mention one other thing in Montreuil was this therefore phone-booth therefore which had therefore erm therefore a therefore an image like a, a diagram or a, a sort of relief design of a therefore phone therefore over the keypads of the phone therefore the keypads?! therefore the keypad therefore the buttons on the phone therefore erm therefore which was a grid of three-by-four therefore buttons therefore erm therefore I took therefore I guess it was dark then it was evening so it's a much darker image therefore and therefore I think that's all that happened in France yeah and then therefore no therefore because ok we got on the therefore road again the next day and started driving to therefore

10

Toulouse and therefore so yeah Toulouse the next day we stopped in Toulouse and I went for a walk as soon as we got to the hotel therefore and therefore saw a sign for a roundabout which is three arrows therefore going in a circle again, pointing at each other therefore the point of each one therefore pointing at the end of each one therefore and therefore oh therefore then what? Mmm therefore Toulouse we went therefore we drove to Madrid and therefore Madrid has these big balls on the motorway by the erm therefore tollbooth things to pay to use the roads therefore and therefore they look like big red beachballs or something

11

erm therefore they go in lines of one big one, two small ones, one big one, two small ones etcetera therefore erm therefore they had a kind of jagged pattern on them as well which therefore was similar to the therefore I guess firstly they were similar to the Ben-Day dots if you got the Ben-Day dots and therefore er strung them out in a line therefore and put them out of order somehow so it was big therefore small small big, small small big etcetera and therefore the just the jagged design sl- was slightly reminiscent of therefore the therefore colour wheel therefore weird mural thing that I think has a question mark in the centre but I can't remember and therefore I mean I can't quite tell on the photo but anyway, Madrid therefore I think that was just at the border of France and therefore

12

Madrid and then we got to Madrid I guess? I can't think therefore and therefore there was therefore I got in the lift therefore I went to the Prado Museum and therefore I was in the lift and therefore that had these therefore this circular patterned floor therefore with a hu- a big bulge in it for some reason therefore erm therefore so there's this sort of circular bump therefore rising up therefore un- from underneath this material that was also therefore decorated I guess therefore with circles therefore that I think serve the practical use of therefore of being non-slip therefore and therefore also therefore in Madrid therefore I saw therefore a large therefore

13

hotel and in front of the hotel were these lampshades that are made up of therefore six lamps splitting off from one stem therefore so they're quite like therefore poppy seed heads or erm therefore those dandelion therefore heads once you blow all the seeds off or therefore something like that therefore which of course reminded me of therefore the circular dots therefore animation of Nicholas Parsons' mouth and of the therefore iPhone and the therefore church therefore window therefore and then therefore I got on a bus to the airport in Madrid therefore

14

and therefore the bus window therefore had not only the same dots as the bus window in London therefore the- the ones going in differing sizes but it also had this therefore this new thing which was a screen therefore erm therefore the screen made up text therefore advertising something on the outside of the bus therefore and therefore that intersected nicely with the therefore halftone dots therefore I still don't know what they're for therefore I think they may reduce flare or it may be to tell you that the glass is safety glass or that it's therefore laminate or it might just be for decoration but I don't therefore I don't know if therefore it would be just for decoration therefore erm therefore something else

15

about decoration what was I thinking therefore about the erm therefore decoration therefore I guess therefore I guess therefore that the ones on the lift floor aren't for decoration therefore I think the ones therefore the big bowls on the motorway were therefore jagged so you notice them better, like the design was jagged so you notice them better therefore so I'm not sure if that's decoration either therefore erm therefore so therefore Madrid therefore got to the airport and therefore came back to London therefore I think therefore yeah, I came back to London therefore and while I was in London I saw therefore er therefore

16

I didn't really see anything erm therefore London, oh yeah, London I was back in London for about two days and then I went to therefore Hull therefore I went to Hull therefore and then to the Lake District to Cumbria where therefore I saw therefore a piece of sheep shit that someone had stood in therefore a, I was going to call it a pat but its not therefore really a sheep pat its just therefore sheep droppings that had been stood on and the print therefore was remarkably similar to the therefore design of the phone booth in Montreuil therefore less like less than a week earlier and therefore

17

I'm sure there was something else in the Lake District oh and also erm therefore there's an umbrella therefore m- my dad has a colourful umbrella therefore that's a bit like the colour wheel again therefore and therefore we were therefore me and my sister therefore and I think my mum was taking photos of me and my sister spinning the umbrella therefore so you got this blurred colour wheel which was a bit like the therefore the one in a mac therefore when something's loading and of course like therefore the loading signs in the iPhone and therefore iPlayer and the roundabout and the window and therefore the therefore dots therefore

18

the dots therefore what else? therefore oh and also in Cumbria I bought a bag of googley eyes therefore in a stationery shop therefore and therefore also in Cumbria I therefore I'd I therefore photographed the googley eyes therefore in a halftone formation therefore like the windows therefore like all the windows therefore and I therefore also took a photo through the screen on my mum's car therefore one of the screens you can therefore slide up by the window of the passenger seat to block out the sun therefore took a photo of a field therefore through that therefore which of course was similar to the Madrid bus that intersected with the halftone dots which were like the London bus therefore

19

and therefore then therefore went back from Cumbria to Hull therefore took a daytrip to Leeds therefore in the Henry Moore Institute in Leeds there was a window covered in a metal erm grate therefore circular metal grate therefore so I took a photo through that grate therefore of the yard next to the Henry Moore Institute Galleries and therefore that was similar to therefore everything else and therefore also therefore got back to Hull therefore and got a bus back from therefore Hull which also had a circular logo of the bus in the same kind of mesh print of the therefore

20

bus in Madrid and therefore that bus in Hull of course also had a Ben-Day dot kind of design along the bottom of the windows therefore slightly different though I think therefore maybe one two three therefore one two three one two therefore mmm therefore I'm not sure, I think therefore I think it was three high therefore three high therefore yeah, it was different because the Madrid one therefore was five high, I think therefore and therefore I therefore once there was therefore oh and there was another one through the window therefore of my Mum's car that I noticed the therefore they do a similar thing with mesh therefore stuff on the window behind the wing therefore behind the mirror, the mirror

21

for the driver to see behind them therefore the one in the windscreen and therefore then I got a train back to Hull therefore no therefore then I got a train from Hull therefore back to London and remembered therefore no therefore hang on therefore I saw therefore the matchbox in the toilet in London and I photographed the edge of that because it was therefore similar dots to all the dots and then I remembered this therefore pegboard I bought from a charity shop therefore that's like the peg the t- therefore text pegboard things you can therefore that you of- that you see in cafes and things and erm therefore yeah I therefore I used therefore I used the pegboard therefore

22

I took a photo of the pegboard therefore and therefore oh, I forgot to talk about the gun therefore there's this gun therefore that I also saw in Leeds therefore in the Royal Armouries Museum therefore which is a knuckleduster and a revolver and a knife all in one and the therefore four holes for the fingers for the knuckleduster were very similar to the f- therefore the dots in Nicholas Parsons' mouth therefore and all the other dots therefore and therefore then finally therefore I therefore in London I remembered the pegboard therefore I collaged together photos of everything I've just described therefore I had them printed in halftone therefore dots therefore on a Risograph therefore and therefore the resulting print I laid over the pegboard

23

just the holes of the pegboard therefore and punched through every hole therefore with a pencil.

RACHAEL ALLEN

Goonhilly

It is 1968 and there's the woman before my mother
behind that flimsy bank glass. She is called Miss Heather
and is a delicately translucent clerk, rinsed out but luminous
with hope. One work evening, dating, you are to take her
to that forest of satellites, where the future ideas of us are mocking you
from behind whacked-out nuclear trees.

As the evening sun greets those farcical disks
hold the small of her back and draw her gently to you
(smelling Lily of the Valley and copper).
She asks about radar and you will conclude it is dangerous
and feeling the weight of a memory about to happen
you tell her so: isn't anything we can't see?

from 4chan Poems
(4chan is the largest imageboard on the web)

Random
/b/

Boxxy you are the home of the anonymous. I liked to read
on you all my false news it went across your head like The
Financial District and how you glowed with it. I got Tippex
and painted you as an angel on my childhood rucksack and
wore you proudly to school – you've got the kind of fame of
girls who killed other girls in childhood. I wonder if you've
ever seen lampposts in LA? Do they have crabs where you
are? Sometimes everyone thinks you're dead. I saw a
rainbow today but it had nothing on you. Your eyes held
entire months of teenage summers when my skin smelt of a
scented diary from the garden centre or an Impulse set from
Safeways, anyway I think where we lost you was somewhere
in the Californian sun squint and glare

232

Cute/Male
/cm/

When we play *The Simpsons* game where I find an episode of *The Simpsons* that is like real life I think about the presence of that squeeze of our shared childhood spent however many miles apart and I imagine us both rooted to a Sunday television with porcelain swans a baby gumming on a cork coaster with mottled animals on it – aching bored afternoons spent grappling with our siblings – this was when our lives were never ending, gazing out of windows into suburbs where the pink dusk settles like a trapping net. Maybe once our eyes met through a satellite or something I think maybe that's too romantic – how about you give me a picture of a verge of grass and a stream I'll show you there we are those tiny dots

Social
/soc/

The reason is probably because she started to watch all these day programmes first about Eileen Wurnos and then about murderers in general but she really loved the show called *The Unthinkable – Children who Kill and What Motivates Them* she'd tell me about the murders the intricate planning and 'aren't they heartless' as though challenging me and while ironing, so the steam would fatten and cloud her face

but the other reason is probably my father who was a library of frustrations but didn't drink – instead he ate arguments until his stomach bloated like a cupcake's foamy middle because he was *exhausted* with all of us but once that calmed down they went back to normal like maybe child-killers and mini-strokes are modern lobotomies but I was scarred for life that's probably two of the reasons

Transportation
/t/

Mother says 'Why ask and re-ask questions!' but I'm so often unsure of the question asked especially when it's the models of cars and you must understand I had lessons for a very long time and I still don't know the difference between one shift and another. Before traffic lights and crowd control people used to march grinning right in front of the bonnet straight into traffic! Like how I once saw so many translucent frogs being swept downstream glassy-eyed and knowing towards the open gritted mouth of a drain their eyes were so resigned that I even gave some a little push the driving instructor gave me similar looks of resignation lorries never seem so big in stasis what was the question?

Rapidshares
/ɾ/

Gina G was the pathway to enlightenment and adulthood another of the pathways was my pink faux-snake-skin halter neck top that came free with a magazine and I shimmied it on it was skinny and violently pink like someone embarrassed. Feeling older, I thought thirty, and drinking too much Sprite when someone shouted from across the beery carpets that 'that top looks like something you'd get free from a magazine' and for some reason I was insulted and girls that strutted and gathered like pigeons patted my back and we puffed out our flat chests for the rest of the evening skittering on our low heels playing at adulthood and anger and all around me was *ooh ahh* and *de de da da da* and a tacky smell of sweet that could have been lipgloss or just as easily the encroaching ledge of age

KATHARINE KILALEA

Hennecker's Ditch

           I stood at the station
like the pages of a book
whose words suddenly start to swim.

Wow. The rain. Rose beetles.

Formal lines of broad-leaved
deciduous trees
ran the length of the platform.

Ickira trecketre stedenthal, said the train.
Slow down please, said the road.
Sometimes you get lucky, said the estate agent
    onto his mobile phone,
it all depends on the seller.

Dear Circus,
Past the thicket, through the window,
the painéd months are coming for us —

See the bluff, the headland, announcing
the presence of water.
See the moths...

The trees walk backwards into the dark.

                *   *   *

Hello? Hello? The snow comes in sobs.
Dogs sob.
Cars sob across town.

Dear Circus,
When you found me
I was a rickety house.

There was a yellow light and a blanket
    folded up on the stoep
and the yellow light – *Dear Circus* –
was a night-blooming flower.

We pushed a chest of drawers against the door.
It's nice now that the corridor's empty.
A necklace. Vacant. Light wrecked the road.

Dear Circus,
We took off our clothes
and did cocaine for three weeks.

The washing machine shook so badly
that a man asleep four floors down reached out
    to hold it:
Shut that dirty little mouth of yours...

*   *   *

Hennecker's Ditch.

You'll never find it, he said over dinner,
a black lobster and bottle of vinegar,
unless, unless...

Blackened,
the dog tilts his head from beneath
    the canopy of the Karoo tree.
Look at my face, he said. Can you see what
    I'm thinking?

A red jersey. Bot bot bot.
Séveral breezes.
Boats on the water were moving at different speeds.
The baker took a portable radio
    into the garden
to listen to the cricket
in the shade of the bougainvillea.
Tick-a-tick-ooh, tick-a-tick-ah.

It was cloudy but hot. We were moving
    as shadows.

Three times he came upstairs and made love to her
then went back down and read his book.
The air was blood temperature
    and the consistency of blood.

Look at my face, he said.
I see you. I see you. I see you
    in our murky bath
I see you in our black and white bath like a cat.

*   *   *

Barbed wire around the fisheries.
A letter from the municipality
Come closer, sir. Step into my office.

Above the harbour, tin roofs and cranes.
Henry? he said. Hello? Henry? he said.
What's been happening in Dog Town these days?
The Audi keys lay heavy on the table.
Aaaaah Henry, he said. How wonderful it is
    to see you.
The mists came down. The moon was bright.
Collectors searched the night market
    with flashlights, and the wind outside,
with its slight chill, howled.
Henry, the breezes – they bolt across the open market
like meatballs, Henry,
like windmills, Henry,
like policemen, Henry, apprehending criminals.

A man in a collared shirt put a cigarette
to his mouth
and looked at his watch.
And what happened then?
He wore a street hat. He wore a street hat
and carried a belt over one arm.
And what happened afterwards?

Tell her... I think he has given up.
Tell her... I know now, this is what I've been afraid of
    all my life.

237

He closed the door and came in.
He closed the door and the sound of the bathwater dimmed.

*   *   *

Thirty-one back gardens.
Thirty-one back gardens overlooking
    the backs
of thirty-one houses.
Thirty-one houses looking out over the sea.
And the sea – *of course it was* – was marbled
and contorting.

Are you sleeping? – Yes.
Figures in yellow mackintoshes make their way
along the coastal path.
And what then, what if I were to ask,
How much longer?
If I were to say, How much further?
It's just
I have used up all my reserves.

There was a yellow light
and a blanket folded up on the stoep.
The light was burning dimly now.
By that time,
the light had begun to flicker.

He opened the door and fastened
    his lonely shadow,
and she fastened hers
and sat on the chair.

I think we are in the middle, aren't we.
He said, I think we may be.
We certainly aren't at the beginning anymore.

*   *   *

The moon was acting strangely.
The moon was moving fast.
It was cloudy but hot.

Electricity cables gathered round a pole
like the roof of a marquee.

He wore a gold vagina on his chest.
He had gold lining on the flaps of his jackét.
She lay her head against the window and sang a song
    by Silvio Rodriguéz
wearing ten gold balls on a chain around her neck.

Dear Circus,
Sometimes we are just so full of emotion.

And what happened then?
And what happened afterwards?
Chicken bones and Pick 'n' Pay receipts.
We were moving as shadows.
And the only light
    was the light from the bakery.

A lampshade swings above the window.
Tick-a-tick-ooh, tick-a-tick-ah
We have no history. Nothing has passed between us.

A hundred years pass like this.

Dear Circus,
I need to see more glass!
I need to see more glass!
This has to be more gentle.

from House for the Study of Water

1 *Whatever you love most dearly*

My dearest brother, last night
I saw water playing in the pond
where the women were swimming.
I was stationed in the House for
the Study of Water amid parapets

and ruby red columns under the
open sky. I was with a man. His
name was Curtis. It was muggy
outside. He said: *it wants to be a
storm.* I said, *it (the water) held
no more shape than a dream.* He
is so much better than me. I have
so much confusion. I lay on my
stomach and made notes in pencil.
From the veranda in front of the
waiting room I can see the entire
garden, including the river, and
further, the shapes of people I
I knew, including you. I'd like to
get closer but what the hell. In
any case, I can almost hear you
saying to yourself, *he always was
an over-ambitious but timorous
child* to which I can add only the
assurance that now I am a man
and nothing in a man's life is
more certain than his being too
timid or too stupid or something.
It goes without saying: a man can-
not have intercourse with a river.
But what then can he hope for?
If you do not know, she says, *why then
do you not ask? You want to
stay with me? To come away with
me on holiday? To live with me in
my house?* The truth is, if I could,
I would have followed her perm-
anently and without resistance. Or
did you expect me to just lie here
like a corpse?

RICHARD PARKER

from ~~R.T.A. Parker's 99 Short Sonnets About Evil~~

LXIV

IT is | mindless! | Practice?
Every | word de | creases
My skill'n | facil | ity,

My memes | are stale | or are
No memes. | Before, | I faced
A world | about | which I

Felt just | contempt; | now I'm
Before | myself | – ev'ry
Conned-con | struction | honied.

LXV

BERRIG | an; an | angle
Charmer | would you | clear my
Depos | its in | your bank

Of *werdzzz*; | my hairs | fluffi
Er now | that you've | gone from
Town – I'm | left here | to mis

Behave / | behave | with all
Of our | rigging | still in
Terwtined; | my head, | your sheets.

LXVI

IF you're | such a | fertile
Field for | poems | then I'm
Cleggy | with ape | shit, and

Jumping | & just | amazed
At all | the great | stuff we've
Got a | going | round us

– Will you | rest your | head its
Fever | on mmmine | , because,
It's all | full of | those holes.

LXVII

IF your | fingers | were there
Gently | trembling | then I
Was ab | solute | by a

Flutter; | or more | like a
Spasm – | *precar* | *'yus heart!*
I am | hungry | ; I was

Hungry | then, but | now I'd
Break bread | & beans | to sink
Into | your cheeks | my teeth.

LXVIII

SHOWER | ING you | in my

Cruddi | ness or | I'm the
Receipt | ticker | ticking
All night | every | night; tuck

My shoes | away – | for all
Alter | ity | affronts
Our sly | commin | gling.

LXIX

EVERY | little | last bit
Of us | *YEARNS* to | be a
Part; passed | growing, | careful

Setting | pattern | into
Pattern, | now the | pieces
They go | crazy | like you,

Your bones! | Crazed be- | bones! That
'Ll still | rattle | when I'm
Gone. Read | these then, | will you?

LXX

WILL you | practise | *LONGEURS*
Still when | you've lost | the old
Place, when | your skin | sack's half

Off & | you're out | calling –
Never | quite out | calling –
The wilds | back in? | Let me

Into | you, once, | into
The grey | innards, | those that
Revolve | ever | glist'ning.

LXXI

Glisten | , my pup, | in far
Darkened | cove, lost | hill track
Or at | point of | dawn &

Sky – I'll | perish | from long
Looking | for you | before
I raise | my eyes | from your

Glisten | in my | inner;
The glow | weak & | fading
But such | a long | half-life.

LXXII

If I | were a | wiser
Man I'd | get phys | ical
With your | meta | physics;

Grow a | perma | nent hat;
I'd, not | quite fi | nally
Able | once & | for all

To just | distract | myself
From my | inner | mounting
Turmoil, | turn-tail | & flap.

LXXIII

Abso | lutely | *no* flights!
It's a | different | logic,
Baby | follow | me through,

Because | that's where | I'll be
Going | &, let | me tell
You – damn!, | it'll | be slight.

Once more | for the | end of
The last | good time, | once more
To stress | about | futures.

SAM RIVIERE

from 81 Austerities

Crisis Poem

In 3 years I have been awarded
£48,000 by various funding bodies
councils and publishing houses
for my contributions to the art
and I would like to acknowledge
the initiatives put in place
by the government and the rigorous
assessment criteria under which
my work has thrived since 2008
I have written 20 or 21 poems
developed a taste for sushi
decent wine bought my acquaintances
many beers many of whom have
never worked a day in their lives
how would you like to touch my palm
and divine how long my working
week has been mostly I watch films
and stare and try to decide what
to wear speaking as a poet I would
rather blow my brains out than run
out of credit as the biographer
of the famously unresolved
50's poet-suicide has commented
capital is the index of meaning
anything is better than stealing
from the Co-Op with a clotted heart
without it you don't survive

Sad Dads of the Girlfriends

I wonder did you think beyond this point
of whole days to dream of what
like a bright key dropped straight
to the bottom of a well your spectacles
warping programmes in the sitting room
you finally use where evenings tighten
to a funnel the TV's zap-line equals sleep
and later to wake for an hour thinking clearly
your silences like streetlights coming on
your stories slowly going nowhere past them
O daughters come away from the windows
lie down here and tell me what you've spent.

Cuts

I can see that things have gotten pretty bad
our way of life threatened by financiers
assortments of phoneys and opportunists
and very soon the things we cherish most
will likely be taken from us the wine
from our cellars our silk gowns and opium
but tell me what do you expect Chung Ling Soo
much ridiculed conjurer of the court and last
of the dynasty of brooms to do about it?

Year of the Rabbit

there is no purer form of advertising
than writing a poem
that's what the monk told me
if I were a conceptual artist
I would make high-budget trailers
of john updike novels but no actual movie
the scene where angstrom drives towards
the end of his life down a street in the suburbs
lined with a type of tree he's never bothered
to identify and laden with white blossoms
reflecting slickly in the windscreen
I would fade in the music
as the old song was fading out
keeping the backing vocals at the same distance
kind of balancing the silence
the word RABBIT appears in 10 foot cambria

I'm a Buddhist This Is Enlightenment

I hate when life like an autobahn explains itself
also when the news presenters share a little joke
alluding to the private world of showbiz bullshit
so Giles had to say 'I can't relate to this' I liked
when Aki whispered something in the pool hall
that remains unknown to most of the universe
and then 'what I just said I'll never say again'
O I'm trying very hard to remember a word
with 'I' and 'O' in it a good amount of mystery
for a Saturday like meeting a really cute couple
or when words touch each other in strange places
like drinking & biography or sex & cheesecake
if I test each object on my desk with heat
under my hand with heat the right one will reply

Heavily

Today is a day of zero connectivity
I brush my teeth and dunk my face in water
which is what you wash your breasts with
I want to use the exact same soap
and drink orange juice probably from Spain
now there is a gelid light in the kitchen
& outside the same air we all have
to breathe the day is in some kind of tank
all I will do is think of increasingly
horrible things to tell you striking the side
of my head for a new image there is no
competing with the spectacular & obvious
am I not a child at the opera of emotions

Buffering 15%

you aren't thinking clearly as you enter the bank
on the day leslie nielsen dies
the coldest december 'in living memory'
mark's badge reads
'have a good time all the time'
maybe you should think about getting a motto
maybe you should think about painting the fridge blue again
maybe then you'd feel less like the shape of a person
suggested by the fall of light on a bookcase
you find you're thinking a lot about your friend the monk
who won't share with you his secret
to be sure he is a very complex gentleman
but hardly deep even *if he can burn leaves*
with nothing but the power of his mind
he is a remorseless self-publicist
maybe that's his secret
or his secret is he doesn't have one
he claims to remember where he buried

a live beetle in a matchbox
but afflicted as you are with awful memories
you're not sure you believe him
filling out the paying-in slip is difficult
maybe you should stop growing your fingernails
'shhh' he went this morning
pretending to be listening

Nobody Famous

This is me eating not 1 not 2 but 3 pancakes
this is me having breakfast in america in paris
with my creepy associates
this is me punching a photographer
this is me listening to my ansaphone messages
these are my new converse all****s
this is me logging into my email
I type my password 40 times a day
what kind of effect is that having
here I am inside the reptile house
this is me examining the roofs on my street
to see on which the snow has melted meaning
the neighbours are growing hydroponic skunk
this is me playing dolphin olympics
this is me reading akhmatova while listening
to arthur russell and the feeling is mutual
this is me planning my comeback
cutting my hair at 20 to 4 in the morning
here I am in a wet field as a clown tells me to 'get real'
here are my eyes suddenly in the train window
this is me surrounded by the sounds of cheap suits
these are my reviews they may contain spoilers
this is me smoking a moth for 10 dollars
this is me having my extremely nuanced feelings
overwhelmed by pop music and kind of enjoying it
this is me trying to remember a word
this is me watching a clip of a hipster being struck

in the head by a pigeon and laughing too loudly
this is me in the grip of my jealousies
this is me pointing at a rainbow
here I am running back and forth along the train
showing the rainbow to my fellow passengers
this is me glancing down at my outfit
every 5 minutes it seems I can't help it
here I am listening to the 7th symphony
this is me in public putting on a 2nd pair of sunglasses
because I feel suddenly like crying
here I am defining my personal space.

KATE POTTS

The Runt

He was one of the last when the talents
were handed out – skulking as usual, purple fists clenched and held low.

The other gods jostled and elbowed for their powers:
muscular flight, velveteen invisibility, the whittled cogs and pulleys

of super-strength. His own gift was small,
misshapen like a dried-up bean, a dulled skin-curl of tan leather.

He held it to his ear and heard – death rattle,
a distant meddling of breeze in grass, grating of worn and hollowed bones.

He cupped it always – little, ugly pod – in his broad palm, in his pocket.
Nothing, it seemed, transpired. The other gods tautened,

grew luminous, their bodies swollen, platinum. They inhaled weather-systems,
spat hurricanes, cantankerous on waking.

They impersonated mountain ranges with the angles of their sleeping knees,
their hips' curl. Often they sacked cities

as they stumbled, dozy, out for a morning piss, drew planets from their orbits
with the storm-force of their swatting, oiled wings.

They didn't notice him, remaining where they all began,
digging his potatoes, listing as the skies boomed orange with their mid-air tiffs

and thundered curses. His own, stranger talent befell him
slowly, with the odd geometry of waking in an unfamiliar room.

With passing years, his hands hardened like stale bread,
the skin shrinking and tautening to walnut-shell. The other gods glowed on,

ripened even, aped the marble of their pale statues
in the city squares, their youthful sadnesses long gone. He felt his sinews

shift and shorten. A day's wood gathering or heavy digging brought on
strong sensation, the stinging weep and welling

of the low autumn sun in the muscles of his arms and shoulders, in his veins.
His siblings' grand spats, beheadings, heroic doings

became, to him, as distant as his own concocted tales, their giant bodies empty
and unlovable as glass, their voices honed

and spun to undecipherable frequencies. At day's end he'd gather up
his spade and scythe, stand his clay feet

steady on the earth and scour the open skies. At dusk the marsh was heady
with sound and darkening, strung with shocks of bluing water.

The lowlands crackled and spat, peppered the air with flocks of wild, diving
birds in strange, excited rhythm and the lone, moon-faced owls

in the dark yews chanted out their own monastic answering. He found,
noticing the dropping sun one harvest night, he had

no memory of that other life, the story of his boyhood – only white noise,
the odd grand smash of godly thunderbolts. No faces, and no names.

Un-History

I have studied evacuees, rationing, *the Maginot Line, British Cinema of the 1940s.*
I'm young, graduate, able; a cataloguer of behaviour as if an interloper at the
zoo. I busy the rememberers with questions, screen-clips of David Niven's
pluck, kohl-black fighter-planes stuttering out over the English Channel – a
mirroring seam of rucked silver. My falseness, my foolishness, razes to a blush
of chaff and dust. The past turns itself up in ironware and sensory ticks, the
shallows of faces, their hallows and bones, wellings in breath. It's told how
friends and sweethearts met to plan a party and the house was hit. None
survived. On Sunday, their wedge of empty pews bowed with an absent mass
of haunches, macintoshes, winter boots. The congregation would not see or
speak of it. Farther back, in 'the last place on earth God made and forgot to
finish' the Jarrow men, washed red-rare, hungry in their Sunday suits, marched
off for parliament. Everyone's brother trumpeted in a dance band. Everyone
practised the lindy for the church-hall hop, would walk an hour to the office,
or factory, or home to stay in darning stockings or sewing a box-pleat, weeding
the garden vegetable plot. Sex was first a dicey, incorrigible thing, best performed
in the dark or out on the commons, like witchery, and never safe until after
the wedding. Those girls, squiffy or mickey-finn'd, who did it with soldiers
and swelled, bellies like beanpods, were quietly disappeared.

In all this, there will be one who joined the Eastern fleet
and never saw the bombs hit home, who –
nineteen, from Leytonstone,
a rack-ribbed tug of body – saw Africa and Singapore.

The sea-reflected light made all mass cut-out sharp;
the green of the land was so green he thought it painted on. He remembers,
most of all, the flying fish. They'd shoal and hang like scaled spirits, fatted
   dragonflies
kissing the boat's bows. Their falling back pitted the ocean's glass like rain.

He saw himself grow backwards to a scorched and stringy boy,
back to the old cheek and nous, the skies shook out, slackening each day.
He'd never thought he had the right.

SARAH KELLY

from **aperture**

that's dust
through the shaft there
hanging along time strands
as tinsel

settles to a down
   pressure just
enough load
must close in
on

or measure softer

sometimes glitter
is harsh
and grey's weight
a calmer
I suspend in

evening
through the draft there
close in
on   blocking out breeze by bitter breeze by
ink for brittle
stained pad-knee-lap   let us   move with the windows
where those corners get
a natural light
come to standing
               say
  'held'

bring things back
to the room

from Cables / to the telescopes

1

like loves like
like listening
we tire of the
trespass
playing it by
your ear
provides a
protocol for the
selection of mine

11

the line I keep forgetting
deleting, matching
        to the telescopes then
to mechanise the rhythm
of rocking arms on
authored ledge

15

armed with her shadows
failing to appropriately
account
for the relativity
of trying

16

the accent I
take to
translate here
is an inquest
nothing spoken
is taken
less than our place
as guest

25

in the place where
we doubted

it was definitely the
differences to save
curling and lined up
  when you were dead you
welcomed it because
no one made it
    like that anymore

22

a preoccupation with a mouth
– whilst I try to
talk of permeation I
waste it on ivory all
skeletal the soil of them
sustainable in some structure sense
  chip at it, the movement
you wish for
because space outlives a hole

'If it is easier...'

if it is easier
to ask forgiveness
than permission
seek us
only as the
imperative creates
its situation
this was set to
settle as this
task addressed
tempted by
ideals of
motherless memory

in the moment
of crash, that
that is broken
bends, apologies
blend in at prophecy

edge and
fulfil the
disquiet

admission to your
singular responsibility
is no more
mentioned than
remembered as
granted

'I write to you...'

I write to you at a slant
so that
the tilt-touch
of the incision will
be less invasive when our
strings are pulled
from our middles
– disconnected we will
be holed but in a
sewable sense and all
drips will drip down
with less spill and
more directing

'I do not miss...'

I do not miss or wish
I say
you come nonetheless
to join   here

we are all reply
    stamped upon each
other as sure

as the question
quarrels its deliver, its
deal with the
progressed or
   the protesters

I hold you at
our edges

                   because you stretch
                   so fiercely

and from these,
from these
places
take all
that we may need

'brighter / sense is...'

brighter
sense is
a secondary hope
just as the sink sashays
about with its fill
and you foster the intent
to sway by me
in sic in obstruction or
fleeing that
the jacket of her

oyez at our
opening
stilt my own
bathing rite
how ceremonious
you looked in
that sideway sleep
with the lock to
hide your mouth
from in an
overspill murmur

SANDEEP PARMAR

Amanuensis at the Chromatic Gate

The sea and sky that aspire   unseasonably   to an unaccountable hue
         of solid reasoning, averse to the long-winded nostalgia
and metaphysics of mother-in-laws, cloaked in wind
        attenuated by a previous century, rise
                ascendant in a spine of Bayer blue.

Footed like its master in steel   the exile's preference
        – an imagined elsewhere – flutes its plumes in ochre
and blushes with notable reticence. Delayed here
     the refugee   12.5 tons of leaden metal
          slowly tallies its accounts
as the locals declare it an eyesore.

Integrate? With this face?

The Gate hangs clean against the undeciduous shore.
The earth refuses to modernise.
The vision erodes under the hand that built it.

The Saltonstall Family

The prolonged façade   of velvet bedcurtains   pinafores and sleeves
     matched by the mother   who is matched to the task of dying
and father – careless reprobate in black – severs the picture.

The elder sister fastens the younger by the wrist, warns
do not interfere   with the red and white of it.

One intimacy too many –
     the glove their father drops into his own mother's pale hand.
It oils.

Father's hat is what will disturb the girl in later years   it is too large
and this will trouble her   the way the dead woman should

The way the too stiff baby in her mother's arms should
The way the certitude of family portraits should,

unpicking themselves in airless rooms.

Taniwha at Whatipu

...I remember the bay that never was
And stand like stone and cannot turn away.
                    JAMES K. BAXTER, 'The Bay'

Fiesome and button-gunny   the awed tailors
chew their needles   to see you borne out, weathering for beauty.

This is hard-earned sibilance.
The earthly mantle that comes with a hero's death.

The chorus mares its black singing.   From the shore
white-hearted celibates   line up like tall breakers

crown for the pearls you hang in each ear.
The moon as celebrant divides the remaining hours into loaves,

makes oaths of stone as women do.

Against Chaos
(after Jagjit Singh)

Love could not have sent you, in this shroud of song,
To wield against death your hollow flute, tuned to chaos.

Whatever the Ancients said, matter holds the world
to its bargain of hard frost. But life soon forgets chaos.

He who has not strode the full length of age, has counted
then lost count of days that swallow, like fever, dark chaos.

And you, strange company in the backseat of childhood,
propped on the raft of memory like some god of chaos,

You threaten to drown me: wind through palmed streets.
Oracle of grief. The vagrant dance of figures in chaos

carting trash over tarmac. Stench of Popeye's Chicken,
the Capitol Records building, injecting light and chaos

into the LA sky. That paper boat in rainwater, rushing, dives
out of my reach and old women give no order here to chaos,

nor calm with their familiar tales. Your voice follows me
into and out of the wrong houses, riding my heels in chaos

as if to say that every half-remembered element I've forged
in glass is only the replicate, dying shadow of love's chaos

that once spoken, is like a poison dropped in the mouth
of song, turning it dolorous and black. I've eaten this chaos,

its paroxysm of birth, and seen it uncoil from the faces
of loved ones, into sickness and distance and loss. Chaos

that hounds – that drums its fingers on the window like rain –
who will not forget me and permit me to reach across

thirty years for the child peering out over the very same
landscape, day after day. Yellowing day, that day of chaos

where you are still sounding your warning (though I was too
young). To be left with the bitter heaviness of song, its chaos.

SIMON TURNER

five sections from **The house at the edge of the woods**

No one is sure who built the house at the edge of the woods, but its foundations are said to be ancient, a single block of obsidian plunging miles into the earth. Its structure has been compromised by the tunnelling of the vast, blind, limbless creatures which nest within it. Some say the oldest, deepest tunnels, abandoned by their builders for centuries, are flooded with rivers of boiling sperm, and that these deposits are responsible for the tropical conditions in the gardens surrounding the house. Even in the depths of winter you can see tomatoes and lemons, squashes and plums, thriving just a few feet away from where the snow halts at the foot of the hills, clumps of it heaped in the black and corrugated earth like torn, discarded clothing.

*

The front door to the house at the edge of the woods was garish with decorations for the feast day of Eudora the Unconscionable. A garland of blossom and rosehips hung from the knocker, and communion wafers, pilfered from the charred and fibrous ruins of a local church, were pasted to the lintel with a mortar of semen and bone-dust. I sat on the front porch in a rickety chair contemplating a horde of minute bones I had gathered that morning, a small contribution to the Noonday Pyre which the others were erecting in a nearby clearing. I could hear the sounds of their labour, a resonant tumult of clattering branches, hoarse raised voices, and bone striking bone. The light was woozy and viscous, smothering the woods like a blanket of sap. Three black birds with bald and scabrous faces landed on the roof and began to mutter their dark occluded language in defiance of the noonday sun.

*

One morning I woke to find the flower head of an enormous heliotrope draped across the wooden steps leading up to the house at the edge of the woods: an offering for the Vegetable King, no doubt. It was early spring, the air still chilly and clear, and the petals had collapsed a little in the overnight cold. Some petals had shrivelled and fallen away completely, lying scattered across the path like a series of undiscovered sex crimes. I began to gather them up in my arms, and looked down towards the lake where the laundry women were at work singing lewd songs from the last war as they smacked their sullied underthings against the froth-bothered stones at the water's edge.

*

Searching for firewood, I found in a clearing a heap of detritus – twigs and feathers, hair and bone, some scraps of shredded leather – concealing a clutch of eleven eggs. These were strangely veined, with pliable translucent skins, and emitted a low hum like the engines of a distant plane flying high above a bombed-out city. Returning to the house at the edge of the woods with my basket full of kindling, I saw as I approached a young woman with pale skin and thick black hair falling across her shoulders, sitting on the porch steps. She was naked from the waist up, and in her arms was cradling, as if it were a sleeping infant, a spider the size of a kitten, which suckled gently but persistently at her left breast. Not wanting to interrupt, I halted, but the young mother had already heard my footsteps, and glanced in my direction. Her eyes were a deep unbroken amber, her lips a delirious rouge. Carefully, she put down her bundle, which scurried away into the lightless underbrush, and rose to her feet. Her breasts were a star-chart of pinpricks where the spider had bitten in the exuberance of its feeding; each nipple wept a delicate rivulet of mingled milk and blood. She hummed once, almost inaudibly – it might have been her name – and began to walk towards me, unbearably slowly, her cheeks and jaw-line pulsating with the motion of hidden mouth-parts, which clicked and chattered with inscrutable intent.

*

Last week, a film crew from The City arrived at the house at the edge of the woods, full of questions concerning the people who choose to live this far from the hub of civilisation. What are they like? What are their customs, their clothing, their habits, their gods? I was happy to oblige them with answers, and over mugs of warm rice wine, as the sunlight deepened to the colour of an over-ripe plum, I told them about the hand-to-mouth existence of the bone-whittlers who lived on the eastern slopes of the nearby hills, and spun elaborate yarns about the spider-farms that thronged the lower woods, lavishing particular detail upon the delicate manner in which the young village girls harvested the silk, reeling it in gently around their index fingers until their hands resembled strange translucent bundles of candyfloss. The director grew wide-eyed, smiling indulgently as I explained to her that the people of the plains refused to eat root vegetables or drink from wells, believing that anything that was drawn from the earth was of the devil's brood. They depended solely on wheat for their livelihood, and water from the river for their drink: ergot and cholera were rife. After an evening's worth of such stories I sent the film crew home with reels and reels of taped interviews in their rucksacks, digitally edited and ready for immediate broadcast to an audience back in The City thirsty for tales of the strange exotic lives of the upland primitives.

Every word I told them was a lie.

SIDDHARTHA BOSE

Mediterranean

I

She lifts ships with
seadrip in her eyelash –

foam grows in hairshades, her forearm
brinks like a precipice.

In eye she gave me her
crinkle of hair, clothed in
aubergines.

Cooked me, fed me horsemeat.

I grew to a cyclops. In
iron I fashioned my drift of world,
logging dreams, one-by-one,
jutting them like fishing nets in Mediterranean.

Now, fog lifts. She waves me away
in granita sip. Facing two-by-two, we spoke the
art of war in a square by a bookstore, fitted in gargoyles,
ambling.

I lived through scars in my teeth, mountain-ridged.
I storied her, foiling the
stab of whiskey, vomit-fresh in a bar basin
somewhere in Chicago.

II

Now, I give her my lizard skin, plumed. My
ashtray of a laugh, stunned.
I slip beneath her footsteps. Coil.

She will sail, anchorfresh,
cigarette-smoked, free.

My heart will be a sock, washing-machined.

My skull splits in the colour of three dreams –
redcoated, seadeep, scarecrowed.

Black electricity wires my lung. Burns

eye, alone,
still.

Storyboard

Car, white Ambassador,   enters New Market,
    Calcutta.   Woman gets out with
girl of ten, boy of five.

Sweating like meat, they smile.

Mother gets out with   girl of ten,
    boy of five.   Father's head stays
in,   cooked in summer heat. Herd of

moustachioed men   yell to help park car,
    cumbersome. Mosquitoes hover like
vultures in   puddles of rain.

Girl holds mother's   hand, boy
    skips round.   Car jerks forward
back, father   lifts eyebrow at
        potbellied policeman,

casually squashing his male child.
Voices swell like bellies.

Wife opens mouth,   does not
    scream. Men,   tongues wriggling,

on seeing the dead,   its head a
    spade with little hairs, and

not knowing,   smash carwindows.

Cop who saw crime,   stops tamasha,
   makes order. Crowd falls
silent.   Father's head hits
                              steering wheel.

Saris, wraps of   festering fruit,
   float wide free of web,
sweat of fume,   in summer

hovered over   by impending monsoon.
   Milk-heavy.
                    Fade to black.

STEPHEN EMMERSON

The Causeway

The black strops calling name in the second before 20 minutes at least of this bullshit. Active tannins redolent with the foam of procurement, or I see the kids dig deep as an act of balance. & all across town on the causeways and the underpass until rain. There is no law here nothing governing our terms, though Wednesday sits with Wednesday & I'm interested in you you know. To build up the manufacture of our tools or when John sits in Starbucks it's a lifestyle choice I suppose. & all this talk of politics is a mask.

It's the naming of things and the confusion that goes along with it that stops us suddenly talking of destruction, or writing a letter to Rimbaud after dinner or to Milton after coffee – &, well, yes, I believe it is possible to be so exact under the circumstances.

Anything from 12 to 20 foot, & the other thing we had in common was the Actionists, and especially the myth about Schwarzkogler though it aroused suspicion in the entry below us. A prominent figure in Europe the time the page ripped on a page about time & it caused a rift… & anyway it's pretty cheap here so dont worry about it. In space time I ordered milk because I believe that's what we'll all drink in the future and no one likes to dwell on the past without making a pun about dairy but it's all relevant and at the end of the day I just want your cheek of it – get out – I love you.

What Glow Subtle. In any business you need to know if it sells, so on this occasion I'll have to kiss you goodbye & all that if you're broke. But I do worry, & pasteurisation just isn't funny which ever way you look at it. One day the truth about his castration will be out and your USP will be worthless.

& the first time I went to her house I felt totally out of place & realised just how the first readers of exactly where I am felt. The wallpaper even tore its nuts on the revised menu & told me that men, real men, weren't supposed to feel like this. She couldn't believe that anyone didn't notice the paper and how it was the same paper as the one on the advert, & I guess that's where we really differed & for the first time we differed.

& the pure cack of the Ocean counting up under the doorway at her house where the chips become serious snapshots or pick up lost in continued mechanics. If anyone mentions Ophelia then Lorazepam is a baby trapped in the room. So to feel like this is to believe that we're already different.

Nothing like a joke to remain serious.

Everything is made out of papier-mâché which leaves a bad taste in the cat's mouth & I really must stop biting my nails. Taking photos for generations wont fix the machine but over time salt water can achieve pretty much the same outcome. Learning the lesson softly softly & the fear of it appearing on YouTube administered by rivalry. Passion is becoming toxic.

Where we are sitting chewing skin cells & the mad hatter sets the table expecting a tip, it is not likely but I take my camera everywhere these days. In these dimensions and being associated with the uneducated there is a cycle of bleeding & prevention. What is the point of reading if they look behind me and substitute gender with cellophane. It's what we've already learnt & I move closer to you & appreciate your delicacy of touch. There are specific sentences that require a response, anyone worrying mouthed as the dream begins & a tape recording snaps on the head. The colour will deepen and the body will become a train.

Every chance is a near win, calculated to protect should you fall on the rails in a tunnel. Thank you guys & they gave me a landslide, sick of tolerance or the body understanding sweat shops in relation to tone will deepen & neuro-transmitter dopamine. Not that you ask the right questions, 'incarcerate' commercial dealers or swallow evolution hard-wire out of order carrier. You throw the dice paranoia or just put a plaster on the cut.

Eyes years biography jerk, the guns in between her teeth. Landscape is a history book barely read, that anyone argues The News is an unmarried mother or that we still have to do what we have to don't create celebrity strangers hand.

We play right into the box. My silence in relation to the topography of where I live. Reading the paper you would be forgiven, were forgiven, the limbic system the horses working away. To make sense of the label or the next instal-ment of the book which is the first time reading where you are in context without exception.

¶

Never saw it. Be honest. Ridicule marks
scupper dead mobile in the queue for benefits.
Relating the death of parents to this affair, an
incredible balance of economy and psychopathic
behaviour. How I can be sure that anything I
say isn't related hiding from politicians heads
pantry dusk & fame. Scratching the back of
window licking the black iron door the grate.
When he decided to be Venus only the mystery
of filling a room, planning to give up oh the
speeches the Jesus tomorrow swathe. A lot of
the time I can't think of any words at all, letters
reverse drizzle sucking fingers and if two
words appear next to each other then what
does it thick & dirty years. Go to the Dr made
out of bronze, it's a looking through books for
hours pages burnt and there is something really
beautiful about you it's the distance I know
but hell. Silence for a bit then holding it
tight, composed.

¶

& kids throwing petrol into cellars skimming the text for a phrase & listening
to the priest for all they can to pick up some trace of betrayal. They kept
saying it was women who were more bloodthirsty at beginning to get used to
it but the fact of radar equals saint deployed naked structures & C see through
artery territorial sorrow. & your toilet was a daguerreotype that evening facing
the red sun on my shoulder dying mind bitten.

I reckon it's the fate of all communities to destroy the roads in and the roads
out, & this way assuming a sort of reliquary a disease. If we were up front
from the getting ready to change then it would have constituted a significant
message across borders and the mad nuns in a tiny box, so happy.

The nearest thing I'd seen to it before was a photo of the back of the eye &
when you recognise in the thing thats seen, the picture of the receptor that
sees it. I called you the other night and it was in that moment, when the
electricity kicked the light out of dark & doctored with salt how you express
what you feel being utterly in that gap. It's where the ghost happens, it's
bringing the images back to us.

¶

Whether it's blood or just a
conversation, or even ancestors
flax on a ribbon. I don't even know
what revolution means anymore
just that language orders the body.
If you could just show that you had
the commitment, I mean if you
could confirm our time severed lover,
a nothing puzzle, a factory on your
your shoulder. So what. & then the
words repeated for nothing.

¶

I won 50 quid on a scratchcard the other day and I'm not taking any chances on
directions to when the hairs on our cheeks begin sparking. When the hypnotist
starts I'm going, a symbol of the old regime, to discover what happened to him
& stand by not wishing to change.

We have accumulated meaning over the years, not temporally but structurally
& if the words we speak, the auras, the related terms trailing far behind were
visible. If they were visible we would lose ourselves, disappear uncontrollable
& yet pretend to exist to each other. If you want to sit in the bathroom all
night go ahead, if only to prove that we do have something in common.

language,
                    the performative
aspects of adrenaline force it,   copied
over / into faith with instructions

                    Affrayed Cash Sputter

he said he was sceptical,   but futures
are based on such doubt
                              nothing new

                                   assuming that
                    all politics work like
          that

& of course eventually the hours cleanse themselves of him, unfolding with the almostnothingatallness of feathers – when like you know – it's heartbreaking & so it is, & has to be, but Paula said the car is eating the dark faster than you can colour it in.

STRESSING   out

    remaining cardigan /

                skiving at last
road gives out to exhaustion / Faustian
handshake, torn gland postulate &
while   *listen*

        Telephone Disarmed

          Wednesday Bones

       I usually do it for a couple
   of hours &
         then leave

As if a premature girder the white jewel sinking in an ocean. Blood sanction. I cannot speak to you but all the wood in the house becomes human.

Acid-light. The cubical we're in. A storm traces the trajectory of our arguments willing him to begin again. Touching the dead hair, home on a wave, completed wire graffiti & the righteous power our servants all polluting cryptic hammers telephone. Photographs demand an explanation by their nature & the call the nowhere changed. Automatic silence. The spoils. The vigorous prison potential or eating sand in the park where they used to engineer ghosts & disquiet. Then literature abandoned nothing structures moaning the dust of bricks an absolute mockery & time snaps in your dress / I'm drunk as hell & running out of excuses.

TAMARIN NORWOOD

Anyway I ran at the tree again

Anyway I ran at the tree again
Headlong.
Still nothing.
Still no trepanation.

Nothing pierces, again
so the eyeballs are staying blunt
and the ink that pools under the surface
collects, pressed up against the film.
These eyes are full already.

We're moving house too soon
I cannot get everything in.

Beasts

A hole in the carpet you are:
        A lion!

This is a burst of action and a coup.
This lion, this carpet lion will prowl about
The upholstery in disguise
        as a paisley
And stow succinctly itself away
To some end.

The upholstery pales.

Alexandra

You haven't
quite
understood
how that cushion goes.

Yes
it is too big for the chair
but make it look causal.

Press it a bit.

Slips

sips
of breath
grains
the thin moths
italic

Afterwards there are always legs.
The legs need collecting and setting straight
one beside the other, sometimes in socks.
They're apologies, these legs: always still there.

STUART CALTON

5 Merits in the Liberty Bodice

I

Pegged out, golden strap
torn peg on unbreakable
disinvested spout loom on
gather when shut out bellow
hearth on, bread; healthful pin

out consecutively cushion spout
dashed, spout: numinous prewash
outbound clinch pegging
up it wake out strapless and
put, retaining ankle, put pin

through bolt of on thread nylon
its blue spout retainer peg
it against to fence now wither
home leg takes begging out to the
slimline laundry blindspot.

Unbreakable suspended buttons
disinvest the inconvenience
is a martyr of you waking up life
streams in and completely put out
broken on niggling is the imputed

hung clothesline violently rained
off at it against to fence then
face turned up towards the
sunlight you can jostle in line, wakeful
drops harry in dry brightness.

II

The image is as of a bright day
discarded flecking jotted on
fibres rain down starch split into
turned off vaporising plastic
hatch box, the cube is discomforted,

shrinks. Vertical wobble sides
semi-upright and its own level
best gradient is not finely
calibrated so that the plastic red
nub is basically inexpensive, is

your glottis flapping in the
block fabric conditioner offsets
when breath inhales, lingering and
drawn in across the hearth tourniquet.
Press down on the nub now, a

diagonally bisected cone of mist
shreds out. Using your thumb,
gradually decrease the assertion
you made of pressure onto the
inexpensive nub you are. When

the mist left the nozzle has
come to rest lightly spray on. The
body is like a liner, glide off
onto the foam-rubber encasement
the iron body wedge reigns in.

III

Listen out to the wind the
blanket sways in target
weight brand. And spinning
wildly there is a fence
there, relax bird wing clip

out over the scrub. Stare
straight into your mirror.
Imagine a straight line
from the inner edge of the eyes'
iris paint on. The warmth

will begin instantly and is
the natural rubbed lipline in.
Now imagine a line band. Love
them or hate them nail.
The line band drawn from

each outer edge of the doily
to converge above the left
eye and drill through the
nail is jewelry. Rootlifting
to the fence basin or

then set with topcoat, the
wrist pivot bold, trenchant;
squeaking round the bowl.
See the plastic holster in trees in
front grips the blanket.

IV

The flame resistant fabric is
soaking all out wired up
wretchedly in an aluminum
rib shaped out of the drum
you rotate like a sex worry.

The rack is a solid line and
boiler hum approximates the
bobbling you shave off, collected
indoors like the vertical spray
out and the sacrifice to dry that.

The drum is a model brain-scan
and mashed in exploded rags
you wrench from the bright rib
trench curvature uniformly
punctured, the resistant fabric.

Over the grille you
lift from its rectangular socket
clanging laminate metal pronged and
torn inwards at the four compass
points. Look at the capped

ignition medal the flame bursts
around. Prevent heart enamel to
split damage as scouring leaves a
dense fabric of scratches. Try
to think of sacrifice as an investment.

V

Everybody up against the
fence smack the wind there
plastic orange teething wet
pincer has its ingress form
against the line pressed into it.

Flip over the trigger nozzle, an
elliptical invert balcony of
ceramic the bonded surfactant
cuts through. Hair poke on. Disinvest
the need for a separate

cloth, permanently. In a certain
point, clip spin wildly over the cooker
hood the see-through platform
wither transversely under the
not wither stiff halfed bulbous

gun nozzle hood frosting, grip
inhale stubborn grease, exhale
5% Ether Glycol sling the tube
capillary draw: on, out: numinous
then dries up. The appearance

tailored tape reinforcements
merit is reduce need for Amphoteric
suffer in your life which wells
up the miniature capillary hose
wick, kick it out the nose plunger.

S.J. FOWLER

from Incidents of Anti-Semitism

#25

thought of as not a man
then it could be anything, blue murder
a whole year, a remark, some women
from the past – blowing through again
carrying nothing – a champion, a belt
loved as a speared belly
left on the mantle place in the event
a fire – books left behind, in the toilet
here it looks at you with a flush
a torch that burns – a death of battery
the red light enfolds a stick, growing
it was two people, all parties, getting
divorced slowly and painfully and diminished

#52

rattle, so I am offended, like a snake
what use is without a mindfulness of mindfulness?
is the one cannot listen? how this is a foot
to not have returned a handwritten
letter but to practise listening in the city
were it not a ledger of badges being lowered
& detonations of impulses from the throats of idiots
of noise, like a baby being born with a cord around its neck
not sad, it would be said, to be massive – a sound all the
more enormous as it has grown from a tiny thing

the city strangles a sound of dying
when it is merely tired

from **Minimum Security Prison Dentistry**

tomtit

my knife was once
a wooden spoon
now it is a knife

my shank is a knife
penetrating & remaining, ensconced
beneath the left lower rib

the floating rib
the consulate of Adam
is neighboured
by the spoon of cold
porridge

screw

wetwork
     or babychanging
     on the hour
     of orphanhood
     & self-deception
     or beyond it
     a sadder
     & wetter trust
     would have been more suitable
     for this line
of work

tattoos

I have atatattoos shaped
like a Whistle
a cock & a weathervein
& a warbird screaming
tearing talons at coy carp scales
the fish swims south
& is unsullied

I am Britain
& in Britain we don't bugger
the weakbirds against their will
our resolve is far more resolving

from Recipes

a recipe for Bramley apfel pie

// a signing on
// an excess of time
// cider
// curbing Sharon until she earns her pocket money

a recipe for Gamman steaks

// an overly academicised intelligence without a sense of general emotional
empathy
// a minefield of unconfronted personal issues
// an aggressive overambition within the confines of an obscure industrial
biscuit factory
// the horror pain at having shins cracked with some object or other, and an
oncoming depression at being raped in revenge

a recipe for Caesar Salad

// a weak wrist, nobel peace prize for two Liberian women
// a suckling fx, cutting it out of the stomach to determine its gender
// a limp salad
// marriage; as if it was the 50s, a huge error, as if you had no choice but all
as a metaphor for inhumanity that bathes the rest of borough in the light of
being ungrateful

a recipe for Pistachio Baklawa

// a turtle, overturned legs up like a beetle
// a debaunched watermelon drill
// a warm cave, a house of friends
// sirens, a contorted face screaming 'art school'

from **Fights**

(cartographic record)

(Caledfwlch)

in
1976
garryfrid
d a nine-year-
old-boy discove
red this sword w
hile walking his dog
he found it in the riv
er swale at gilling
west gary was la
ter awarded
a blue peter
badge for his
discovery a
nd he and the swo
rd appeared on the bbc programme
a blue peter badge is awarded to children
whoappearonbluepe
terunusually
the sword
was awarded a badge of its own

TIM COCKBURN

To a Stranger in Company

Guessing what draws you, what draws me to you
is the shape your courage makes, now, from here,
and my faith, if you like, is that however distance
like grass should obscure it, it will betray,
as a scorched field in summer the site of a former church,
an impression at least of that patient construction.

Immediately on Waking

I had a dream my two girls, grown up,
with their intelligent eyes and nuanced, searching faces,
stalked up to me at Christmas, or something very like Christmas,
and their faces said, 'Dad, we're sorry it didn't work out with mum,
but we've forgiven her.' And I beckoned them come hither,
and fond of me as they are, with that wry, faux reluctance
best becoming intelligent women, they came hither,
and my look said, 'So you should forgive her, girls,
she's a marvelous woman and if we're being honest
I should never have let her get on my bus in the first place,
knowing what I know about Cockburns before me,
about rocks melting with the sun
and everyone getting under the table when the phone rang;
I should have wound down my SORRY NOT IN SERVICE sign,
switched off my interior lights and driven straight back to the depot,
but you know, girls, your mother was only cold like anyone
and probably not any less selfish, and I was selfish too
and I wanted to love and fuck your mother always;
so I took her little ticket from her, which was furry from use,
and she took my little ticket from me,
which also was furry from use, and off we went.

And we laughed and cried and mostly cried aboard my bus
as it rattled along, just holding together on the faint promise
of the sort of destination one hopes, upon reaching, to concede,
with a wry faux reluctance best becoming intelligent women,
was certainly there all along. And whether it was or not,
look at you two, you're perfectly wonderful
and you've got the knack of living – that's all your mother –
she hates that sort of talk too, but it's Christmas, girls,
or something very like Christmas, and I can be as camp and weary
as I please, and can't a man draw the loveliness of women
around himself like sand if he wants to?' At which point
their two boyfriends, who I knew in the dream were fond of each other,
came in, each enjoying the other's company,
but, it being late and they being men, wanting only really
to draw the loveliness of women around themselves like sand,
and my girls kissed my cheeks, first the eldest, then the youngest,
and smiled at me, and I smiled too and my smile said,
'Go to them, girls, it is to them you should go.'

Deco

I love you because you are, like love,
a flimsy and preposterous thing,
like a deco bedside cabinet
whose gold trim is coming away,
whose quilted sides are yellow and punctured,
but that you buy anyhow,
if only because, among the serious junk,
its cheerful stab at flair seems
a certain defiance, a retort.

Sex and the City

walking to a garage not because
you want anything but because
at home everyone is shoving into each other

staring at a carton of juice
which shows an orange skipping with a cane
and two grapes laughing at the orange

Appearances in the Bentinck Hotel

Sometimes in going to pick something up,
however casually certain your fingers it is one thing,
looking may show it to be another,
just as sometimes in telling someone you love them,
however casually certain your tongue the words are true,
on the ear they may fall as forced or artificial,
and in saying them you may come to realise you don't,
or not as you thought, and it will seem
a kind of sneakiness on the part of the words,
as it does on the part of my lager, when playing pool
I swig from it and it is not my lager
but your lager top, or even in coming to write a poem,
when it shrugs at you from the page and says,
No poem here, only the bones of one at best,
and those you reject as too deliberate or too cute,
since always it is possible that for forty minutes
exactly my lager is a lager, on my ears on my tongue
to the touch I love you, and this is the Bentinck Hotel.

TOBY MARTINEZ DE LAS RIVAS

The Clean Versus The Psoriatic Body

The body as image of the state, violated and violating.

Broken and brought to heel in its northernmost parts, and the dykes like scars
in the hindquarters, wasta est.

The moon above Alston, which is an anagram of the end, where my heart was
lost.

That hé said: I do will it, and meant it.

Your head, de Comines.

The exultant, levelling teeth of the harrow biting at the meat of this rayless
heaven.

Torn open, suzerain.

My little sons are lain out side by side in midwinter, the light barely born, that
it might not burn.

And my bride has lain with another.

Not bough snow, nor flawless mirror of the fall, nor allergic to September.

Not an iconoclast, not an islander, not England in miniature.

Nor does he hear how the sea hisses, that shall salt and scorn and whiten me.

From the runnels in spate at Alston, petal, where my heart was lost, to the bare,
shaking Levels.

My citadels, and my drowned folds.

My fields, my arms, my brutalist heartland, the corporations of London that
humbled Napoleon.

Penitential Psalm

Tenderly

Out of the shallows, horizonless, unbroken, the impenitent, vertical
body tenders its asperities

                                        to blinding waters.

None to anoint it, looking out towards Huish and the dismal strato-
cumuli.

O, hark at! The helicopterish whap | whap of goose wings.

                                        Shall I thrust

my own head under, inhale the shattered meniscus,   *ghost-cases of larvae*
                                                                 fixed to stems in the
                                                                 vacancy of self-
the third clause held indefinitely to spite your transformational   *possession*
grammar?

Fierce joy that is like retching, undo me. As a dead polity,

brick by brick, stitch by stitch, the squat, feudal tower at Langport,
or the drowned mole in this baptismal water, claws subtly
demonstrative

of admonishment, supplication, *woefully arrayed*.   *My tender heartroot*
                                                                 for thee brake:

My tender heartroot for you in the brake of thorns,
            and the desperate purchase of this falling metre, Laura.

Simonsburn

The yews like sentinels, divested of life, bristling with dull pods or cherries
of blood,

at the lych gate, in the city of the dead.

One day, I shall have a daughter I will call out *Honey* to,

or *Oh, Hon*,

phonemes beyond approximation in the strict textures of print, half exaltant
or dramatic address, half strangulation.

Oh, the feminised rhetoric of pleading, knees cleft in the unlight
at Simonsburn, the poisonous frill of nettles purring in the wind.

Dire and beautiful is the male voice in its unmanning: Alessandro Moreschi,
Hostia et Precis, from faraway and through static.

Stripped of its sexual function, something cries through the open mouth *Óh*,

Óh, Óh, unrepeatably, consubstantial with desire. Believe me,
in the carnal paradise, you still can dance with terrific abandon.

Annulment

I feared the water: the shadows and spawn resurrecting
in dark light, the glory-stare through low broken cloud.
Genuflecting among the basal leaves of withering hare-
bells, I saw and see the barred and agile God ravenous
in his snowdrift of feathers tearing at the plucked anus,
prolific eye engulfing the days, the years turned briefly
to a psalmody of rotor blades behind the sheltering hill.
And something else: the prodigious bellowing of cows
in the yard planting their bulks and straining after their
penned weans: that still reaches me from a way aways.

TOM CHIVERS

Poem as Diminishing Return

: simply gutted technocrats no longer
dropping smileys & molesting one another

w/ grace of two Poles and a Czech
plumbing future kitchenettes

then 'staying on'. Take what you can;
this poem is an act of desperation:

skint but mobile, planed and
sculptural yet, like a spice, ground

and noseward. Naked at a window,
Colombo inspects his swollen bollocks.

Good eye captures slightly purple tinge
around the fluffy perineum.

Tomorrow and tomorrow, he starts,
we shall launch like mortars, like

a broadside, and an unmanned drone
will soar above the mountains

and the valleys that are you and me
or at least some gurning pug

in the gents who was forced
to climb down from an initial, dodgy

faith in the truth.

Security

Trick or Treaters are not all kids as

campers are not all happy and I wish

the banks would just start lending or

improve their customer service you know

I have to use a plastic keypad just to

check my balance which is invaluable

in the fight against fraud so when

you bowled towards me outside Bank

in the costume of the dead that is to say

masked and painted I had to ask the value

of that feint of pure hostility you are

clearly having fun which is a good thing

don't let me stop you

on my island none of this would be true

The Herbals

Pale globe inset,
you hive.

To crumble yr vision
into backstreets is to
interrupt certain large
unwieldy (or rather
profitable) structures

& who
would
desire
that kind
of mental
collapse.

In any city or text-based
practice to be confined
in such articulated coffins
collapses desire & its
attainment causing

sweat
to
gush.

Now if unit cost declines
& free creative expression
requires a constant hum
please define yr target

market
or at
least
revert
to type.

I am frequently asked
for directions & am
too polite to shake
you from yr dreaming

left
left again
right at the end –

You & I,
alone in a node I barely
recognise –

towers
turn
&
shimmer.

Censorious streets,
how you suckle me!

Router is a deep blue.
Certain interests of a
mercantile nature
such as speed and
theft.

You've worked out how to get here?
Timing's key.
Through snowfall,
radio cars,
bank collapse
the visionary
comes –

cherished pathways
back-mutate
to nodes.

Insist the marshes, the herbals.
Static blends.
Blue is righteous accident.

Pastel turns
and we unfold like
an aircraft hangar
in a field of gold
translucent rape.
My name is Simon.
I am your train guard, yr
personal shopper.
Hardware
flocks. Green
beyond limits. Cartilage
locks a vista –

light spilt across a
mechanised trackway,
Eileen House
absorbs the solar
flares. Petulant orb
commanding eyelines,
level and rise.
Spliced in
international waters,
the body, you told them,
was still inside you.

Pale globe inset,
you hive.
Resist the flatscreen,
heavenly musics;
turning towards
a mirrored wall.

Yes, pulse thickens

You

Silver   orange   blue

Pine release

Puerta Pollenca, Mallorca
January 2010

walked into the mountains (actually
rain: rain on path   rain on dogs
rain falling in the bay through sun)

    direction of   ie. towards   the
fuming mountains   (also, on crown
of Hitler Youth till slick)   where the mist
(a kind of purple)   clung or shrouded
whatever   and (it fell on our faces and
hands)   made to stop and go left
(pine release, very wet)   at the fence-line
even though I didn't see any military
personnel or smart bombs and correctly
identified the tiny bird that was flying
        in the storm

                    when the mountain
was biggest   (I saw a crane, you
a house, it was pouring) on the bypass
with four lanes   two for local traffic
direction of   i.e. towards

KEI MILLER

Some Definitions for Night

the time which follows evening like the next carriage of a train.   A justification for candles and by extension love whose pronouncement is made easier in dark spaces, over small flickering flames and a cascade of wax.   Night is a storing place for creatures that have not been named yet; a mammalogist says of a purple, rhombus-shaped creature – it's *as if it just stepped out of night where it had been hiding.*   Night is a habitat for dreams, the acre of forest inside us.   Night cannot be measured by the second or the hour hand. It is its own time, requiring only that we breathe deeply.   Night is a large womb, a spectacularly bloated pregnancy. Entire planets are born from night.   And night is an opening chapter I am yet to write; it will include peeniwallies, the terrible red-eyed Rolling Calf, and the following instruction: turn these pages slowly – push the sun down, down, below the horizon – and a story will come to steal your breath.

The Law Concerning Mermaids

There was once a law concerning mermaids. My friend thinks it a wondrous thing – that the British Empire was so thorough it had invented a law for everything. And in this law it was decreed: were any to be found in their usual spots, showing off like dolphins, sunbathing on rocks – they would no longer belong to themselves. And maybe this is the problem with empires: how they have forced us to live in a world lacking in mermaids – mermaids who understood that they simply were, and did not need permission to exist or to be beautiful. The law concerning mermaids only caused mermaids to pass a law concerning man: that they would never again cross our boundaries of sand; never again lift their torsos up from the surf; never again wave at sailors, salt dripping from their curls; would never again enter our dry and stifling world.

12 Notes For A Light Song of Light

I

A light song of light is not sung
in the light; what would be the point?
A light song of light swells up in dark
times, in wolf time and knife time,
in knuckle and blood times; it hums
a small tune in daytime, but saves
its full voice for the midnight.

II

A light song of light spits from its mouth
the things that occasionally gather:
the dull taste of morning and cobwebs
(you would not believe their thickness),
and the strangest word – caranapa –
so much larger than its letters, a Maroon
of a word, and a word so silent
it is the opposite of song.

III

A light song of light occasionally stutters.
This is par for the course.
There is no need for concern
no need for bed-rest or vitamins
no need to take your song in
to the song specialist for treatment.

IV

But were you to take your light song in
for a thorough checking-up, a blood screening,
you might discover your song has cancer,
HIV, diabetes, is going blind in its left eye.
You may not have strength to sing
your song for this season or the next.
But a light song of light cannot be
held back. It cannot wait on health
or its perfect occasion.

V

A light song of light meditates in the morning,
does yoga once a week, accepts the law
of karma. It may not worship in a synagogue
it may not worship in a balmyard
but still it believes in a clean heart
in righteous living and the general
avoidance of pork. It would like to touch
your feet, pronounce a blessing
before you go:
> Jah guide and protect always.
> Selah.
> Ashe.
> Ashe.

VI

A light song of light will summon daffodils,
bluebells and strawberries, humming birds;
will summon silver, the shine of sequins,
the gold of rings – and the dreadful luminosity
of everything we had been told to close
our eyes to (because they had no sharp
edges, because they could not be wielded
against our enemies) will be called back into service –
retired weapons that have no memory of war,
or that they could fight, or that they could win.

VII

A light song of light is not reggae,
not calypso, not mento or zouk,
not a common song from a common island,
not a song whose trail you have followed for umpteen years,
a song trembled from the single tooth of
the Singerman – the Singerman who had beat his tune
out from a sheet of zinc
and how it surprised you, the thin bellies
from which music could be drawn.
You did not know then that his song came
at the price of history and cane
and the terrible breadth of oceans: a price
which, even now, you cannot fully consider.

VIII

A light song of light don't talk
the way I talk most days.
To tell the truth I never know at first
what this country was goi do me –
how I would start hearing myself
through the ears of others,
how I would start putting words on a scale
and exchange the ones I think in
for the ones I think you will understand,
till it become natural, this slow careful way
of talking, this talk like the walk of a man
who find himself on a street he never born to,
who trying hard to look like nothing
not bothering him. And maybe nothing wrong
with a false talk like that, but that
is no way to sing.

IX

A light song of light is not understood completely
not in the moment it is sung
and maybe not for months after.
But it sings with a faith common
in those who never lost their accents
who talk their talk knowing, tssst
you may not catch everything but chu –
you will catch enough.
And if you don't catch nothing
then something wrong with your ears –
they been tuned to de wrong frequency.

X

A light song of light tells knock-knock jokes
and tells them in order
to illustrate the most heart-breaking points.
It is not that the song
does not know the weight of sadness;
it is not that the song
does not take things seriously;
it is not that the song
needs to write one hundred times on a chalkboard –
I will be heavy,
I will be heavy, I will be heavy, I will be heavy...

XI

A light song of light is distant cousin
to songs we sing in bath tubs,
is related then, by accident, to water
and to soap and to square white tiles
that bounce sound one from another,
is related also to rain and to blankets
and to the little things we say
to get us through the hurricane.

XII

A light song of light says thank you
to the paper it is written on –
this most solid evidence of its existence
however thin. Sometimes though,
a light song of light wishes it were written
on material even thinner, the shaft of morning
that slides through a shut window.
A light song of light believes nothing
is so substantial as light, and
that light is unstoppable,
and that light is all.

A Parting Song

May your portion be blue
        May your portion be sky
May your portion be light,
        Goodbye.

And may your portion be song
        Whose notes never die
And may the music be sweet,
        Goodbye.

And may your portion be soft
        And may your portion be love
Yes, may your portion be love
        And may your portion be soft
And may the soft lift you high
        And may your portion be sky
Goodbye.

LAURA ELLIOTT

Nowhere Near

11.00am.

light as white space or light as weight
light as process
moving toward touch
here is light coming through
transitional
here is light complete
leaning touching blessing
the wall with its white cheek
kissing surfaces butter
here is hollow light
whistling through a bottleneck

      1.49pm.

      that was yesterday
      tracing a circle on my hand
      ink run over and over the same line
      until it stains today we try again
      but never together
      today I wear an S instead
      look too closely at the pattern of my skin
      see if it fits and what else

3.10pm.

watching glass through glass
and its opposite white flash
skim across the floorboards
difficult gradations of light
bleach and blend
a touch that matters – as in matter –
sometimes the green arc out-of-focus leaves

just aren't enough company
think about cloud cover and how
this should shudder

A Compositional Arrangement (that) Persists

bones bristle like whiskers
in your teeth she is delighted
the plates match little blue waves
pulsing between you

the construction of a meal
one table two chairs the table
is glass/wood and assembled
on top are various plates full
of foods with rinds and crusts
and bones and furs foods
that require utensils precision
and care to unwrap you can
learn a lot about a person
from the way they use their
instruments prepare their plate
compose their sentences

saucers stacked on the lid
of the table a tank fish float on air
rearrange the dishes fish spin
on discs of ocean

but if the table is made of
i) wood then details such as
the colour of the plates
and the clarity of the food
the tonal qualities of the plate
arrangement gradually alter

the atmosphere of the table
(think about subtle shade
variations draw attention
to particular areas dynamics
connections between people)

    place the plates below
      the table blue flares through glass
like gasps of breath
        beneath the surface

and if the table is made of
ii) glass then the plates are also
to be made of glass and
the gentle digestion used
to reveal _____
beneath the table or this be
enacted more slowly and
the plates are made of porcelain
and same as above (i) attention
to colour moving softly into
(ii) skin beneath glass for
the practice these are the only rules

    below the foam frills say something
      silver say anything open we are so far
in hold your breath
        she says and dives

It is Always about the Distant Claims on Appearances

what is it about the journey that holds you
so lightless shuddering into nowhere
clenching dark inside the car
even the stars
in their own way deny us
portioned by glass fixed
on the strained horizon

there are gaps in everything
you show me in your vests in your eyes
in your letters
I fix these shapes in pictures
or make semblances from stones
how can you doubt
that specificity

we have lost each other driving through
farmlands closed fields breathing fibres of gold
russet leaves the textures
of everything we can't see
richer on the skin imagine
being wrapped in this night long enough
to feel its ripening body

I want to make it possible to want
something (un)true I want you to be
(un)sure of me
this drawing was (not) taken
from life this stone is (a replica)
painted to resemble that stone (why
do you) believe me

go back to the wheels faltering
was it nothing
at all your face emptied maybe
a hint of dial lights
but you were not there
do not lay claim do not lay anything
down we could share

you say this is (not)
the way mornings should feel
                    we are noticing surfaces
                    and hurting them testing the limits of
                    (y)our perception did you see did you
(want to) see here underneath
are fingerprints

            your hand in my lap in starlight no
            we knew nothing of stars
perhaps a struggle so sure of ourselves
eventually light rushing yellow
unbounded out and
                up and everything
                hurtling unclasped

                    the difference (in touch)
                    weighs nothing but
                              your voice hollows nearing
                              truth (I feel) your difference
                              drawing deep
                    from its stone (here
                    is what we know)

THOMAS IRONMONGER

The Smatcher *from bottom to top*

the end.
the ditch, before
traction slips towards
cannot grip the final bend;
column wrenching its calloused hand
to contain this speed and steering
revolutions, enough double-drop clutch,
a bald, peerless, outcrop of rock, needing more
to beat the hill, reach the dark woods crowning
groups of chilled spectators scream
with swinging croup, exhausted smoke,
tires and spokes churn the muddy climb,
before the starter's whistle shrieks like a life between teeth,
Old engines loosen their throats, digesting the morning air

Olympic Ode

Strophe

In these rubble days, newly rebuilt about the zero
        grounds where the King and Queen of Dinero
lost their battle with the Boeings:
I ask of you: listen to the stars singing
        of the great dignitaries shifting shape,
encroaching around beauty. As lexicographer Green expects:
        Bunga Bunga will not become absorbed

Antistrophe

by the fats of our language.
Instead, I implore you: listen out for the sound
        of the Bolt beating the sea from a tropical cloud,
stripping the world record of hundredths of seconds
as if they were clothes from a child. Of recent legends
        it is said that justice is hard to gauge,
that violence no longer gives by the strength of Satan's wrists

Epode

that illusion is the new religion. Such was this
        that the thick moustache of Saddam
exposed upon a screen, contrasted with the greens of his
rope hung face; that the iris of Osama
was broken on command from Obama.
But please, do not worry, you needn't have to strain,
        these harmonies have been tuned
automatically. And look further still, for how prevalent the food!
How bright the summers! How generous the rain!

RACHEL WARRINER

continued...

continued...
straight painted terracotta
pointgothic
cartoon faced
taste clicking when
'grounded in reality'
we come here to
type like Quasimodo.
story turning
like the last day with
folds in your shirt
peacock jaded
to our eyes
Christ compare while
scroll nodding
hope lies youth &
see you Francis

an ode to gravity:
you bring me down
but i like it

silence
pretty pencil case sparks
Plutarch's fire
right blurred
under the arches
your red tacit dress
of gilabbey silk
cites sewing lessons for children
[circa 1910]
gaffer tape old oak
in moments of difficulty
digress in bed
in grain

Prologue

from Fine Lament

redwine and sift
sink into this
safe keeping
thought guarded
by glycerine
and deep screams
no need for politics

costumed out of
consequence
hark back
permed and pernicious
to frivolity rules
in dark blue
scraping the frame

three stories of
prophetic wall holding
hidden in fiction
suburbia our
soft furnished strictures
distract through
melodramadaydreams

20.11.10

from Eleven Days

stuck in the snug
unfinished &
unrepeatable
walking into lungs
we bring mega-celebrities
to show excess
as walls crumble
and you crawl
back into bed
benefit breakdance
protects industry
for wasters
in pointlessly named
lupins
on the run
now as yesterday's news
discredited and dishevelled
in fraction humiliation
we sign on remote
to the best party in Dublin
on the day that the
injurious mother-fuckers
walked in
with economic
wish fulfillment
playing in their ears
cathartic slide
as i hallucinate
our escape
through these steel walls
we are sold
down the river
and drift off smiling

OLLIE EVANS

St Aquinas & Co.
after Paradiso X

My turn to wheel
the banquet but.
Who can see beyond
the sun?

      Belief, believe
our language but bite
off the image branch.
Nouns taste less
when salted with verbs
and you're still licking
for shape.

Look up their skirts,
transgendering
dancers of light
answering thirst.

This circle is not
literal but literate,
like letters are
themselves.

The luna part is past
and my ultra tear
is urge, tintinnabulating,
disposting spirits unarmouring
this turgid rota,
render voices on voices
I now tamper into doted
note form.

this non knowable inging

I believed I know
save only them ineveryinging there,
above, where

seven and thirst
sound the same
ring.

Belacqua

after Purgatorio IV

    Quando, poor dilettante, over a dull year
parks a new lap, all tender. Few intend to
air poor ole' Quando, so old he caused over ten
    requests at a legato, quelled and kept – escorted...
As such I was busy decoding these lines (1 thru 12)
into my tongue, that I failed whilst typing,
    to notice the sun shoot up fifty in the sky.
We came on camel back to crawl the postern
on our knees and scrape through scramble up
    the Jordan slate where my foot slots in creases
cut with salt bolts stained a few worlds ago.
The violin rests pressed untouched. From here,
    the lowest altitude in the world, I arch my neck
back and slit my eyes to where rock and blue
indistinguish eachother – eyes up to the nothing
    peak. I have no wings. My spare answer
was to clay my skin from a moulded jar and lie
on the beauty water whilst salt nebulates
    beneath my body – finger rests on snooze, a
gain, head up, but back flat. Less move.
To wade back to my surrogate on shore
    I stand with the dead sea at my ears
and levitate on borrowed wings. No need
to tread. Before I know it, we're gone.
    I feel the salt mineral through my skin.
We're waiting for nothing. Ah...

MARIANNE MORRIS

Who Not to Speak To

The sky is threaded with tree limbs
and electric lines
and the crosshatch detail of cranes,
train lines and more trees.
The direction of each thing bleeds into the direction
of another thing,
making the directions subjective and laughable.
This a metaphor for purpose, which is

<surely all of those things>.
You say instinctively that this
is what you want to hear,

and I try to hear you out but aren't you
dying to ask me something
inappropriate?

*If you prefer, we can wait
until there is nothing left to say
and the hostess sends everybody home.*

The limp clouds are puddles holding watery sunlight,
and so many awful things have happened
that

the radio enunciates the toll,

and the place
and the proper name
                as if it was all just shipping news.
                And in a way, it is, because
the core is always the same.
Battered fish pose as nourishment as
a girl on her tip-toes leans over the pier, wondering what's all
that stuff in the sand:

        (Enormous toxic mutant fish,
        a discontinued dumpster,
        the fin of a mythological whale)

SUCH PASSIONS   ABOUND
in the CYBERSPHERE !

On the <u>Have Your Say website</u>,

Pitt-Palin **Pacified** Rice Thatcher's

face is *embroiled* in a **botox debate** about one

hundred and sixty four people having a debate debate

about the <u>Have Your stick insect Say</u>

debate where a good cross-section of social strata are

embroiled in a **patriotic** debate

about themselves,

a digital mirror sputters,

the lines rage aimless,

the passion is aimless.

I just want some language I can trust I can
trust the announcement that all the lines are working

as if that were news
   and
      in a way
         it is.

   <OFTEN THE LINES ARE DOWN DUE TO A ~~SELFISH~~
~~CUNT~~ PERSON UNDER A TRAIN>

Even something as filmic and flimsy as *'love you'*

can feel like a proxy debacle, preferring the sex

   and the city and the rotten erotic

   indulgence of authorised porn

      to yourself (?)

FILMIC INTERLUDE:

<In the language of storytelling>
I enter the retail space

I AM HOPEFUL with anecdotes, charm, and energy

NO ONE WILL COME BECAUSE I don't want to destroy
anything

I just want my items to envelope you,

look!

<u>I HAVE BOUGHT YOU</u>

a plant,

a bottle,

and a dimmer switch.

Lullaby Never Work

Downstairs the little voice cries in anguish
at having been born recently, enough
to anguish anyone, anguish
dulled in the safety of
passing years, sleeps
repressed and is occasionally
      articulated in the vapour of dreams.
The thing that makes you smoke when you are
already coughing up blood, the rare dream of satis
leading to inevitable immolation on the pyre, good
bye husband and with you myself, you were all that I am.
Vexing games played against conscious will, one:
                              The Defence
Secretary eats the fish eyes and the eyes breed in the
Defence Secretary's belly and then pop out of the De-
fence Secretary's skin, a thousandfish-sight breaking the
demonstration staged by the Defence Secretary's flesh.
            All of the eyes blink in unison, you
can hear the gulp of the wetted epidermis.
            Vexing games [...], two:
The seating arrangement was 'done' by
the butterfly swarming on her face as it ate
serotonin from a doggy bag of past envy.
Then the weird fact of pets being owned and their
polystyrene beds and the shit of the world fairly ablaze,
the usefulness of latex, rubberised veins, and lithium,
then you lick salt off the blancmange. Dying Alone
runs down your leg, as the voices of men cook
in oil against your chest where the hurt is caked,
clasping the unconscious minnow.
           Dying Alone curls itself round your thigh. To
finally fuck standing up, that will be the death of me. I hope
you feel the same way too, then we can get the cheapest
ironing-board and lip-synch in the aisle to something awful
as our double-paean to death is formulated in the privacy
of our shared thoughts, milk in our
mouths like the good old days. This
is a choice, but it's not exactly your
fault. Just go to work, it's easier that way. The droll
insufficiency of wages pings like static in a pyjama top.

De Sade's Law

Amongst the angels that season frog-tying was the cool thing to
do and they would exchange. Frog ties which were long green
strips made from dead frogs, the skin cured and moulded until
supple.
                They were expensive because everyone wanted one.
They were inexpensive because everyone had one.
They were inexpensive because everyone wanted one.
They were expensive because everyone had one.

The trouble was, you inattentive lovers, one of victory.

The fuck-you is remonstrance for the
violence of your dullness, the violence of your numbness, your easy
forgetfulness of injustice, your efficient hoovering up of flesh
blown from Fallujah to the front page, and then the
mince pies and larks.
    A template of blown wind through the mouth of a cloud,
blushing into the mirror that curves up like beef powder
as impacted and hard-hitting as the
checkpoint in Baghdad, it shoots first and says 'do you
have any ID' afterwards. In English. Monotone.

Fish have more trust in them*selves*.

Your friend Jimmy Blair would be a more sensible choice] would be hard-pressed to
say, in public, perhaps over some mince pies and mulled wine, that he
doesn't give a shit about injustice on a world scale (leaping forms of angels, their ankles

                frog-tied

their aprons lactating); but it would be
easy for Jimmy Blair to say that he thinks the poem is a cunt. There is no quotient
       of lust.
No one else needs to know where it is that you feel that particular pain.

You Put the Fiancé in Financier

Come on don't leave me just yet, if I haven't figured it out. Come back for one more kiss that will turn into fruit trees. Not to wish for the metaphor overmuch. But at night when the tunnels are coaxing with curled fingers slogans in colours and wishing and I've looked up at the sky only to find it filled with Canary Wharf, the red dashes of light comforting as the night closes in, and would like to bed down in there under the desk with you, in our blanket of wasted 30gsm, and steal ruined, pasty kisses like sleep returning after too long away but the goal is not sleep or nature or money it's just making sure we never get there, then? We get paid, probably, I don't know I guess like I said it's not about the goal. And down the street you weave amongst the trees with blossoms, inviting the rain to flood your front room. The leaves trying to get in the front door, with the balance sheets thinly resting amongst the shoe trees, I guess there are things we are asked to carry in our hearts and the asking is so gently put that we do or that there is something inherently sexual about forward interest rate curves. It's your life, as you like it. It is me too that wants the key, sucker for mythology and advertising and those workdrinksjewelleryfuckers who think everything is fabulous.

BIOGRAPHICAL NOTES

Who are you? The pen-dragon.
Again. Nothing new on this earth.
The same old song and dance.
Notes from the deepest space.

Rachael Allen was born in Cornwall and studied at Goldsmiths, University of London. She is the co-founder of poetry collective Clinic Presents. She reviews for *Ambit* magazine and has written for *Granta online*. Her poetry has appeared in *The Salt Book of Younger Poets* and *Night&Day*. ➤ 232

Andrew Bailey was born in London and raised in Northwich and Preston. He studied at the universities of Nottingham and Sheffield, lived in London for several years, and now lives in Sussex. He was one of the original editors for the Poetry Archive, and has also worked for the Poetry Society, Poetry International Web and a handful of fringe theatre companies. His poems have appeared widely, online and offline, and a first collection, *Zeal*, was published by Enitharmon in 2012. He was the 2005 winner of the Geoffrey Dearmer Prize. ➤ 55

Emily Berry grew up in London and studied English Literature at Leeds University, and Creative and Life Writing at Goldsmiths College. She is a co-editor of the anthology series Stop Sharpening Your Knives and a contributor to *The Breakfast Bible*, a compendium of breakfasts. She won an Eric Gregory Award in 2008 and her first full-length collection of poems is forthcoming from Faber. ➤ 112

Ben Borek was born in London in 1980. His verse-novel, *Donjong Heights*, was published by Egg Box in 2007. Other work has been anthologised in *City State* (Penned in the Margins) and *London: a History in Verse* (HUP). A new verse-novel is forthcoming. He has read work throughout the UK, and in Europe, as well as on BBC Radio. He lives in London/Warsaw. ➤ 78

Siddhartha Bose was born in 1979. He is a poet, playwright and performer based in London. His first collection, *Kalagora*, appeared in 2010 (Penned in the Margins). He has been featured on BBC 4 (TV), BBC Radio 3 and *Times Online*. He has written, performed and toured a play, also entitled *Kalagora*, which completed an acclaimed run at Edinburgh Festival Fringe 2011. Sid is a Leverhulme Fellow in Drama at the University of London. His new play, *London's Perverted Children*, premièred in July 2012. www.kalagora.com ➤ 264

Elizabeth-Jane Burnett is a poet specialising in experimental writing and performance. She holds a BA in English from Oxford and an MA and PhD in Contemporary Poetics from Royal Holloway, University of London. The poems in this anthology feature in a collection of ecopoetics called *oh-zones* (Knives, Forks and Spoons, 2012) which considers issues of environment and activism. She currently teaches Creative Writing at the University of Northampton. ➢ 123

James Byrne's most recent poetry collection is *Blood/Sugar*, published by Arc in 2009. He co-edited *Bones Will Crow: 15 Contemporary Burmese Poets*, the first anthology of Burmese poetry ever to be published in the West (Arc, 2012) and *Voice Recognition: 21 Poets for the 21st Century* (Bloodaxe, 2009). His most recent anthology project is *The Wolf: A Decade* (The Wolf Editions, 2012). He was a Stein Fellow ('Extraordinary International Scholar') at New York University in 2009-11. ➢ 136

Stuart Calton, born in 1979, is a call-centre worker, poet and revolutionary Marxist. He has published four volumes of poetry with Barque Press. These are *Sheep Walk Cut* (2003), *The Bench Graft* (2004), *The Corn Mother* (2006) and *Three Reveries* (2009). *United Snap Up* was self-published in 2004. Under the name T.H.F. Drenching, he is an improvising Dictaphonist, a composer of musique concrète and runs Council of Drent Recordings (www.councilofdrent.com). The short domestic cycle included here is previously unpublished. ➢ 274

Melanie Challenger was born in 1977. She won an Eric Gregory Award for her first collection, *Galatea* (Salt, 2006), and was shortlisted for a Forward Prize for Best First Collection. She is the author of one work of non-fiction, *On Extinction* (Granta, 2011). ➢ 197

Tom Chivers was born in 1983 in South London. He is a writer, editor and literary arts producer. His publications include *How To Build A City* (Salt, 2009), *The Terrors* (Nine Arches Press, 2009; shortlisted for the Michael Marks Award) and, as editor, the anthologies *Generation Txt*, *City State*, *Stress Fractures* and *Adventures in Form* (Penned in the Margins, 2006-12). In 2009 Radio 4 broadcast his documentary about the poet Barry MacSweeney. He received an Eric Gregory Award in 2011. He is currently working on ADRIFT: a commission from Cape Farewell to explore the changing environment of the city. ➢ 289

Tim Cockburn was born in Banbury, and raised in Nottingham. His pamphlet, *Appearances in the Bentinck Hotel*, was published by Salt in 2011. He is grateful to the editors of the following publications, in which poems have appeared previously or are forthcoming: *Clinic, Five Dials, Mercy, Poetry Review, Stop Sharpening Your Knives*. ➢ 282

Rebecca Cremin was born in 1983, hails from Ireland by way of the world and currently lives in London. She is currently undergoing a practice-based PhD at Royal Holloway investigating site specific and feminist performance poetics. She is a founding member of the poetic collective PRESS FREE PRESS. Her publications include *LAY'D* from Veer and *Cutting Movement* from The Knives Forks and Spoons Press. Her performances take place in galleries, pubs, on council estates, in her bedroom, in the street, in the book and on the page. ➤ 74

Emily Critchley holds a PhD in contemporary American women's poetry and philosophy from the University of Cambridge. She is the author of several critical articles – on poetry, philosophy and feminism – and several poetry chapbooks. Her *Selected Writing, Love / All That / & OK*, was published by Penned in the Margins in 2011. She teaches English and Creative Writing at the University of Greenwich, London. A new book is forthcoming from Egg Box. ➤ 120

Jo Crot lives in Edinburgh and 'was born 15 April, 2006'. Say hiya – franciscrot @gmail.com / @jolwalton / @franciscrot /sadpress.wordpress.com / franciscrot. tumblr.com. See also Jo L Walton, *Invocation* (Critical Documents), Harvey Joseph & Lindsay James, *Sea Adventures, or, Pond Life* (RunAmokPress), Megan Sword & Timpani Skullface, *Superior City Song* (Critical Documents), Colleen Hind, *Lots of Poems* (Intercapillary Space), Brad Ox, *Leaden Sausagefust Annals* (Passim Press), Pocahontis Mildew & Colleen Hind, *We Are Real* (Critical Documents), Joseph Walton, *Harmony* (Critical Documents), Francis Crot, *Prets in Persia* (Veer), Francis Crot, *The Cuntomatic* (yt communication), Look Robots, *Only a Christian Boy Can Kill Christmas* (Mountain) and Walt Walton, *Gramma's Kinda Old Honey* (Rat Nuh-uh-uh Press). 'Poetsplain' is part of *DP*, co-authored with Justin Katko (www.plantarchy.us). ➤ 148

Patrick Coyle was born in Hull in 1983. He is an artist who lives and works in London, and completed his BA (Hons) Fine Art at Byam Shaw, University of the Arts London (2005) and MFA Art Writing at Goldsmiths, University of London (2010). Recent exhibitions include ICA London, Toomer Labzda Gallery, New York; Pippy Houldsworth Gallery, London, Hayward Concrete Café, London; and A Foundation, Liverpool. He has recently given performances at various venues including ICA, Zabludowicz Collection, Spike Island, and Flat Time House. www.patrickcoyle.info ➤ 222

Amy De'Ath was born in Suffolk in 1985 and lives in Vancouver, Canada, where she is a doctoral student at Simon Fraser University, and works on the poetics journal *West Coast Line*. She previously lived and worked in London, where she was recently Poet-in-Residence at the University of Surrey. Her publications include *Caribou* (Bad Press, 2011), *Erec & Enide* (Salt, 2010), and *Andromeda / The World Works for Me* (Crater Press, 2010). ➤ 62

Toby Martinez de las Rivas was born in 1978 and studied History and Archaeology at Durham. He received an Eric Gregory Award in 2005 and the Andrew Waterhouse Award from New Writing North in 2008. He lives in Córdoba, Andalucía. His Faber New Poets pamphlet appeared in 2009, and his first collection, *Terror*, will be published by Faber in 2013. ➤ 285

Laura Elliott was born in 1987, studied at Norwich University College of the Arts, and has since completed her MA in Poetry at the University of East Anglia. She won the Café Writers Norfolk Commission in 2009, her debut pamphlet, *Bridge* (Gatehouse Press) was subsequently published in 2010. Her work has featured in various publications, including most recently *The Best British Poetry 2011* (Salt). She writes in response to contemporary visual arts, her poetry speaks from the borderlands between sensation and communication. ➤ 300

Stephen Emmerson is the author of *Telegraphic Transcriptions* (Dept Press), *Poems found at the scene of a murder* (Zimzalla), *The Last Ward* (Very Small Kitchen), *A never ending poem...* (Zimzalla), *Pharmacopoetics* (An Apple Pie edition), and *No Ideas but in things* (KFS). He lives in London. ➤ 267

Amy Evans grew up on the Isle of Wight and lives in London. Her first pamphlet, *Collecting Shells*, was published with Oystercatcher Press in 2011. She is one of four women poets commissioned to write for Veer Book's *VierSome #01* (2012). Her poetry and collages feature in *Shearsman*, *Jacket*, *M58* and *Openned* magazines, *Women's Studies Quarterly* and in the anthologies *Sea Pie* (Shearsman, 2012) and *In Place of Love and Country* (Crater Press, 2013). She was a Visiting Lecturer at King's College London where she is currently completing a PhD on Robert Duncan and women poets, and co-edited *The Unruly Garden: Robert Duncan and Eric Mottram, Letters and Essays* (Peter Lang, 2007). She works as a classical singer and singing teacher. ➤ 51

Ollie Evans, born in 1987, is a performer, poet and puppeteer from London. His first booklet of poetry, *Stutter Studies*, was published by Department Press in 2011, followed by two books of experimental homophonic translations of Rilke, *Dashed Booked a Builder* (Redceilings Press, 2012) and *Dante, The Chomedy* (Holdfire, 2013). He has had poetry published in the *International Egg & Poultry Review*, *Depart*, *Anything Anymore Anywhere* and *Spine*. He is currently working on a PhD about 'Performance and *Finnegans Wake*' at Birkbeck College. He blogs at orte.tumblr.com ➤ 310

S.J. Fowler, born in 1983, has published four poetry collections, having had poetry, performance and conceptual art commissioned from the Tate, Mercy, Penned in the Margins, Jerwood Charitable Foundation and the London Sinfonietta. He is poetry editor at *3am magazine*, Lyrikline and is the curator of the Maintenant series and the Enemies project. He has performed across Europe and been translated into nine languages. He works for the British Museum and as a martial arts instructor.. www.sjfowlerpoetry. com | www.blutkitt.blogspot. com | www.maintenant.co.uk ➤ 278

Miriam Gamble is from Belfast, and now lives in Edinburgh. She won an Eric Gregory Award in 2007 and published a pamphlet, *This Man's Town*, with tall-lighthouse in 2008. Her first full collection, *The Squirrels Are Dead*, published by Bloodaxe, won her a Somerset Maugham Award in 2011; she has also won the Ireland Chair of Poetry Bursary Award and the Vincent Buckley Poetry Prize. She lectures in Creative Writing by Online Learning at the University of Edinburgh. ➤ 85

Jim Goar received an MFA from Naropa University and studied Jack Spicer's *The Holy Grail* for the critical component of his PhD at the University of East Anglia. In 2010, Reality Street brought out his first full-length collection, *Seoul Bus Poems*. A second book, *The Louisiana Purchase* (2011), is available from Rose Metal Press. The poems in *Dear World* are from the manuscript *The Dustbowl;* '#10' originally appeared in *#NewWriting*. ➤ 126

Matthew Gregory was born in Suffolk, in 1984, and studied at Norwich School of Art & Design and Goldsmiths. In 2010 he received an Eric Gregory Award. His work has appeared in publications like *London Review of Books*, *Poetry London*, *Poetry Review*, *The Best British Poetry 2011* (Salt) and *S/S/Y/K* anthologies, and has been aired on BBC radio.. ➤ 132

Elizabeth Guthrie is a poet and performer living in London researching for a practice-based PhD in text and performance at UEL. She is a co-editor of Livestock Editions. Her work has appeared in various journals including *Onedit, Requited, Bombay Gin, Pinstripe Fedora*, and *Open Letter*. She has a pamphlet, *X Portraits*, out through Crater Press, a chapbook, *Yellow and Red*, through Black Lodge Press, and the collaborative chapbook with Andrew K. Peterson, Between Here and the Telescopes, through Slumgullion Press, and is poet in residence at the Centre for Creative Collaboration in London. ➤ 105

Emily Hasler was born in Felixstowe, Suffolk, in 1985, and studied at the University of Warwick. In 2009 she came second in the Edwin Morgan International Poetry Competition. Her poems have appeared in many magazines and anthologies, including *The Rialto, Poetry Salzburg* and *The Best British*

Poetry 2011 (Salt). Her debut pamphlet *Natural Histories* was published by Salt in 2011. She lives and works in London. ➤ 142

Oli Hazzard was born in Bristol in 1986. He studied English at University College London and the University of Bristol, and is currently working towards a DPhil at the University of Oxford. His first collection, *Between Two Windows*, was published by Carcanet in 2012. ➤ 206

Colin Herd was born in Stirling in 1985 and now lives in Edinburgh. His first full-length book *too ok* was published in 2011 by BlazeVOX and his first pamphlet *like*, in 2010 by The Knives, Forks and Spoons Press. ➤ 96

Holly Hopkins currently lives in South London. Her poems have appeared in *Poetry Review, The Rialto, The North* and *Magma*. Her work has also been anthologised in *Birdbook* (Sidekick Books), *Captains' Tower* (Seren Books), *Herbarium* (Capsule Press), *Lung Jazz: Young British Poets for Oxfam* (Cinnamon Press) and *Hampstead Companion* (Couplet Books). She received an Eric Gregory Award in 2011. ➤ 147

Sarah Howe was born in Hong Kong in 1983. A former Foyle Young Poet of the Year, she won an Eric Gregory Award in 2010. Her pamphlet, *A Certain Chinese Encyclopedia*, is available from tall-lighthouse. Her work has been anthologised in *The Salt Book of Younger Poets* (2011), *Best British Poetry* (2012) and broadcast on BBC Radio 3. She is a Research Fellow at Gonville and Caius College, Cambridge, where she teaches Renaissance literature. ➤ 89

Thomas Ironmonger was born in 1982, grew up in Kent, and lives in London. In 2010 he completed an MA in Creative Writing at Goldsmiths. He is a cofounder of Nightingale Poetry (www.nightingalepoetry.com), an agency specialising in the production of bespoke poems. ➤ 305

Meirion Jordan was born in 1985. He is a Welsh poet from Cwmllynfell, in the upper Swansea Valley. He studied mathematics at Oxford, where he won the Newdigate Prize, before taking an MA in Creative Writing and a PhD at the University of East Anglia. His first collection, *Moonrise* (Seren), was short-listed for the Forward Prize for Best First Collection in 2009, and his pamphlet *Strangers Hall* was shortlisted for an East Anglia Book of the Year award. His latest collection, *Regeneration*, was published by Seren in 2012. ➤ 220

Sarah Kelly is currently based in Buenos Aires and London. Her first chap-book, *locklines*, was published in 2010 (Knivesforksandspoons Press) and further work can be found in *Better than Language: An Anthology* (Ganzfeld Press, 2011) among various other print and online journals and magazines in the UK and North America. Recently her work increasingly involves the medium of paper which she makes by hand and explores playing with the body and surfaces of both text and page. She has exhibited in several galleries in Buenos Aires and in 'Visual Poetics' at the Poetry Library, London, February 2013. ➤ 254

Luke Kennard, born in 1981, is a poet and writer of fiction. He won an Eric Gregory Award in 2005. His prose poems collection *The Solex Brothers* (2005) was followed by three collections from Salt, *The Harbour Beyond the Movie* (2007), which was shortlisted for the Forward Prize for Best Collection, *The Migraine Hotel* (2009) and *A Lost Expression* (2012). He lectures at the University of Birmingham. ➤ 161

Katharine Kilalea moved from South Africa to London in 2005 to study for an MA in Creative Writing at the University of East Anglia. Her first book, *One Eye'd Leigh* (Carcanet, 2009) was shortlisted for the Costa Poetry Award and longlisted for the Dylan Thomas Prize for writers under 30. She has received Arts Council Awards for poetry, and her poems have appeared in publications including Carcanet's *New Poetries V*, *Best British Poetry 2011* and the *2010 Forward Prize Anthology*. ➤ 235

Laura Kilbride was born in 1988, and is in the second year of her doctorate, preparing a thesis on 'Swinburne's Style'. Her first pamphlet, *ERRATA*, came out from Tipped Press in 2011. With Rosa Van Hensbergen she co-edits *The Paper Nautilus Magazine*. She lives and works in Cambridge. ➤ 66

Michael Kindellan's chapbooks include *Charles Baudelaire* (Bad Press, 2005), *Word is Born with Reitha Pattison* (Arehouse, 2006), *Not love* (Barque, 2009), *Crater 1* (Crater, 2010), and *Financial Times* (No Press, 2011). He is currently an Alexander von Humboldt post-doctoral research fellow at the Universität Bayreuth. ➤ 210

Ágnes Lehóczky holds a PhD from University of East Anglia. Her poetry collections in English, *Budapest to Babel* (2008) and *Rememberer* (2011) were published by Egg Box. She won the Jane Martin Prize for Poetry at Girton College in 2011. Her collection of essays on the poetry of Ágnes Nemes Nagy, *Poetry, the Geometry of Living Substance*, was published in 2011 by Cambridge Scholars. She teaches creative writing at the University of Sheffield. ➤ 45

Frances Leviston was born in 1982. She read English at St Hilda's College, Oxford, and has an MA in Writing from Sheffield Hallam University. In 2006 she received an Eric Gregory Award from the Society of Authors. *Public Dream*, her first collection, was published in 2007 by Picador and shortlisted for the T.S. Eliot Prize, the Forward Prize for Best First Collection and the

Jerwood–Aldeburgh First Collection Prize. She works as a freelance writing tutor and reviews new poetry for the *Guardian*. ➤ 116

Éireann Lorsung was born in 1980 in Minneapolis, where she lived until 2006. She holds an MFA from the University of Minnesota, and did her PhD at the University of Nottingham. Her first book, *Music For Landing Planes By*, was published by Milkweed Editions in 2007; *Her book* is forthcoming from Milkweed in 2013. She co-runs MIEL, a micropress (miel-books.com), and edits 111O (111oh.com). ➤ 33

Chris McCabe has published three poetry collections: *The Hutton Inquiry* (Salt, 2005), *Zeppelins* (Salt, 2008) and *THE RESTRUCTURE* (Salt, 2012). His work has been recorded by The Poetry Archive and anthologised in *Identity Parade* (Bloodaxe, 2010), *The Best British Poetry 2011* (Salt, 2011) and *Adventures in Form* (Penned in the Margins, 2012). His play *Shad Thames, Broken Wharf* was performed at The London Word Festival and published by Penned in the Margins in 2010. He works as a librarian at the Poetry Library, London ➤ 109

Michael McKimm was born in 1983 in Belfast and now lives in London. A graduate of the Warwick Writing Programme, he is an Eric Gregory Award winner, was an International Writing Fellow at the University of Iowa, and in 2012 received a writing grant from Arts Council England. He has published one collection, *Still This Need* (Heaventree Press, 2009). His work has appeared in anthologies and magazines in the UK, Ireland and the USA, including *Best of Irish Poetry 2010* (Southword Editions, 2009) and *Best British Poetry 2012* (Salt, 2012). www.michaelmckimm.co.uk ➤ 90

Fabian Macpherson was born in London in 1984. His *Song from A Waspshire Lad* was recently published as a Crater Press broadside. Other poems have appeared in *yt communication bulletin, QUID, Hi Zero* and *Intercapillary Space*. In 2011, he completed a PhD at University College London on late 19th-century political verse, a thicket of lost utopias. ➤ 139

mendoza is a London-based poet from Northumberland, founder of the *ninerrors poetry series* and editor of *FREAKLUNG* poetry zine. Investigating identity through poetic practice, mendoza writes and performs under several personas including Linus Slug and Elffish Jon. mendoza's poems reference Northumbrian history, and North-East dialect as well as insect folklore and mythology. The idea of containment is explored through self-defined boundaries in the form of the nine-line poem, examining the tension that exists between the interior and exterior 'self'. ➤ 200

James Midgley was born in 1986. His poems have appeared in journals such as *Fuselit, Kenyon Review, Magma, Poetry Review, New Welsh Review, The Rialto, Shearsman Magazine* and *The Warwick Review*, and in anthologies such as *The Salt Book of Younger Poets* and *Lung Jazz*. In 2008 he received an Eric Gregory Award. ➤ 57

Kei Miller is a Jamaican poet and novelist. He has been an International Writing Fellow at the University of Iowa and presently teaches at Glasgow University. His most recent books are his novel, *The Last Warner Woman* (Weidenfeld & Nicolson, 2010), and his anthology *New Caribbean Poetry* (2007) and poetry collections *There is an Anger That Moves* (2007) and *A Light Song of Light* (2010) from Carcanet. ➤ 299

Marianne Morris, born in 1981, is the author of *Iran Documents* (Trafficker Press, 2012), *Commitment* (Critical Documents, 2011), *Tutu Muse* (Fly by Night, 2007), and *A New Book From Barque Press, Which They Will Probably Not Print* (Barque Press, 2006). She was the 2008 recipient of the Harper Wood Scholarship for Creative Writing, and was the founding editor of Bad Press. Full-length collections are forthcoming from Egg Box and Enitharmon. ➤ 312, 336

Camilla Nelson is based in south west England. She has recently completed a practice-based PhD entitled *Reading and Writing with a Tree: Practising Nature Writing as Enquiry* at University College Falmouth incorporating Dartington College of Arts. Her poetry has been published by *Shearsman Magazine, The Rialto, Writers Forearm, Cleaves Journal* and *Pomegranate*. www.camillanelson.co.uk ➤ 93

Tamarin Norwood was born in 1981, and is an artist and writer. She has recently shown work at Tate Britain, Modern Art Oxford, Whitechapel Gallery and the London Word Festival. Published titles include *olololo* (MAO & Book Works studio), *was* (LemonMelon), *DO SOMETHING* (ULS), and contributions to *Maintenant: the Camarade Project* (Red Ceilings Press), *Roland* (ICA) and *Timepieces* (Art on the Underground). She studied linguistics at Oxford University, fine art at Central Saint Martins (2007); her MFA art writing at Goldsmiths (2010) was funded by AHRC and she has just begun a Clarendon-funded doctorate in art theory at Oxford University. ➤ 272

Richard Parker, born in 1978, is an academic in Turkey but originally from London. His collection entitled *From The Mountain of California...* appeared through the auspices of Opennal Press in 2010, his pamphlet *China* from Knives, Forks and Spoons, also in 2010. His long poem *The Traveller and The Defence of Heaven* was published by Veer in 2012, and his pamphlet *49* was published by Oystercatcher Press, also in 2012. ~~R.T.A. Parker's 99 Sonnets~~

~~About Evil~~, from which the poems in this anthology are taken, is forthcoming from Ninerrors Press. ➤ 241

Sandeep Parmar received a PhD in English Literature from University College London and an MA in Creative Writing from the University of East Anglia. She edited *The Collected Poems of Hope Mirrlees* (Carcanet, 2011) and *Myth of the Modern Woman*, her study of the unpublished autobiographies of Mina Loy, is due from Continuum in 2013. Her poetry has appeared in the UK and the US and her debut collection, *The Marble Orchard*, was published by Shearsman in 2012. She was a Fellow at Clare Hall, University of Cambridge, in 2011-12, and is now Lecturer in English at the University of Liverpool. ➤ 259

Holly Pester, born in 1982, is a sound poet, artist and researcher based in London. She regularly performs at text, art and poetry events including the Serpentine Poetry Marathon 2009, Text Festival 2011 and dOCUMENTA (13) 2012. She is currently researching 'Speech Matter: Sound Poetry and its and its Recurring Mediations' for a practice-led PhD at Birkbeck, University of London. Her collection of poetry, *Hoofs*, was released with if p then q press in 2010. ➤ 102

Heather Phillipson's poems have been published and broadcast widely. She received an Eric Gregory Award in 2008 and a Faber New Poets Award in 2009. She is also an internationally exhibiting artist, working across video, sound and live events, with recent shows in Switzerland, Sweden, Germany and London. Her first book-length collection, *Instant-flex 718*, is published by Bloodaxe in 2013. ➤ 187

Kate Potts was born in 1978, and worked in music publishing before training as a teacher. She has taught English and Creative Writing at colleges in London for several years. Her pamphlet *Whichever Music* (tall-lighthouse, 2008) was a Poetry Book Society Pamphlet Choice and was shortlisted for a Michael Marks Award. Her first full-length collection, *Pure Hustle*, was published by Bloodaxe in 2011. She is currently working towards a PhD on radio poetry. ➤ 251

Eileen Pun was born in 1980 in New York and now lives in Grasmere, Cumbria. In 2011, she was selected as an Escalator prize-winner by Writers' Centre Norwich and also awarded a writing and research grant by Arts Council England. ➤ 129

Nat Raha was born in 1987 and lives in London. Her poetry includes *polemics for loudhailer* (Veer Books, 2012), *Octet* (Veer Books, 2010) and *countersonnets* (Contraband, forthcoming), and is included in *Better than Language: An Anthology of New Modernist Poetries* (ed. Chris Goode, Ganzfeld, 2011). Her work has also appeared in *Damn The Caesars, The Paper Nautilus, Department*, and her performances include SoundEye (Cork IRE), Crossing the Line, Openned, Cambridge Reading Series, Sussex Poetry Festival, Hi Zero, The Situation Room. She helps out with ninerrors press and is a postgraduate student at the University of Sussex. ➤ 215

Sam Riviere was born in 1981. He co-edits the anthology series Stop/Sharpening/Your/Knives. He received an Eric Gregory Award in 2009. Faber published his debut pamphlet in 2010, and *81 Austerities*, winner of the Forward Prize for Best First Collection, in 2012. ➤ 245

Sophie Robinson was born in 1985. She has an MA in Poetic Practice, a PhD in Queer Phenomenology and Contemporary Poetry from Royal Holloway, University of London. Her first book, *a*, came out from Les Figues press in 2009. Her work has been included in several anthologies including *Infinite Difference: Other Poetries by Women in the UK* (Shearsman 2010), *Voice Recognition: 21 Poets for the 21st Century* (Bloodaxe, 2009) and *The Reality Street Book of Sonnets* (Reality Street 2008). In 2011 she was poet in residence at the V&A Museum. ➤ 190

Hannah Silva is a South West based playwright, poet and theatre maker. She has shown her work internationally and has performed throughout the UK including at Latitude Festival, the Edinburgh Fringe and the London Word Festival. Her solo show *Opposition* toured nationally and was described in a five star review by *What's on Stage* as 'radical, political, courageous'. She is currently directing her play *Hunger* with support from the Jerwood Charitable Foundation and the Arts Council England. http:// hannahsilva.wordpress.com ➤ 144

Angus Sinclair studied at Norwich School of Art & Design and has an MA in Creative Writing from the University of East Anglia. In 2010 he was awarded the Café Writers Norfolk Commission, resulting in the publication of his debut pamphlet *Another Use of Canvas* (Gatehouse Press). ➤ 71

Marcus Slease was born in Portadown, Northern Ireland, and emigrated to Las Vegas at age 12. He has lived all over the world as a teacher of English as a foreign language and is the author of six books of poetry. Recent poetry, flash plays and fiction have appeared in: *Forklift Ohio, Juice is Dead, Radioactive Moat, 3AM Magazine, Thought Catalog, Housefire Books, Metazen, So and So Magazine, Everyday Genius, Spork, InDigest, NAP, Gesture* and *Little White Lies* (among others). Poor Claudia have just released his latest book of poetry *Mu (so) Dream (window)*. He lives in London and blogs (and reblogs) at The House of Zabka: http://marcusslease.tumblr.com ➤ 193

Andrew Spragg is a poet, performer and critic. His books include *The Fleetingest* (Red Ceiling Press, 2011), *Notes for Fatty Cakes* (Anything Anymore Anywhere, 2011) and *cut out* (Dept Press, 2012). To Blart & Kid is due to be published by Like This Press in early 2013. He edits Infinite Editions, a blog that publishes free poetry postcards for download and distribution. ➤ 68

Ben Stainton was born in 1978. His poems have appeared in *Blackbox Manifold*, *The Rialto*, *Magma*; and in the anthologies *Lung Jazz: Young British Poets for Oxfam*, *Coin Opera 2* and *Stop Sharpening Your Knives*. His debut (experimental) pamphlet, *The Backlists*, was published in 2011 by the Knives Forks and Spoons Press. He blogs at Hello, Fig. ➤ 86

Keston Sutherland, born in 1976, is the author of *The Odes to TL61P*, *The Stats on Infinity*, *Stress Position*, *Hot White Andy*, *Neocosis*, *Antifreeze* and other books of poetry, many essays, and a book about Marx and poetry, *Stupefaction: a radical anatomy of phantoms*. He lives in Brighton and works at the University of Sussex. His poetry has been translated into German, French, Greek, Finnish, Czech, Dutch, English and Chinese. He co-edits Barque Press with Andrea Brady and is the editor of *Quid*. ➤ 174

Jonty Tiplady was born in 1976. His first chapbook was published by Barque in 2008 as *Zam Bonk Dip*. He has since published many others since, including *At The School Of Metaphysics*, as well as the sequence *J1*, published online on onedit. He has also published in *Hi Zero!*, *Hot Gun* and *Cambridge Literary Review*. In 2009 he won the Crashaw Prize for his first full-length collection of poetry, also called *Zam Bonk Dip*. ➤ 166

Emily Toder, born in 1981, is the author of *Science* (Coconut Books, 2012), and the pamphlets *I Hear a Boat* (Duets Books, 2011) and *Brushes With* (Tarpaulin Sky, 2010). Her poetry and translations have appeared in various journals and anthologies, among them *jubilat*, *The Rialto*, and the *2011 Pushcart Prize Best of the Small Presses*. She lives in Northampton, USA, where she works in the university archives. ➤ 171

Simon Turner has published two collections of poetry, *You Are Here* (Heaventree, 2007) and *Difficult Second Album* (Nine Arches, 2010). His poetry has appeared in a number of publications, including *The Wolf*, *Tears in the Fence* and *Poetry Salzburg*, and in the anthologies *Dove Release* and *Lung Jazz*. With George Ttoouli, he co-edits *Gists and Piths*, a blogzine dedicated to contemporary poetry. He is currently working on a third collection, as well as a critical study of modern civilian war poetry. ➤ 262

Jack Underwood was born in Norwich in 1984. He graduated from Norwich School of Art and Design in 2005 before completing an MA and PhD in Creative Writing at Goldsmiths College, where he now teaches English Literature and Creative Writing. He won an Eric Gregory Award in 2007 and Faber published his debut pamphlet in 2009. He also teaches at the Poetry School, co-edits the anthology series *Stop Sharpening Your Knives*, and reviews for *Poetry London*. He lives in Hackney. ➤ 204

Ahren Warner was born in 1986. His first collection, *Confer* (Bloodaxe, 2011), was both a Poetry Book Society Recommendation and shortlisted for the Forward Prize for Best First Collection; his second, *Pretty*, is published by Bloodaxe in 2013. He has also published a pocket-book, *Re:*, with Donut Press. He was awarded an Eric Gregory Award in 2010 and an Arts Foundation Fellowship in 2012. ➤ 59

Tom Warner was born in Mansfield, and now lives in Norwich. He won an Eric Gregory Award in 2001, a Faber New Poets Award in 2010, the Escalator Prize in 2011 and the Plough Prize in 2011. A pamphlet of his poetry was published by Faber & Faber in 2010. ➤ 42

Rachel Warriner was born in 1981, and currently lives in Cork, Ireland. She was involved with DEFAULT publishing, and now does poetry things with RunAmok and the SoundEye festival in Cork. She has published poems in *Dusie, International Egg and Poultry Review, Cleaves* and *Hi Zero*. Her chapbooks include *Primary* (2009), *Detritus* (2010), and *Eleven Days* (2011). Her new book, *Fine Lament*, is forthcoming from Critical Documents. ➤ 307

James Wilkes was born in 1980. He has collaborated widely with scientists, artists and musicians to investigate topics such as brain imaging, camouflage, and new approaches to landscape. He has particular interests in using speech and radio as material for poetry, and is currently poet-in-residence with the Speech Communication Lab at UCL's Institute of Cognitive Neuroscience. See www.renscombepress. co.uk and www.thevoxlab.org ➤ 36

Steve Willey was born in 1984, lives in Whitechapel and co-runs Openned (openned.com). His poetry has been anthologised in *Better Than Language* (Ganzfeld, 2011) and *City State* (Penned in the Margins, 2009), and has also appeared in *Yt Communication, Past Simple, Tengen* and *Brand*. He is undertaking doctoral work at Queen Mary, University of London, on Bob Cobbing's per-formances. His recent poems are reflections on a trip in 2009 to the Lajee Center in Aida Refugee Camp, Palestine. ➤ 82

ACKNOWLEDGEMENTS

'and I would like to acknowledge
the initiatives put in place
by the government and the rigorous
assessment criteria under which
my work has thrived since 2008'

The editor would like to thank Jeremy Noel-Tod, Sonja Blum, Ben Borek, Philip Langeskov and Emily Critchley for their major help, patience, thoughts or encouragement during the production of this anthology.

The editor would also like to thank Sam Riviere, Ágnes Lehóczky, Elizabeth-Jane Burnett, Alec Newman, and Joseph Walton for their good chats, assistance or suggestions.

Thanks also to Michael Mackmin at *The Rialto* and to Neil Astley at Blood-axe for the opportunity to put this together. A number of the poems included here were published in three thematic issues of *The Rialto*.

Acknowledgements are due to the following publications where these poems first appeared: **Ben Borek:** 'Bezwlad', *S/S/Y/K/4*; 'A Poem Written Between County Hall and Parliament', *The Rialto*; 'Lavender', *Herbarium*. **Siddhartha Bose:** 'Storyboard', *Tears in the Fence*. **James Byrne:** 'Air Terminals' from *Blood / Sugar* (Arc, 2009). **Tom Chivers:** 'The Herbals', *3:AM Magazine*. **Toby Martinez de las Rivas:** 'Penitential Psalm' in *Poetry Review* (101:4, Winter 2011); 'Simonsburn' in *Clinic II*; 'The Clean Versus the Psoriatic Body' on *The Best American Poetry* website. **Amy Evans:** 'Collecting Shells' was originally published as a pamphlet by Oystercatcher Press in 2011. **Miriam Gamble:** 'Webs', *The Irish Review* (October 2012). **Oli Hazzard:** all poems from *Between Two Windows* (Carcanet Press, 2012), published courtesy of Carcanet Press Ltd. **Holly Hopkins:** 'I Have Chosen To Become A Plasterer', *The North*. **Katharine Kilalea:** 'Hennecker's Ditch' was commissioned by the BBC 3's *The Verb* and has been published in Carcanet's *New Poetries V* and *Best British Poetry 2011* (Salt). **Frances Leviston:** 'A Shrunken Head', *London Review of Books*; 'Story' was commended in the 2008 Arvon Poetry Competition; 'The Historical Voice', *A Tower Miscellany*. **Éireann Lorsung:** 'Grey Century' in the e-anthology *TWO WEEKS* (Linebreak, 2011). **mendoza:** 'Hitherto Hither Green' are 'unassarts' or 'son*nots*', and first appeared in *Onedit 16*; 'Signs for Notation' appeared in a short-run zine to accompany the 2nd Sussex Poetry Festival under the name of Linus Slug. **Sandeep Parmar:** all poems from *The Marble Orchard* (Shearsman, 2012). **Holly Pester:** 'Distance Vision Test', *Hoofs* and in *zimZalla* Object 002. **Kate Potts:** 'The Runt' and 'Un-History' from *Pure Hustle* (Bloodaxe Books, 2011), courtesy of Bloodaxe

Books Ltd. **Eileen Pun:** 'The Armoury', The Rialto, and performed by the BBC Singers SATB Choir, London, in January 2010 and Icarus Ensemble, in January 2011. **Sophie Robinson:** 'animal hospital', *The Salt Book of Younger Poets.* **Hannah Silva:** 'Citadel', *Tears in the Fence.* **Keston Sutherland:** from *Odes to TL61P 2* (Enitharmon Press, 2013). **Ahren Warner:** I, V & XV from *Lutèce, te amo* in *PN Review*, IX & XVIII in *Poetry Review*, all from *Pretty* (Bloodaxe Books, 2013). **Rachel Warriner:** 'Eleven Days' was published by RunAmok in 2011 and *Fine Lament* is available in full from Critical Documents. **Steve Willey:** The third page from *Signals* was first published in the magazine *Tengen* (2012); the second page was recorded with the band Rumour Cubes as a B side to their single *1871* (2012).

acknowledge mine, a home,
at the least, a shore. Seen
wrack
as the scene as
if gone back
and back for more,

                                        IT turned out i got
                                            it dirty or it got dirty
                                                                    its

            hands were dirty variously wreckage
            a needle turns into expanse
                    because it flips about of its
        own accord
      the trembling mannequins   certainly they're happy
                    to turn off the feeding tongue
            the dripping tongue of opinion

━━━━━━━━━━━━━━━━━━━━━━━━━━━━━━
                wants to know who 'they'
                        are in the reasoning
      in the dreaming
            in the let's face it dreaming
                a celebutante with open lips and cheeks
              to munch their fishy lips and cheeks see it
        performed at last for an assembled audience
        Taliban poetry
                        it wasn't more or less political.
                            it was less political.
              just to test and make dirty the word who wants
        political when it could have passion
when it couldn't care whether what it said had
      should invading the insect farm,
              i just longed away about missing you
        to whom would listen soda
    to whom would frothing milkshake

                WE K ARE WHISPERING PAPER
    A STREAM OF BUBBLES THAT ARE WE
        CASCADING UP INTO THE AIR

            REAL RUBBISH. like a salad of whether
                or not the guests at the dinner table made
                                        sense or not
                            sensor knot
                            censor not